The Legacy of Maggie Dixon

The Legacy of Maggie Dixon

A Leader on the Court and in Life

Jack Grubbs

ROWMAN & LITTLEFIELD
Lanham · Boulder · New York · London

Published by Rowman & Littlefield
An imprint of The Rowman & Littlefield Publishing Group, Inc.
4501 Forbes Boulevard, Suite 200, Lanham, Maryland 20706
www.rowman.com

6 Tinworth Street, London, SE11 5AL, United Kingdom

British Library Cataloguing in Publication Information Available

Library of Congress Cataloging-in-Publication Data

Names: Grubbs, John H., 1940– author.
Title: The legacy of Maggie Dixon : a leader on the court and in life / John H. Grubbs.
Description: Lanham, Maryland : Rowman & Littlefield, 2018. | Includes
  bibliographical references and index.
Identifiers: LCCN 2018018754 (print) | LCCN 2018021364 (ebook) | ISBN
  9781538114490 (electronic) | ISBN 9781538114483 (hardcover : alk. paper) | ISBN
  9781538137796 (pbk. : alk. paper)
Subjects: LCSH: Dixon, Maggie, 1977–2006. | United States Military Academy.—
  Basketball. | Basketball coaches—United States—Biography. | Women basketball
  coaches—United States—Biography.
Classification: LCC GV884.D59 (ebook) | LCC GV884.D59 G78 2018 (print) | DDC
  796.323092 [B]—dc23
LC record available at https://lccn.loc.gov/2018018754

♾™ The paper used in this publication meets the minimum requirements of American
National Standard for Information Sciences—Permanence of Paper for Printed Library
Materials, ANSI/NISO Z39.48-1992.

To the women of the 2005–2006 West Point women's basketball team. You have grown into the exact women Maggie Dixon knew you could be.

To the Dixon family—Jim, Marge, Jamie, and Julie—for nurturing and guiding a young woman to an inspirational life of leadership. I wish there were no need for this book.

Contents

Preface

On a quiet New Orleans Wednesday night, March 8, 2006, while surfing the television channels, I landed on ESPN, where two basketball analysts were talking about the National Collegiate Athletic Association (NCAA) Tournament, both men's and women's. I hadn't been watching for more than a minute when one of them made the statement (paraphrased), "If you want to see college basketball in its purest form, take a look at the women's Patriot League Tournament." They switched to the end of the Army (West Point)–Holy Cross championship game. It was an extraordinary game, and the crowd reaction at the end of a one-point thriller almost defied imagination. Win or lose, both teams did themselves proud.

As a graduate of the United States Military Academy, I was intrigued by the Army coach. During 35 years of active duty, I had experienced both the fulfillment of inspirational leadership and the demoralizing effects of toxic leadership. I surmised this particular coach was a pretty positive person, regardless of profession. Margaret Mary "Maggie" Dixon was in her first season at the Military Academy, and I soon found out that not only the team, but also the entire West Point community had fallen in love with her. There was something different about Maggie Dixon. Fascinated by her leadership style, I wrote a short article about her tenure at the academy. In it, I tried to capture why, and how, a person could have such a positive influence on others. This book is a continuation of that original article. It is her West Point story.

Before proceeding, I would like to mention support given to me by the Office of the Chief of Public Affairs–Northeast, Department of the Army, which gave me permission to approach the United States Military Academy for help finding documents, photographs, and interviews with people stationed there. I do not claim that this book is endorsed by or composed with permission of the United States Army. No one needs to worry about the book, as a thread of positive leadership weaves its way through most of the chapters.

I was honored to meet some marvelous people during the last three years. In particular, coach Dave Magarity has been very supportive of my efforts. We've had sit-down sessions and he's invited me to the women's games, to include having access to the locker room prior to games, during halftime, and at game's end. Others, including the players I interviewed, have been open and candid, even to the point of giving me the names of other people who could speak of their relationships with Maggie. Information related to game action, team statistics, and each player's background came from the Office of the Director of Intercollegiate Athletics (ODIA). Team catalogs, photographs, and video media were provided to assist me in researching just how much Maggie Dixon accomplished in the crucible of athletics at a military institution.

On a personal note, I do have a close association with West Point. I entered the United States Military Academy in July 1960, graduating in 1964. I met my wife Judy while a plebe (freshman) at the academy. I later served a three-year tour as an instructor in the Department of Earth, Space, and Graphic Sciences (ES&GS). After returning to the field through battalion command, I was fortunate to be selected to the permanent faculty at the academy, eventually serving as professor and head of the Department of Geography and Environmental Engineering (GEnE). Twenty-two years of my life were spent at West Point; for 16 of those years I served as an officer representative (OR) for either the men's soccer team or the men's basketball team. The duties of an "OR" are discussed later. During the last five years, I returned many times to speak on leadership topics with the Thayer Leader Development Group (TLDG), an organization that uses West Point as a model of inspirational leadership. Cadet life and the educational program have changed significantly since I first walked in the door, but I still have a firm understanding of the inner workings of the academy.

And now, a final comment on Maggie Dixon and the West Point women's basketball team of 2005–2006. Every player on the team understood what a great leader they had in "Coach Dixon." To their way of thinking, Maggie Dixon was the "real deal." As for Maggie, she probably didn't even think about it—she was having too much fun.

Welcome to the story of an inspirational leader—Maggie Dixon.

Foreword

$\mathscr{P}$art of the human spirit includes the ability to eventually move through grief to a place where you are capable of bringing together varying degrees of sadness, softness, and fond memories of a loved one lost too soon. We are a family still on the journey.

On April 6, 2006, we—Jim and Marge Dixon, Jamie Dixon, and Julie Dixon Silva—lost a daughter and younger sister, Margaret Mary "Maggie" Dixon. The suffering from losing Maggie will never end, but we have been able to replace a portion of our grief with the stories that continue to come our way. As a youngster, Maggie was a great kid. She loved many things, not just basketball. She enjoyed poetry, walks in the woods, and people. She turned out to be a beautiful woman, sure in herself and one who enjoyed time spent with others, regardless of age, position, or gender.

Maggie woke up on the morning of April 5, 2006, full of optimism and enthusiasm about her experience at West Point during the previous six months. One of the most upbeat stories in collegiate women's basketball was in full swing on that day. Maggie was absolutely the "Cinderella" of women's collegiate basketball in the United States. She achieved in five months what no other coach, man or woman, had accomplished in the history of men's or women's basketball at West Point. Everything seemed beautiful. And then we lost her.

Many journalists interviewed us in the weeks following her death. To the degree possible, we spoke of our remarkable Maggie. Jamie, speaking for the family, said, "I told them that I would never stop talking of her, and I would always remember the good times we shared." Maggie's inspiring story has survived, even thrived, through the ensuing years. This book—*The Legacy of Maggie Dixon*—has taken us on an emotional journey. As her parents and big brother and sister, we were hesitant to begin it, but are certainly glad we did. The Maggie Dixon of West Point was the same Maggie Dixon we knew since she was a child; the same Maggie Dixon Doug Bruno knew at DePaul University; the same Maggie Dixon who captured the hearts of a military community; and the same Maggie Dixon who brought laughter and a higher sense of purpose to anyone who crossed her path, regardless of the situation. Having met each player and the other coaches on the team, we relate fondly to the stories told over and over. Some stories we knew and seemed to have happened only yesterday; others we never knew but are humbled to know now. She was, and still remains, our hero.

Similar to Maggie's true understanding of the game of basketball and the game of life, Jack Grubbs has found an understanding of who Maggie was as a daughter, a sister, a friend, a coach, and, yes, to many, a hero. He has respectfully brought to life the memories of our Maggie and her incredible march with the West Point women's basketball team. Vivid pictures play out in our minds of the way she brought the Army team together. We found ourselves smiling, laughing, and, every now and then, filled with tears as we turned the pages, reliving the stories of Maggie Dixon years later. For those who did not know Maggie personally, by book's end we believe she will have touched everyone in her own way, and we, her family, are sincerely grateful for the time and energy invested in telling her story. It is one of sadness, but it is also truly inspiring, challenging each and every one of us to take whatever adversity we face "head on."

One way our family faced adversity was through the founding of the Maggie Dixon Classic and our work with the Sudden Cardiac Arrest Foundation (SCAF). There are people thriving today who have suffered sudden cardiac arrest (SCA) but, because of training and defibrillators, survived. We want to urge anyone involved with elementary, middle, and high schools; colleges; and any other system involved with high-intensity physical fitness programs to learn the procedures and procure the equipment needed to save the lives of those who experience SCA. You can contact SCAF at http://www.sca-aware.org. If given the opportunity to attend the Maggie Dixon Classic basketball tournament, take advantage of the Maggie Dixon Heart Health Fair as well. We know Maggie would be proud.

Jamie Dixon
Jim Dixon
Marge Dixon
Julie Dixon Silva

Overtime

February 4, 2006
United States Military Academy
West Point, New York
Early afternoon

𝓜argaret "Maggie" Dixon looked up at the scoreboard. Army 63, Navy 63. The time clock read "0:00." Overtime. A raucous cacophony of band music, foot stomping, and cheering rose to the flat ceiling and bounced off the walls of Christl Arena, the basketball venue for the USMA, named in honor of First Lieutenant Edward C. Christl Jr., class of 1944, former captain of the basketball team who was killed in Austria on 4 May 1945, exactly three days before Germany surrendered to end World War II in Europe.

Four months and one day into her tenure as head coach of the Army women's team, 28-year-old Maggie Dixon learned quickly the nature of the Army–Navy rivalry in sports. At Army, a season without defeating the Midshipmen of the USNA is a losing one. It is the same with Navy. Two weeks earlier, the West Point women had defeated Navy at Annapolis by the comfortable score of 83–69. Just as Army "shot the eyes out of the basket" in the first game, the Cadets did the same at the start of this game. But Navy, as intent on winning as Army, showed zero signs of wilting. Down by as many as 11 points early in the game, the Middies (jargon for the title of the Brigade of Midshipmen) scratched and clawed their way back into the game, taking a two-point lead with 19 seconds to go. At the 11-second mark, Navy's Margaret Knap fouled Army's consensus "best player," Cara Enright. With more than 2,500 fans, a large majority cheering for Army, almost blowing the roof off Christl Arena, the California-born Enright stepped to the line and calmly sank both free throws. Navy took possession of the ball and tried for a game-winning field goal; Army's Margaree "Redd" King blocked the shot. Overtime.

The young, statuesque coach, resplendent in her brown skirt, white silk shirt, smooth brown jacket, and high heels, huddled with the coaching staff. If she weren't so young, Maggie Dixon could easily be mistaken as the CEO of a Fortune 500 company. Following a short discussion with the other coaches, she brushed her collar-length hair to the side and turned her attention to the team surrounding her. She looked intensely into the eyes of the five players sitting on chairs. They would carry the fight to Navy. She spoke, loud enough for the other players and coaches to understand where she could take them. If they could execute the game plan they would win the game. An enthusiastic smile broke across her face as she finished giving them their final marching orders. Maggie Dixon was clear in her instructions during a game. But she many times ended a timeout with a well-known quote: "Have fun." The players nodded their heads, comfortable in the knowledge that their coach had basketball wisdom well beyond her years. Black magic-marker residue covered Maggie's hand from where she had erased tactical instructions on her small whiteboard.

Standing behind the circle of young women, the other coaches had to be impressed with the cool, positive demeanor of a new coach not much older than the seniors (known as "firsties") on the team.

As the players—Cara Enright, Jen Hansen, Alex McGuire, Stefanie Stone, and Megan Vrabel—returned to midcourt, Maggie Dixon, a confident aura in her movements, directed her attention to the 10 players on the court. Prior to arriving on the magnificent campus overlooking the Hudson River, she knew some historical background of the more renowned graduates of the academy but nothing about the nature of the daily purgatory lived by cadets. On this afternoon, Maggie Dixon knew she was with family—in this case, a close-knit military family. Given the closeness of her biological family, such a claim might seem a grand exaggeration. It wasn't. The players were young women willing to do anything for their new coach and teammates. The coaching staff locked into her instructions to the team. The fans—cadets, faculty, staff, and community families—came to support Coach Dixon almost as much as they supported the Army team. Most of the fans had seen coach Maggie Dixon during previous games and wanted her to succeed.

The entire scene most likely seemed surreal to Maggie Dixon. She clearly loved it. So did the kids at the game. Having little knowledge of what a basketball game really was, little girls in their black and gold pom-pom cheerleader outfits with "Army" embroidered on the front, and the little boys with T-shirts defiantly stating "Go Army—Beat Navy," jumped up and down, laughing and genuinely having a wonderful time. Maggie could be serious when needed, but, regardless of the game situation, she always had an upbeat nature, which she shared with anyone and everyone with whom she came into contact.

The game officials took their places. Two teams, both with tough, smart, and genuinely patriotic players, were zeroed in on one mission—win the game. To fans looking down toward the Army bench, Maggie's positive leadership stood out like a neon sign. She had been a history major at the University of San Diego, but most of her understanding of West Point came through the macro lens of textbooks. That afternoon, she belonged to West Point and the team. She still had much to learn, but Maggie had the discipline and determination to know everything possible about the academy. She wanted to see the academy and her players from a perspective of the micro lens of individual human beings. She did not know it at the time, but the history of West Point, and her small but significant part of it, had begun more than two centuries earlier. It started in the year 1778.

Fortress on the Hudson

$\mathcal{E}$arly October waxes beautiful among the mountains and meadows of New York's Lower Hudson Valley. Leaves dress the forests rising above the Hudson River in assorted hues of orange and yellow, and the rocky highlands bask in the last vestiges of autumnal warmth. Few places on earth are more beautiful. But the warmth and the breathtaking leaves won't last—they never do. By winter, scudding gray clouds, naked trees, bitter winds, and, eventually, ice and snow envelop the highlands standing sentinel over the Revolutionary War chokepoint on the Hudson River known as West Point.

Approximately 50 miles due north of New York City the Hudson River takes a sharp turn to the west; after a few hundred feet, the river turns again due north toward Albany. Mountains rise more than 1,300 feet on both sides of the river. The sharp turn and small width of the river at that location rendered the geography strategically important for both the Americans and the British. Bristling winds and turbulent currents make the river always interesting and sometimes very dangerous to waterborne traffic. Thus, during the American Revolution, it represented a major strategic position on the Hudson River: Whoever controlled the chokepoint controlled the Hudson River.

In 1778, General George Washington, who declared West Point to be the "key to the continent," sought the services of Thaddeus Kosciuszko, a hero of the Battle of Saratoga, to design fortifications on the higher elevations on the west side of the river. From this "west point" above the river, Continental soldiers built numerous forts, firing locations for artillery, and even an iron-linked chain across the Hudson River to stop British waterborne movement. The harsh winter of 1777–1778 provided Continental general Samuel Holden Parsons the ability to cross the frozen Hudson and occupy the fortifications for the colonists. Since the initial occupation date of January

27, 1778, West Point has been the oldest continually manned military installation in the United States.

Following the Revolutionary War, Washington and other prominent individuals realized the need to train and educate a cohort of American engineers and artillerists. At their urging, then-president Thomas Jefferson signed into law the establishment of the United States Military Academy on March 16, 1802.

For the first few years, the quality of education and the discipline of the cadets were mediocre at best. Cadets were as young as 10 and as old as 37. The curriculum was disjointed, and some cadets graduated in as little as six months; others took as many as six years. Colonel Sylvanus Thayer arrived as superintendent in 1817, with the specific mission to improve every facet of the cadet experience. During his 16-year tenure, Thayer upgraded the academic curriculum, particularly in civil engineering; instilled stronger military discipline; notably the demerit system; instituted a summer encampment program; and formed the basis for honorable conduct via the first Cadet Honor Code. He mandated that the academic system be designed in a manner requiring daily homework, daily recitation, and small class size.

Known as the "Thayer Method," the system still bears a great resemblance to his vision of academic excellence. The civil engineering nature of the curriculum reflected the natural reality that most of the civil works projects (roads, bridges, railroads) in the great move west were led by West Point graduates. Throughout time, the academy—more often than not known as "West Point"—became famous as an institution graduating outstanding engineers and military leaders. During the Civil War, most of the Union generals and a significant number of Confederate generals were graduates of the USMA.

Adding to a culture of "leading by example" was Douglas MacArthur, class of 1903, who served as superintendent during the period 1919–1922. Highly decorated in World War I (and later in World War II), the former "First Captain" (the top-ranking cadet in the Corps of Cadets) and number-one graduate in his class, MacArthur improved upon military discipline, Thayer's cadet honor system, the academic program, cadet physical fitness, and team athletics. Today, physical fitness is a core value of life at West Point. MacArthur, during his time as superintendent, stated the linkage between athletics and leading in combat: "Upon the fields of friendly strife are sown the seeds that, upon other fields, on other days, will bear the fruits of victory."[1]

Since the end of the 19th century, cadet athletic teams have competed throughout the United States and, on occasion, in foreign countries. In 1890, the Navy team challenged Army to a game of football. An interesting side note comes from the fact that the Navy "challenge" was actually initiated by West Point cadet Dennis Michie (pronounced "Mike-ee"); Michie's initial efforts to play Navy had been scuttled by the Military Academy's Academic Board. Navy played football as far back as 1879. Much different than the game of today, no helmets or protective shoulder pads were used. In their first foray into battle, Michie's West Point team was soundly beaten by the Midshipmen, 24–0. The cadets were far better prepared for the second encounter in 1891, winning, 32–16, at Annapolis.

Throughout time, other sports were brought to the forefront, including basketball, baseball, wrestling, soccer, tennis, golf, swimming and diving, squash, track and field, lacrosse, rugby, sprint football, cross-country, and gymnastics. Since not all cadets could compete at the intercollegiate level, fitness was maintained through physical education courses in boxing, swimming, wrestling, and gymnastics. At the intramural level, company teams (of approximately 120 cadets) competed in many of the same sports as those at the intercollegiate level; in some cases, the competition was as fierce as existed among the major universities throughout the nation. Club sports included handball, orienteering, and volleyball. Without question, the men of West Point were physically prepared to lead the young soldiers of the U.S. Army.

And then life at the USMA changed forever.

On October 8, 1975, President Gerald Ford signed Public Law 94-106, opening of admittance of women to the country's military academies.[2] Senior military leadership, in the academies and well beyond, felt war fighting was a mission strictly belonging to males. The attitude, "women will come to West Point, or any other service academy on the day it snows in hell," prevailed at every level of the military. But, especially in the military, the "Rule of Law" is paramount to the lifeblood of our country. Thus, the entire chain of command was ordered to "salute and implement the law."

Early on the morning of July 7, 1976, 119 women entered an institution that for the previous 174 years had been all-male.[3] Keying on the existing attitudes of the senior leaders, many of the male cadets in the upper three classes treated the incoming women with total acrimony. On graduation day 1980, 62 women received their diplomas and commissions as second lieutenants in the U.S. Army. The road to graduation for the class of 1980 and the following two classes had been extremely rough, but, since that hot summer day, the women have excelled as cadets, army officers, and leaders of American society. And for the early classes with female cadets, it was in basketball that West Point had its first women's collegiate athletic team.

In the first year with female cadets, basketball was handled as a club sport. Since the first varsity team took to the court, women's basketball at West Point has gone through periods of feast and famine. Known as the "Sugar Smacks" (based on the fact that first-year cadets, plebes, were often called "smackheads"), the 1977–1978 women's basketball team, coached by Joseph Ciampi, had a more-than-satisfactory season, finishing at 18–5; a year later, the team posted a 21–5 record. Other great seasons included the 1983–1984, team at 25–3, under the coaching of Harold Johnson, and a 20-win season in 1987–1988, with Lynn Chiavaro at the helm. On the downside, in the 15 seasons beginning in 1990–1991, Army suffered through nine losing campaigns, including less than 10 wins for six-straight seasons from 1994 to 2000.

The academy selected Sherri Abbey-Nowatzki as coach beginning with the 1998–1999 season. In 2004–2005, the Army team registered a 15–13 record, including two wins over archrival Navy. With a solid cohort coming back, led by returning sophomore ("yearling") Cara Enright, both the Patriot League Rookie of the Year and All-Patriot League second team, Army had potential. But it also had turmoil.

During the summer of 2005, the wheels began to come off the buggy. Tensions between Coach Abbey-Nowatzki and the leadership team for athletics moved past the critical stage. Although given a contract extension after the 2004–2005 season, Abbey-Nowatzki was suspended from her coaching duties in early September. Her contract with Army terminated at the end of the month. No formal reason for her departure was given to the public. Whatever the reason for the suspension, Army needed to canvas the country for a new coach.

Immediately.

· 3 ·

The Search Begins

*C*oach Sherri Abbey-Nowatzki's departure had nothing personal to do with Maggie Dixon. To her credit, Abbey-Nowatzki brought the women's team from four-straight losing seasons, featuring a 1–25 collapse in 1996–1997, to two winning seasons, a trip to the Patriot League championship game in 2003 (where they lost to Holy Cross, 78–65), four losing seasons, and one even season (14–14) in 2003–2004. Regardless of the coach, recruiting athletes in any sport in 2005 was difficult at the five national service academies (United States Military Academy [USMA], United States Naval Academy [USNA], United States Air Force Academy [USAFA], United States Coast Guard Academy [USCGA], and United States Merchant Marine Academy [USMMA]).

In 2005, applications to the three major academies had taken a nosedive: USMA was down 9 percent, USNA 20 percent, and USAFA a staggering 23 percent.[1] The reason was simple: The Global War on Terror (GWOT) had started to enter a stalemate phase. Too many military members had been killed in action. Although West Point fared better in overall applications, the Navy and Air Force academies had an easier pathway to successful athletic recruiting. In terms of pure perceptions, the Naval Academy boasts of world cruises, aircraft carriers, and jet fighters, while basking in the never-ending glow of Tom Cruise and the movie *Top Gun*. The Air Force Academy met athletic recruiting goals with visions of living the good life and flying jet fighters. For the USMA, moms and dads know which academy sees most of its graduates in places where few vacations are taken—places such as Afghanistan and Iraq. A caveat is the reality of former midshipmen who branched to the Marine Corps or the Navy Seals (Sea, Air, and Land) also serving multiple tours in combat.

But, almost stranger than fiction, applications to all the academies from high school men and women have risen by the thousands recently, and for the class of 2020, less than one in 10 applicants were admitted to West Point and Annapolis. Since the infamous events of 9/11, virtually every candidate for West Point applied with the knowledge he or she could come face-to-face with real combat. On the upside, West Point is one of, if not *the*, finest leadership institutions in the world and continues to attract thousands of candidates for admission. On the downside, top-rated athletes, especially those with valid dreams of becoming professional players, see other options and most often go elsewhere. So, the bottom line remains that matriculation to West Point carries the reality of going to war—and that fact dominates many kitchen-table college discussions in American households. It's only natural; for coaches at Army, it's tough.

Abbey-Nowatzki's suspension and eventual resignation left the Army women's team in a lurch. The team had lost four seniors (known as "firsties") to graduation, one junior (known as "cows"), and four sophomores (known as "yearlings"), for differing reasons. Of the 10 announced incoming recruits (the "plebes"), five decided not to come to the academy at all. To top it off, three assistant coaches—Lorraine Morrissey, Keith Abbey, and Liz O'Brien—were departing for other opportunities. Fortunately, Lieutenant Colonel Jennifer (Jen) Fleming, a 1990 graduate and former team captain, would stay with the team, along with Kelly Flahive, who moved from basketball operations director, and Craig Madzinski, new to the program.

Then there was Major Kim Kawamoto. A 1992 graduate, Kawamoto worked with the team in both an official and unofficial capacity. The two-time American Women's Sports Federation All-America selection and inductee into the Army Athletic Association Hall of Fame was another major asset to the team. She still held the academy record for assists in a game (16), assists for a season (234), assists for a career (796), steals in a game (10), and steals for a career (287). In 2005, she was serving a regular army duty assignment as senior woman administrator in the ODIA. Kawamoto worked with female cadets of all sports and in many areas, one of which was issues concerning the women's basketball team. When time allowed, she often attended practices. She still loved the game.

Also, Colonel Donna Brazil, USMA class of 1983, volunteered to serve as the head officer representative (OR) for the team. A former high school basketball player herself, she had both the right temperament and the background to be real "value added" to the coaching staff. The OR is akin to being somewhat of a "den mother" whose charge is to ensure the players follow the "straight and narrow," assist them with academics and military requirements, and serve as a sounding board for anyone having personal problems. As a senior officer and a permanent professor (the Army equivalence to being tenured) at the academy, Brazil had many other duties aside from those related to the women's basketball team. Thus, she had a cohort of younger officers who had volunteered as assistant ORs to help ease her load. The OR system works well at West Point. More about Colonel Brazil later.

With but six weeks before the start of the new season, the team and, for that matter, the academy faced immense pressure to find a new coach. The one absolute in the situation was clear to everyone associated with Army women's basketball: Whoever they selected as the next women's coach needed to show up with a magic wand.

Because time was crucial, Kevin Anderson, the director of intercollegiate athletics, and Gene Marshall, the deputy director, took over efforts to find a solid coach on short notice. They were the search committee. Anderson's background suited him well for his position; he grew up involved in athletics since he was a kid in San Francisco. He was a multisport athlete at Abraham Lincoln High School and a 1979 graduate of San Francisco State University with a degree in political science. His path to the USMA was unique.

Anderson spent some time coaching at the high school level before diversifying his talents. His first foray into corporate administration came with his attendance and graduation from the Xerox Corporation's New Manager School and the Xerox Marketing School. Given his background, Anderson moved up rapidly, including serving as director of annual giving for the Stanford University Athletics Department, executive associate athletic director for external affairs at the University of California, and, before coming to West Point, executive associate athletic director at Oregon State. He was named Army's director of athletics on December 13, 2004. Marshall joined the ODIA in July 2005.

Although relatively new to West Point, Anderson understood a hard, clear fact—little time existed before a new coach needed to be on campus, arriving on day one and being ready to coach in less than two weeks. Anderson notified the academy's superintendent, Lieutenant General William J. Lennox Jr., of the situation with women's basketball; in the same discussion, Anderson presented his plan to find a new coach. Both agreed to a national search strategy. Interviews with the finalists would include the team. Because Anderson and Marshall constituted a miniature search committee, they decided players from each class would meet with the finalists and give their recommendations to Anderson. He met with the seniors and informed them that the entire team would be part of the interview process. "We want to know the team's view of each candidate and who you recommend for coach," he said. That he wanted, and valued, their input left them elated. They also carried great respect for Gene Marshall, who would be working with Anderson while concurrently overseeing the individual workouts and strength programs of the players.

On the national stage, word travels fast. In short order, Army had a sizable stable of candidates to consider. Most were young and talented, male and female. Several were quite impressive. Four candidates were invited to the academy for an official visit. One of them approached her candidacy with the same fervor that led to her being hired as an assistant women's basketball coach at DePaul University. Her name: Margaret Mary "Maggie" Dixon.

Born on May 9, 1977, in North Hollywood, California, Maggie Dixon was not destined to be a basketball player and coach. One of two daughters—Julie being eight years older—of Jim and Marge Dixon, Maggie also had a brother, Jamie, older by 12 years. As a youngster, Maggie did not have a burning desire to become a great basketball player. Her main association with basketball came through her admiration for Jamie, who she adored whether or not he ever played the game. He was her big brother and that was all that mattered. Along with her parents, she watched him play basketball in high school and, later on via satellite dish, at Texas Christian University (TCU). During the summer, Jamie and Maggie would shoot baskets in the backyard.

As a preteen, Maggie had a growth spurt, giving her an opportunity to play basketball in high school. As a freshman at Immaculate Heart High School, Maggie was in no way a star on the team and played sparingly. For her sophomore year, she transferred to a larger high school, Notre Dame, and decided to try out for basketball. Unfortunately, state rules dictated those students changing high schools had to wait a full year before playing at the new school. But, during her junior year, Maggie began to gain a real feel for the game. Still, she loved the arts, music, and dancing as much as playing basketball; in a nutshell, Maggie Dixon was a Renaissance girl. She made friends across the spectrum of activities and was as happy as a kid could be. Bit by bit, Maggie's interests turned more and more toward basketball. The only downside to her improvement on the high school court came from Jamie being unable to see Maggie play more than a couple of times because of his professional career; he had been selected by the Washington Bullets in the 1987 National Basketball Association (NBA) draft and played with the Lacrosse Catbirds of the Continental Basketball Association (CBA), and also in New Zealand.

One specific indication of a growing confluence of basketball lives between Jamie and Maggie came during Jamie's early coaching career. He was hired to assist in running a summer basketball camp. He thought the camp would be ideal for his youngest sister.

Jamie mentioned the camp to Maggie. "Maggie," he said, "some of my buddies are going to run a basketball camp. Would you be interested in going to it?" For Maggie, barely in her early teens, being around her big brother always stood out for her. She asked Jamie about the girls. "Are there a lot of girls?"

Jamie, not really knowing the answer, made a reasonable guess. "Sure, it's for boys and girls."

When they arrived at the camp, both Jamie and Maggie looked around and counted heads: boy, boy, boy, boy . . . and on and on with only boys. Jamie sheepishly asked Maggie if she wanted to go home.

"No way. I'll just be the only girl," she answered.

She was the only girl and loved every minute of the camp. She really enjoyed playing basketball with the boys and, more importantly, got to be around her big brother. Maggie not only loved being around Jamie, but also she could hold her head high, knowing she had held her own playing with and against the boys.

Her late-blooming high school basketball career at Notre Dame High School gave Maggie a shot at playing varsity basketball at the University of San Diego (USD). At 5-foot-11 and in possession of a gifted and growing "feel" for the game, Maggie flourished at USD; she lettered all four years and was selected as team captain during her senior year of 1998–1999. To this day, Maggie remains among the top-ranked USD players in field goal percentage for a season, with a solid 52 percent. It was good enough to get her a shot at playing professionally in the Women's National Basketball Association (WNBA). She tried out with the Los Angeles Sparks but was cut in May 2000. The bad news for Maggie was being cut; the good news was her knowledge of the game and her world-class determination. Near-perfect interpersonal skills, high energy, and just a touch of pizzazz gives one the recipe for being a great basketball coach. That description fit Maggie Dixon to a "T." The DePaul University Blue Demons would be the first team to encounter the improbable young woman from California.

· 4 ·

The Bruno Connection

The disappointment in being let go by the WNBA did little to slow Maggie down. After being cut from the Sparks, Maggie was free to do whatever she wanted—at least until she had no money. The timing turned out to be perfect. Maggie had a close friend, Jackie Liautaud, who she roomed with during her freshman and sophomore years at USD. Prior to college, they had only known one another through playing basketball against each other from grade school through high school. Both matriculated to USD and crossed paths at the beginning of their freshman years. Maggie was playing basketball, Jackie was not.

It was late May when Jackie's brother agreed to drive her to Chicago. At the last moment, he had to cancel taking the trip at all. What to do? Jackie called Maggie and asked if she wanted to take a trip to the Windy City.

Maggie responded with an eager thumbs-up. Earlier, she had sent her resume to the head coach at DePaul University in Chicago. Meeting him in person was the best of all situations. She packed her bags, jumped into Jackie's car, and the two of them headed northeast. Maggie said over and over, "This is great. My best chance is to see the coach person-to-person." Maggie was locked and loaded to land a coaching position with the DePaul University Blue Demons basketball team.

The Doug Bruno–Maggie Dixon connection unfolded in an unorthodox manner. It was a classic matter of one of the undervalued principles of leadership: perseverance. And perseverance leads to a story.

Coach Doug Bruno was looking forward to an evening with the guys. He needed a break, and they needed a break. It is a given in the life of a basketball coach—at least for most successful coaches—that work is a grinding, nonstop experience for nine months out of the year. Coaching is packaged in developing individual skills; practicing before the start of a season; maintaining the grueling pace of playing almost 30 games during a regular season (including travel for half of the games); playing deep into a conference tournament; and, if both good and fortunate, playing in the single-elimination NCAA Tournament against 63 other teams. It is not easy. Each team in the tournament is on the same mission—win six games in a row.

For Bruno, it was the Friday before the Memorial Day weekend in 2000. He was enjoying a warm shower, the only one he had ever taken on a Friday night in the old Alumni Hall. A 1950s structural derelict, Alumni Hall was scheduled for demolition the next month. It was, in Bruno's words, a "ghost house." Fortunately, the team moved to the DePaul Athletic Center in 2000. Life was busy. Life was good.

To his dismay, one of the employees, Blair Banwart, knocked on the door, interrupting Bruno's revelry, and yelled.

"Hey, Coach Bruno. You've got two 6-foot-3 girls standing at half court. They want to talk to you."

"Damn it," said the DePaul coach, less than pleased. He recruited 6-foot-3 girls out of high school to play for the Blue Demons. But he certainly did not need to talk to some girls on his first Friday night of freedom in nine months.

He grudgingly responded, "Tell them I'll be up in 10 minutes. But I don't have a lot of time."

Ten minutes later, he met the two "girls" at center court. The two "girls" were really two "women," and only Jackie was 6-foot-3. Maggie stood maybe 5-foot-11, no more.

As he walked up to them, Maggie Dixon, a genuine smile on her face, reached out with her hand. She introduced herself to Coach Bruno and introduced Jackie as well. She told him of the cross-country trip from California and that her only purpose of the trip was to discuss her application for a coaching position. She made it clear from the beginning that she was sure she would be a good fit.

Doug Bruno grew up a basketball junkie. He played high school basketball in Chicago at Quigley Preparatory Seminary South. He matriculated to DePaul, lettering in his final three years and starting his final two years. His coach was the legendary Ray Meyer. Following his playing days, Bruno coached boys basketball at the high school level. In 1976, he accepted the head coaching job for the women's basketball program at DePaul. In two years, he compiled a record of 27–16, with the team winning 16 games in 1977–1978. He left DePaul and coached the Chicago Hustle, a professional women's team, for two years before becoming an assistant men's coach at

Loyola University Chicago. Bruno returned to his alma mater as head coach of the women's basketball team in 1988. The rest is history—Doug Bruno is, to this day, one of the premier college coaches in women's basketball. He knows women's basketball, and he knows team-building for both the coaches and players.

Bruno, following a short pause bordering somewhere between consternation and disbelief, answered stoically with, "Look, I've got things to do tonight."

Without hesitation, Maggie showed how transparent a person she was, responding, "Well, I would be glad to come with you."

Bruno, as diplomatically as possible, nixed the idea of her joining the guys for that night, but her openness put a little hook into his psyche. He thought for a moment before answering. "Tell you what. I can give you about 15 minutes tomorrow. Can you be here at nine in the morning? But, remember, I only have a few minutes."

She happily acknowledged his time constraints and indicated that she would be back at exactly nine o'clock in the morning.

Bruno did have a great night out; so did Maggie and Jackie. Maggie was thrilled at the possibility she might end up a coach at DePaul University. The Blue Demons—what an honor. Jackie got a kick out of watching Maggie's enthusiasm.

The next morning, Maggie arrived on time, looking as fresh as can be. Jackie waited outside in her car.

Bruno's plan called for driving to Michigan Saturday morning and spending the weekend with family. He absolutely did not need impediments.

His first words to Maggie included a reference to his not having a position. "I don't have a job opening. So, before we go any further, let's just talk stuff. Let's talk basketball."

The interview ended up lasting almost three hours and 15 minutes. Within a few minutes, Bruno found Maggie to be very savvy in her knowledge of the game. That she even received the opportunity to try out for the Sparks was a good sign. Before long, Bruno found himself enjoying the discussion. Maggie Dixon was unique. He couldn't quite put his finger on what made her stand out so much, but she certainly was marching to her own drum. She knew many of the intricacies of the game. He liked her, but the numbers were not in her favor. They talked more about each of their perceptions of the duties of an assistant coach and the interactions among the coaching staff.

Another strike against Maggie was Bruno's conservative principle of the "sanctity of his staff." In his words, "I don't hire on a whim. The staff chemistry is necessary before team chemistry." Putting it bluntly, he said, "I will not simply hire someone off the street." His personal view of the right assistant coach for DePaul University was straightforward: "I don't want an assistant coach to be a clone of me. I want differences. But, in a disagreement there has to be agreeability, not division."

Well into their meeting, Bruno changed the subject.

"Maggie, what else do you like to do? What goes on in your spare time?"

Maggie surprised Coach Bruno. She told him how much she enjoyed taking a walk in the woods, reading poetry, and meeting new people.

"Do you like to go out to dinner?" he questioned.

Again, Maggie answered with an enthusiastic smile. She told Bruno how much she enjoyed the company of other people, regardless of positions of responsibility or events attended. She was very much a social animal. Bruno saw a sense of seriousness not noticed before when she added that she was a hard worker who could always be counted on to arrive at work on time.

Doug Bruno, by this time very impressed with Maggie, thought of a possibility. He related,

> Tell you what. I run basketball camps during the summer. In our organi-zation, we have a position of what I call "dorm mom." If you take it, you would have responsibility for keeping the campers under control. Having peace and quiet will be a major challenge, and you would be the central authority figure. In the position, you will interact with 200 kids—and that means 400 parents. It is a big job.

Maggie agreed to give his offer considerable thought. "How soon do you need to know?" she asked.

He responded, "Pretty soon. Consider it on your way back to California."

Maggie said she would let him know soon and thanked him for the con-siderable amount of time he gave her. The morning discussion pleased both Coach Bruno and the energetic young California woman.

Jackie waited the three hours, wondering what was going on. Finally, Maggie, almost flustered, walked over to her friend.

"Jackie, I don't believe it," Maggie said, trying to keep herself under control. "I think I've been offered a job. Oh, my gosh. I might be a DePaul coach pretty soon."

Jackie smiled, thrilled at the possibility of Maggie's receiving a coaching position, especially since she had invited Maggie to take the drive to Chicago. Maybe some things are just meant to be.

The next step belonged to Maggie.

Maggie returned to California by train. It was the appropriate mode of travel for someone who was so full of life and always game to try something new.

Once back in California, Maggie returned to the free life of a college graduate without a job. Aside from activities consisting of walking in the woods or reading poetry, Maggie loved shopping, with shoes ranking highest on her list. A few years later, Bruno explained her as being an "eclectic dresser." She was an eclectic person in the finest sense of the word. She didn't feel trapped by the current fad. She spent her time pondering the life of an assistant basketball coach at a premier school like DePaul University. A reasonable decision might have been to stay in California and seek opportunities in the Golden State. But, in her case, Maggie went out on the proverbial limb.

She knew any possibility of ending up at DePaul on a full-time basis would have to be through the doorway of being the dorm mom at a Doug Bruno basketball camp. Her soul-searching included many questions. Since her first meeting with Coach Bruno and her time on the train, and day and night since returning to California, the possibilities had been churning in her head. She knew he needed to know soon—and the clock ticked on.

Maggie loved to shop, and it so happened that one of those serendipitous "moments in time" popped up. She happened to be browsing a White Elephant Shop and found a T-shirt with the lettering, "Doug Bruno Camp" on the front. Maggie read it to be a sign pushing her toward a career as a college basketball coach. Who knows? It could very well be that the basketball camp might be an ignitor for a career with the DePaul Blue Demons. She sent it to Bruno, along with a note: "I would love to be a dorm mom for your summer basketball camp." And so, the Bruno–Dixon journey began in earnest. And, as a tidbit about her persona, she never mentioned she was the kid sister of the well-known men's coach at the University of Pittsburgh, Jamie Dixon.

As much as the coaches and counselors enjoyed coaching the young kids, it was a grueling process: rise early in the morning, make sure beds are made and the kids ready for breakfast at the right time, coach throughout the day with little time off for a noontime meal, and make plans for the next day. The 200 campers and 400 parents seemed more like 2,000 campers and 4,000 parents.

Coach Bruno saw more in the camp than bouncing a ball. He once said in an interview, "You learn about people in a basketball camp. After watching coaches and staff for eight to 15 hours a day, I pretty much know what kind of people they are. Almost all of my coaches worked very hard." If a camp coach did not work hard, chances were the coach would not work in a Bruno camp for long.

He continued, "It's hard to define. Working a basketball camp is not easy, and it's certainly not linear management. Too much goes on." Speaking of Maggie's position, he added,

> And serving as the dorm mom can lead to chaotic situations. But, because of her ability to communicate with virtually anyone, the chaos around her was invisible to an outside observer. Her management skills and care of people were out of sight. She survived the chaos and could keep going even though dead tired. On numerous occasions and despite her heavy workload, she would often join the other coaches in teaching the game to the campers. You find out about people in the camp. With Maggie Dixon, I struck gold.

By the end of the summer, Bruno believed Maggie would be a perfect fit for the DePaul Blue Demons. But he had no positions for a new assistant coach. What he did have was a plan.

He went to the DePaul University athletic director and presented the background concerning Maggie Dixon. In an interesting twist of fate, it was Doug Bruno who hired Jean Lenti Ponsetto as his first assistant coach; it was Lenti Ponsetto who, several years later, hired Doug Bruno to return to DePaul as the Blue Demons women's head coach. What goes around comes around. Bruno asked if Dixon could be given a grad-assistant position with the team. Lenti Ponsetto is a creative woman. While not able to add a formal position to the coaching staff, she was able to put together a grad-assistant position for $8,000. The move allowed Maggie to get "into the system." But, to help Maggie to survive, Bruno touched base with a close friend, Mr. Artie Greco, to find her a waitress position. She spent the year working the tables at Greco's restaurant, Sorriso's, where the finest in authentic southern Italian cuisine could be found. Lawyers and business chiefs dined at Sorriso's with great regularity. With the grad-assistant pay of $8,000 and some pretty solid tips, Maggie survived the year.

For Maggie's first year on the staff, Coach Bruno was able to hire her as director of basketball operations. The following year, she was named the recruiting coordinator. Her personality paid handsome dividends for the DePaul recruiting program. In each of the last three seasons Maggie coached at DePaul, the Blue Demons notched at least 20 wins and made the NCAA Tournament. The team recorded an overall record of 72–22 and won its first tournament game in both 2004 and 2005. In 2006, with many of the players Maggie recruited, the Blue Demons made the Sweet 16. Throughout her tenure as an assistant coach, Maggie brought a sense of pure enjoyment to the program. To his way of thinking, in Maggie Dixon he had found a very special person, a person destined for greatness.

For the DePaul 2001–2002 season, a new arrival joined the team. Jana Mathis was to be the new director of operations, the position Maggie had previously held. Maggie and Jana hit it off immediately. Jana, a graduate of DePauw University (sounds somewhat like DePaul, but they are two very different schools), came from the high school coaching ranks. She had been a young participant in Doug Bruno's basketball camps and was a natural choice to join Bruno's DePaul basketball staff. As for being a director of operations, Jana knew little of the position, but she was determined to be up to the task.

Maggie, having just served in the position, reached out and taught Jana, a smart woman, the basics of the job. Jana was eager to learn and carry out her duties. Between the two of them, the learning curve was not steep for Jana. She was proficient after just a couple of weeks. Watching the personal interactions among the coaching staff, Doug Bruno knew his latest pick for an assistant coach had been a good one. Following eight months as director of operations, Jana became an assistant coach. From the day they met, Jana and Maggie were colleagues on a coaching staff that was already solid and would only get better.

The two women became close friends and were famous for putting levity into all things coaching. Both women, unmarried at the time, worked 80-hour weeks and still reserved a little time for enjoying life outside of basketball. Neither Maggie nor Jana were one-trick ponies by any measure; both loved life and good times with anyone and everyone. For as hard as they worked, laughter was a given wherever they went. Coach Bruno often invited the coaches to join him at a local pub for a beer and conversation, usually focusing on basketball. Maggie and Jana enjoyed the camaraderie and social functions of any color.

For a Halloween party, Maggie, a tall woman in most groups, fashioned a costume from some yellow materials she found in one of her closets, put on semi-high-heeled shoes, and came as Big Bird, while Jana, an inch shorter than Maggie, wearing low heels, came as a red lobster. Both were quick on the uptake and could garner belly-busting laughter with a quick retort to any remark. Working the Bruno basketball camps while living in dormitories without air conditioning was physically draining, but the two women found ways to laugh about their position in life—and the steaming rooms they lived in. Despite the marginal living conditions and lengthy work hours, life was good.

If anyone should be tagged the ultimate "multitasker," it would be Maggie Dixon. Jana remembered a recurring story of Maggie, describing her ability to do multiple tasks simultaneously;

> On occasion, Maggie would need to leave practice, attend a function of some sort, and then return to the gym. She would run through a room, throw on a dress, put her earrings on, and brush her hair, talking all the

time. The whole routine took no more than 10 minutes. She would ask, "Do I look alright?" She looked beautiful, simply stunning. Upon returning, if practice was still going on, she would change back into her sweats in five minutes and head back to the gym. How she could pull it off I'll never know. She was so easygoing and efficient.

There is one other important linkage between Maggie and Jana. On October 14, 2003, the Chicago Cubs were hosting the Florida Marlins in game 6 of the National League Championship Series (NLCS). Someone on the DePaul women's basketball team had access to tickets for the game. Given the Cubs 3–2 record in the series, it was a big deal. The Cubs were in position to win the World Series for the first time since 1908. Maggie had a ticket, but she also had the opportunity to spend some time with her brother Jamie and offered her ticket to Jana. Delighted, Jana took the ticket and, grabbing a DePaul sweatshirt, headed out to Wrigley Field, home of the Cubs. Jana didn't know it before the game, but the ticket Maggie gave her would change her life forever.

The game itself is historically significant for being bizarre. In the eighth inning, with the Cubs up 3–0 and only five outs from heading to the World Series, a fan named Steve Bartman almost caught a foul ball, denying Cubs left fielder Moises Alou an opportunity to make the catch. Although the Chicago fans booed Bartman relentlessly on that night and for a long time thereafter, what he did was not considered fan interference; he did exactly what any other fan would have done: try to catch a souvenir. But Chicago went straight downhill, giving up eight runs following the play. The cascading events of the eighth inning doomed the Cubs to baseball purgatory for another year. But, more significantly, during the game, a young man, George Balis, noticed the young woman a couple of rows in front of him. He could not keep his eyes off her. Feeling nervous, young George realized it was now or never. He walked down a couple of rows and introduced himself to Jana.

"Hi, I noticed the DePaul shirt," he quipped. He had a pretty good line, good enough to earn himself some conversation and learn her name. And, if nothing else, he did manage to shake hands with her.

George was clearly smitten with Jana and went on a search to find out more about her. He checked numerous sources, most of them on the internet, and finally tracked her down to the DePaul women's basketball team. He asked her out on a date—to another Cubs game in the spring of 2004. Not knowing whether to trust him, Jana invited Maggie to join her. Maggie went with them to serve as both predictor and protector; she gave Jana a solid thumbs-up for George's behavior. Sure enough, Maggie predicted that great things were in Jana and George's future, and Jana would not need to be protected—George was an honorable man.

Until Maggie left DePaul there was an agreement: Since George had cable television and Maggie didn't, on the nights when Jamie's Pittsburgh Panthers were on George's television, Maggie had a standing invitation to watch his cable television, along with Jana. There were those rough times when both Pittsburgh and *The Bachelor* were on at the same time, and *The Bachelor* took second billing.

By 2004, Maggie was Doug Bruno's top assistant and recruiting coordinator. He mentored her every day both on the court and in one-on-one interactions. Without question, she deemed herself capable of being a successful head coach. Bruno agreed; eventually she would be recruited by some university and move on to a superb career as a head basketball coach. He hated to see her go but knew she was ready to leave the nest of the DePaul basketball program. She wasn't cocky, she was confident. Still, in September 2005, with another season fast approaching, Maggie Dixon remained quite content with her position and looked forward to the upcoming season at DePaul. But, there is the poignant saying, "Life is what happens to you while you're making other plans."

Upon learning of an immediate opening for a head coach at the United States Military Academy, Maggie considered the opportunity. Her first action involved taking a look at the nature of the beast. She pulled articles and historical documents concerning West Point, its history, and the history of the Army women's basketball team. As mentioned earlier, the team history showed some success at the Division II level but very little since becoming a full-time Division I competitor. As best she could, Maggie studied the background of each player, the opponents, the schedule, and the commitments required of cadets (time management and military discipline). She did not watch any game tapes. She also knew the departure of Sherri Abbey-Nowatzki had been related to difficult circumstances.

In short order, Maggie had a fairly solid outsider's understanding of an institution having a juxtaposition of exceptional academics with a male-dominated military culture. The more she plowed through documents related to West Point in general and the team in particular, the more a sense of excitement about a possible "incredible journey" at a one-of-a-kind institution grew within her. But, before submitting a resumé, she did what she always did, and called big brother Jamie. At that time, Jamie knew what he did not know about Army—a lot. He wasn't even sure how many of the cadets were women. One thing he did know, however, was that Army basketball would always bear an unrelenting demand on a cadet's time. But Jamie told Maggie to go ahead and submit a resumé so she could gain experience in interviewing for a head coaching position.

"It's Army," he told her. "It's not the traditional basketball setting."

He understood, for example, that in most high-profile basketball programs, a player takes 12 to 15 credits a semester, but at West Point, the course load is 17 to 24 credits. Classes in calculus, physics, and engineering (required of every cadet at the academy) make the four years at USMA difficult, athlete or not. You simply cannot slide along in academics at West Point. If you do slide, you will soon slide right out the door. And then there's all the regimentation.

"I don't know what to tell you, Maggie," Jamie admitted, "except just be yourself. But, if you're invited to the campus I would recommend you accept the offer to visit. You're not far from a head coaching job on your own merit, and the interview at Army would be a good experience for you." Jamie did not think Army would be the best fit for his young, but determined, sister.

Talking with Doug Bruno was different. Like Jamie, Doug had some reservations about a military academy, but he had great respect for the military. He warned Maggie of the difference between a military school and a "normal" school. He told her,

> You have been a magnificent recruiter, and on the phone, you are charismatic. But at West Point, your Irish blarney won't do it. You will need an organized structure for recruiting. Your gift of gab will be good, but it will only take you so far. The West Point players will be doing more important things.

That being said, and understanding he would lose a great basketball coach and an even better friend, Bruno told Maggie, "Go for it."

He had just given his full endorsement to Maggie's quest to spend her professional career as a women's head basketball coach, even if she was taking a risk known as "West Point."

During an interview years later, Bruno said, "I was totally in favor of her taking the job."

Maggie considered what Jamie and Doug had told her. She talked to close friends. West Point could easily become problematic. But West Point was a national icon—an institution standing for all that is good in America. A decisive woman, Maggie submitted a resumé.

The Search Ends

$\mathcal{O}$n September 24, 2005, Kevin Anderson invited Maggie to interview for the position. She arrived on September 27, staying at the historic Thayer Hotel on the grounds of West Point, standing sentinel over the Hudson River. September at West Point is usually idyllic. The leaves begin the annual change from green to differing hues of orange, red, and yellow. The weather on this day did not disappoint. To Maggie, the campus was even more beautiful than it appeared in catalogs. Granite academic and administrative buildings, statues of graduates who gave so much to the nation, and beautiful old homes, some dating back to the early 1800s, whetted her appetite to know more about this strange institution. Although on a whirlwind visit to West Point, Maggie did have the opportunity to observe a healthy culture of cadet life. She saw cadets in uniform on the way to class or any of myriad other requirements; cadets jogging along sidewalks overlooking the Hudson River; intramural sports being played with the intensity of a national championship contest; and, to her delight, cadets walking alongside officers discussing any of uncountable topics, probably none of which related to basketball or pop culture.

Maggie noticed something else. When walking by the superintendent's (a three-star lieutenant general) home, she could see two long rectangular signs sandwiching the concrete walkway leading into the home's front entrance. The sign on the left read, "GO ARMY," and the sign on the right read, "BEAT NAVY." She found similar sentiments throughout the campus. The dean and the commandant, both brigadier generals (one-star), had flags and banners saying, "Beat Navy." Concrete walls along a tunnel under the main access road (Washington Road) were covered with all the years Army had beat Navy in football. It's the only location on the main campus specifically mentioning only football. In pure unadulterated passion, victory is fought for in all sports. On the bleachers at the huge parade ground known as "The Plain," small black stripes are painted on the bleacher seats in such as manner as to make it possible for someone looking down from high above, for instance, from the Cadet Chapel or an overlook from Highway 9W as it rises on its journey north toward Newburgh, to make out two words: BEAT—NAVY. A block away from The Plain is a four-unit brick home known as the "BEAT NAVY" home. For years, the residents, assigned generally for a three-year tour of duty, made sure a "Beat Navy" sign of some sort was always present. Eventually the home's title was formally designated the "BEAT NAVY" home, and a large metal sign in the front yard signified the exalted position among all the homes at West Point. Throughout the on-post housing areas for the staff and faculty are differing forms of messaging, urging the athletic teams to "take it to the middies."

Beating the men and women from Annapolis was a year-long goal. To Maggie, what she saw felt good. Sure, it was very competitive, but it seemed a healthy competition. Many, although not all, of her doubts about coming to West Point started fading away. The more she understood of the academy and its inhabitants, the more she embraced a possible fit between herself and an institution about which a month earlier she had known practically nothing.

Maggie's interview came in two parts. First, she met with Kevin Anderson, Gene Marshall, and a couple of other key personnel. She answered questions about basketball, interpersonal relationships, the United States Army, and the nature of college athletics at a military academy. Of course, keeping things equal, she had a few questions of her own. Also on the agenda was meeting with the team members.

Her first team interview, with firsties (seniors), was, to say the least, strange. They met in a conference room at the Center for Enhanced Performance at lunchtime. Maggie walked in as the firsties were preparing to have lunch consisting of pink cellophane-wrapped sandwiches and a piece of fruit. To Maggie's astonishment, one of the firsties was in the process of unwrapping her sandwich by attacking the cellophane wrapper with a two-foot-long cadet sabre. Maggie was taken aback at what appeared to be an immature act by someone who should have been the portrait of a military leader. But, in the wink of an eye, Maggie realized she was not dealing with the often ill-stereotypical "military robot," but rather, a smart, energetic, fun-loving young American woman. The only real difference between the firstie and any high-achieving college student was the sabre lady at the table was wearing a military uniform.

Maggie looked around at the young women and said, "Is this what West Point is all about, where one opens lunch with a sword?" Everyone laughed,

Maggie very comfortably and the young women almost as comfortably. The ice had been broken. During an interview later on, Maggie recalled her discussion with Jamie, with the emphasis on West Point not being a normal basketball setting. She related the story of the fun-loving cadet attacking her sandwich, and Maggie thinking, *I just might like this place*. Her thought that day might possibly have been the 2005–2006 American athletic understatement of the year.

The "cellophane attacker" was Michelle "Micky" Katherine Mallette. Similar to Maggie's, Micky's journey to West Point was unusual. Born in Elmira Heights, New York, to James and Kathy Mallette, Micky played basketball for Thomas Edison High School. She loved sports early in her childhood and was naturally gifted in basketball. Micky received numerous high school awards and was the catalyst to an 18–0 season her senior year. Intelligent and disciplined—with the possible exception of her attack on the sandwich—she also excelled in the classroom, graduating as class valedictorian in 2001. Recruited by Army, the University of New Hampshire, and Canisius College, Micky liked the idea of the challenges she would face at West Point while still being able to participate at the Division I level in her sport of choice.

But Micky had major obstacles to overcome. The first came in the form of a torn ACL, suffered in a New York state playoff game. The injury was severe enough to delay her entry to West Point until 2002. Another "kicker" raised its ugly head when Coach Abbey-Nowatzki told Micky, "Either spend the year at the United States Military Academy Preparatory School (USMAPS—pronounced 'yoos-maps') or go elsewhere." USMAPS, similar to the military preparatory schools at the air force and naval academies, provided academic improvement programs in mathematics and English to assist high school athletes and soldiers from the regular army, army reserves, or army national guard to score high on the Scholastic Aptitude Test (SAT) and survive the rigors of an intense, yet outstanding, academic program. For the athletes, USMAPS represented a pseudo "red shirt" year. A final advantage of USMAPS came with the mandate that the "cadet candidates" must adhere to a military life, including inspections, drill, and "customs of the service."

Early on, Micky was not pleased with the "my way or the highway" ultimatum of Coach Abbey-Nowatzki, but she weighed her options and agreed to attend USMAPS. As it turned out, Coach Abbey-Nowatzki led Micky to a good decision. Not only did she enjoy playing basketball for USMAPS, where she was the team's most valuable player, but also Micky met many teammates and other cadet candidates who later became friends during her time at West Point and in the years following graduation.

Micky thrived on challenge, be it in the classroom, on the court, or leading by example in the military life of a West Point cadet. At the start of her firstie year, she was appointed regimental commander of the 2nd Regiment, an organization of approximately 1,100 cadets. The entire Corps of Cadets consisted of just less than 4,400 cadets. At the top of the cadet chain of command were the brigade commander, the deputy brigade commander, and the four regimental commanders. In cadet life, as a regimental commander, Micky Mallette stood at the pinnacle of success. But, despite her leadership strengths, as a basketball player Mallette was as unsure of the future as any other player.

The interview unfolded into a smorgasbord of possibilities. For starters, Maggie certainly brought her "A" game.

Early on, Ashley (affectionately named "Smash" by her teammates) Magnani asked an important, but rhetorical, question: "You can say the right things, but can you be the right person?"

The firsties remember her answer almost perfectly:

> I hope by the end of our time here you will have significant insight into my character, my intentions, and my ability to inspire each one of our players. I realize I have much more to learn about West Point, but I have put a lot of effort in understanding just what makes West Point tick the way it does.

A solid answer for a very candid question. The interview turned to enthusiastic discussion in which the word *possibilities* loomed large.

Maggie knew the names and backgrounds of the entire Army team. One by one, she made some light remarks to each player, commenting often about a player's hometown, basketball background, or interests. A huge factor in her favor was her unexpected understanding of the academic program. Unlike programs found in other universities and colleges, West Point has a unique system of wickets to pass through on the way to graduation. The academic program[1] for the class of 2009 offered more than 40 majors across a continuum, from philosophy, economics, leadership, history, foreign language, mathematics, chemistry, physics, and computer science to the aerospace, civil, electrical, environmental, mechanical, and systems engineering programs. If a cadet wanted to major in philosophy, no problem; however, the philosophy major still had to take required technical courses (e.g., a three-course engineering sequence—mathematics, physics, chemistry). Conversely, an engineering major needed courses in philosophy, foreign language, English, law, and history, to name a few. Because of the number of technical courses taken, all graduates receive a bachelor of science (BSE) degree upon graduation. For the engineering accredited programs, a minimum of 13 courses are required.

Maggie was also well aware of the academic process of classes at the academy. For example, there exists a "one-day, two-day" schedule in which cadet activities, including academics, would cycle through a two-day period. On a "one" day, half of the plebe (freshman) class might have a specific lesson in mathematical modeling, while the other half would have a class in chemistry; on a "two" day, the plebes would simply switch class topics. The third day would be another "one" day. The process continues to this day throughout each semester.

One of the firsties asked Maggie about her understanding of the difficulties of playing a Division I sport at West Point. For Maggie, the question was a gift. Time pressures and, thus, time management, are enormous issues at West Point. Maggie understood and supported the requirement stating that playing a sport does not allow an athlete to underperform (known as "stacking arms" in military jargon) in any individual course or to not pursue a major. Having studied the cadet schedule and the academic program, Maggie juxtaposed them against the upcoming basketball schedule and developed a plan not only providing a preview of practices, but also listing those periods of time she could give them to help them with academics.

"Here are the dates I can give you two days off." She pulled out her concept of time management. Without skipping a beat, Maggie continued to explain her understanding of the major competitors for a cadet's time. After covering her knowledge of the composite requirements related to athletics, academics, clubs, military training, and other "predators," Maggie pulled out her plan to find a way for the women to have some "down time." The firsties recalled being awed at her preparation. They saw firsthand what it really meant to be organized. In organizational skills, Maggie was off the charts. The interview ended much too soon. Maggie thanked the young women and walked out of the room. The players sat there, partly in a daze and partly on the road to a mental destination called "Euphoria."

Then Ashley "Smash" Magnani spoke up. "How about that? Did you notice she knew us by name and knew our backgrounds? She's incredible."

The others collectively said, "That's it. She's the one."

Years later, Smash summed it up well. "Part of it was her honesty. You knew she would do the best she possibly could. You could feel her positive intensity. She had fire in her eyes."

For Megan Vrabel, the entire episode seemed surreal. She had struggled through three difficult years on the team, and Maggie, even if only for Megan's last year, represented a new beginning. Megan reflected on the interview. "The other candidates were good, very good, but Maggie started bonding with the firsties before the interview was complete. It wasn't so much that she knew basketball inside and out, or that she had obvious organizational skills. It boiled down to the fact that in half an hour I trusted her." Building and maintaining trust is a hallmark of an inspirational leader.

For that first group, the selection was unanimous—Maggie was their top choice. The same result played out for the underclass teammates as well.

"We received the scoop from the firsties. They told us about her, and we were excited to meet her," said Joanne Carelus, a cow (junior) backup guard/forward out of Saint Dominic High School, Westbury, New York. She worked as hard as anyone on the team, yet still occupied a position at the end of the bench. She realized the team recommendation would be crucial in bringing in the best possible person as coach, and time was not an ally. Of the interview, Joanne (also known as "Jo," "Jo-Jo," or "Joey") remembered, "She told us about herself, her family, and her basketball background. Of West Point, she told us, 'I want to join the experience.' That statement meant a lot to us. Coach Dixon was a breath of fresh air." Jo-Jo's sentiment was echoed by her classmates. Maggie Dixon was exactly what the doctor ordered.

Anna Wilson was impressed by Maggie's ability to talk about things in life other than basketball. "She really wanted to know about our day-to-day life."

Few people in American society have an inkling about the daily life of a cadet. Consider the following schedule:

0500–0615: Wake up. One can choose when they want to wake up, as long as they are ready to go for formation.

0650: Breakfast formation

0700: Breakfast

0730–1145: Classes. Classes are 55 minutes each, and there are 15-minute breaks in between class periods.

1205: Lunch formation/lunch

1250: Dean's Hour. Dean's Hour may just be some free time to study or get ready for other classes, or there may be a mandatory briefing or meeting to attend.

1355–1600: Classes

1610–1800: Collegiate athletics/company athletics/drill/study/workout time/unit training time. This varies with the time of year and what is going on during the week.

1800–1930: Duties and dinner. Dinners are mandatory for plebes on Mondays, Wednesdays, and Thursdays. Plebes have duties every day.

1930–2130: Evening study period. There is mandatory study for academic courses.

2130–2330: Perform duties, clean room, and free time

2330: Taps

2400: Lights out

Day in and day out, the schedule dictates every cadet's life down to the minute. It is unrelenting, and it is carved into stone. That Maggie Dixon knew and understood the cadet schedule blew the cadets away. They were stunned.

Maggie's interactions with the yearlings (sophomores) and plebes were somewhat different; they were a little reticent about asking questions, which was somewhat to be expected. The yearlings were only four months out of plebe year, and the plebes had only been at West Point for a little more than three months. The plebes were clearly in the mode of answering questions, not asking them. Maggie took the bull by the horns, telling them about her background, her love and understanding of the game, and the plans she had already prepared.

Stefanie Stone, a 5-foot-11 yearling forward, is quiet by nature. Add in the fact that she played exactly one minute the previous season, in a blowout win against Central Connecticut, and you have reasons not to ask questions. Along with Stefanie, Natalie Schmidt also logged one game, but at least she had six minutes of playing time. The other two yearlings had seen plenty of action, and they did ask some questions.

Cara Enright, a 5-foot-10 guard, was the 2004–2005 Patriot League Rookie of the Year and Patriot League Second Team selection. Hailing from Norco, California, she came in with a good billing and did not disappoint. In high school, she was elected captain of the Rosary High School basketball team for three straight years. Of many honors, including three-time pick as all-league and twice selected as all-county, Cara was selected most valuable player of the Los Angeles City Section vs. Southern Section All-Star Game. Topping everything off, she was a scholar and a member of the National Honor Society. From a West Point perspective, Enright was exactly the type of player who would flourish at a military academy. And in this case, her attending West Point would help the Army team flourish on the basketball court. Coming off an outstanding plebe season (she scored 370 points and led the team in rebounds five times), Cara wanted to be part of a championship-caliber team.

Margaree "Redd" King, a quick, tough defender, had played in 17 games the previous year and also performed well, more as a defender than an offensive player. She, too, had some questions for the candidate. She and Cara were anticipating major playing time for the upcoming season. Of course, playing time is a function of coaching decisions, not a player's wants and perceived needs.

"How would you run a practice? What would the schedule be? What offense do you run? How do you play defense?" As she had with the other players, Maggie answered each question straight up.

When the question, "How would the practice be broken down?" was asked, Maggie pulled out a sample practice schedule. It was the same one she had shown to the upper two classes. Showing it to the women, Maggie broke down practice sessions into specific time periods, not only for the players, but also the coaches. Stretching, warm-up drills (generally of a competitive nature), skill-building, offense, defense, set plays, trapping, free throws, defeating a full-court press, scrimmaging, and any other facets of being a solid basketball team were laid out as tightly as a military parade.

Following the interview, the four yearlings discussed candidate Dixon.

Stefanie Stone was thrilled at what she heard. Deep in her mind rested a single thought: *Maybe I'll get to play for more than one minute this year. Maybe.*

As for the others, one of them said, "She sounds like she really knows what she's going to do. She has a plan."

Courtney Wright excelled as a multisport player. A three-year letter winner and team captain at Santa Fe High School, she was chosen most valuable player in the New Mexico North–South All-Star Game. Courtney led all players in rebounds in the state of New Mexico her junior and senior years. In track and field, she participated in the 100m dash and 200m run, and, finally, reigned as the state champion in the javelin throw. A fierce competitor, Courtney had a solid perspective of what had just transpired.

"You're absolutely right. Did you notice her passion? I love it."

The most subdued player on the team was plebe Alex McGuire, a gifted athlete from Maryland. At that time, Alex had not asked questions; she just listened. But she was in agreement with the others that Maggie represented the "best fit" for the Army team.

Megan Evans said, "That's it. She's the spark we've been looking for. She knows more about each of us than we know about each other."

The others laughed. Spirits were sky high.

Sarah Anderson, a 6-foot-4 center from Honey Creek, Iowa, exclaimed, "She's unbelievable. I like her and I'll play hard for her."

Years later, Sarah explained the sensing of the plebes accurately.

> To all of us, Maggie was fantastic. She had great energy, passion, and excitement. But she was also very focused. We all loved her right away. We came to West Point with a different coach and, with having just gone through Beast Barracks, still felt very insecure. Right in the middle of the interview we could feel our security return. Absolutely a wondrous change to our perceived future.

Following the interviews, the team gathered as a group and discussed the candidates. Maggie was the landslide choice. Micky Mallette, the other three firsties, and a single representative for each of the lower classes took the team recommendation to Kevin Anderson.

Sarah's comments used the words "Beast Barracks." The term "Beast Barracks" has little meaning outside the academy walls. But, to every graduate (collectively known as the "Long Gray Line"), it brings back many memories, both good and not-so-good. Often shortened to simply "Beast," it is a six-week period of military training and physical fitness. It is tough training from the moment a new cadet walks into the care of upperclass cadets.

Sarah, Megan Evans, Alex McGuire, and Courtney Wright began their four-year journey on June 27, 2005. Destined for the women's basketball team, they received zero special treatment. As a matter of fact, no different than the other new cadets coming from throughout the country (and numerous arrivals from allied countries worldwide), they ran into a proverbial "buzz saw." It's the same with everyone. On reception day, known as "R-Day," the young men and women selected to attend West Point, most with their parents, siblings, and close friends, gather at Eisenhower Hall as close as possible to a specifically appointed time. Arrival times are spread out to preclude large groups waiting in long lines. It works to some degree, but the tendency is for new cadets and families to arrive early, ensuring a wait time for almost everyone. Eventually, these soon-to-be new cadets and their parents are led by an upperclass cadet into one of several staging areas in the huge auditorium, where short briefings are given by the upperclass cadre.

Once the briefing is completed, the cadet-in-charge instructs new cadets and parents, "You have 90 seconds to say goodbye." When the upperclass cadet says "90 seconds," she or he does not mean 91 seconds or 89 seconds. The cadet means 90 seconds—period. Both parents and their offspring have just received a firsthand look at life at the United States Military Academy. While the new cadets are doing their best not to cry, many of the parents, including fathers, sob openly. Certainly, almost everyone has a tear or two that can't be hidden. Their lives have changed forever.

R-day is a blur of activity. The new cadets immediately learn to address upperclassmen with four basic answers ("yes sir/ma'am," "no sir/ma'am," "no excuse ma'am/sir," and "sir/ma'am I do not understand"). They are given haircuts, measured for uniforms, issued uniforms and other military garments, and taught the basic fundamentals of marching. ("When the strike of the drum sounds, your left foot *will* be hitting the ground.") By six o'clock that evening, a parade of approximately 1,300 new cadets and more than 100 upperclassmen occurs. In spite of left feet not always hitting the ground on a drumbeat, parents are stunned by the precision of their sons and daughters. A small downer to the parade is that many of the parents can't recognize their own daughter or son. It is a truly remarkable day.

The remainder of Beast Barracks is filled with the new cadets (who are not recognized as full members of the Corps of Cadets until they successfully complete the summer training) receiving an introduction to basic rifle marksmanship (BRM) (including cleaning, disassembling, and reassembling their weapons); drill and ceremonies; class after class in military culture and customs; physical fitness; and an almost unending list of other requirements. The topics of living an honorable life and the Cadet Honor Code are introduced during Beast Barracks. Nearing the end of Beast, the entire class travels to Lake Frederick, where they bivouac for military combat training. The last night calls for a talent show put on by the plebes. The active minds and pure talent of members of the class of 2009 brought laughter and camaraderie to the entire class.

The final event is the 12-mile march, with weapon and full field pack, from Camp Buckner back to the academy. The new cadets, soon to be recognized no longer as new cadets, are in high spirits and look forward to the Acceptance Day (A-Day) parade and recognition as a full member of the Corps of Cadets. But still, the "yes ma'am, yes sir" mode of life is ever-present.

Dating as far back as the 1980s, West Point leadership has tried, unsuccessfully, to rename the summer training "Cadet Field Training (CFT)." The name "Beast Barracks" is sure to last another 200 years.

The team players gathered to select the candidate they would recommend to Anderson. It was unanimous—Coach Maggie Dixon was the team's choice. The firsties took their recommendation, along with the players' observations of Maggie's enthusiasm, candor, and ability to excel in a military environment. Micky Mallette spoke for the team, stating, "The entire team placed Coach Dixon first in order; she was the best fit for everyone."

In a discussion with Coach Marshall during the search, one of the players told him, "Coach Marshall, we love you, but we've found our coach."

Shortly after the interview process at Army was finished, Maggie attended a friend's wedding in Chicago. While there, she ran into another close friend, Nicci Hays-Fort, at that time the women's coach at Barry University in Miami, Florida. Maggie and Nicci had met during the 2004 Women's Final Four in New Orleans. The following year, both of them, along with Jana Mathis, worked the basketball camps run by Doug Bruno. As for head coaching at a place like West Point, Nicci had some background with the military environment, having been head coach at the Merchant Marine Academy, in Kings Point, New York. She knew there were vast differences between a military school and a civilian school, and wanted to make sure Maggie was on the right track. Although Nicci was proud of Maggie, she had reservations, just as Jamie Dixon had a few days before.

"Are you sure about this?" Nicci asked.

Maggie's response bore in on one simple fact: Even at this early stage of her career, the process of human bonding was well underway.

"They need me," she said.

The conversation continued the next day at a Chicago bar and restaurant. Only this time Doug Bruno joined them. He had a lot to lose were Maggie to leave DePaul University. But he also believed she could handle just about anything coming her way. The same question was repeated.

"Do you really want to do this?"

Both Doug and Nicci discerned an enthusiasm in Maggie's demeanor. Her perspective became crystal clear in her answer.

"I think I can do it. They've been overwhelmed with mass confusion, but they are up to the fight. I want to coach these women. I can make a difference."

The phone call came on October 3, 2005. Kevin Anderson told Maggie, "Maggie, I want to offer you the position as the head coach of the West Point women's basketball team." He did not have to wait long for her response.

She accepted with no hesitation.

Maggie called Jamie that night. She told him about the entire recruiting process related to West Point. The interview with the team and academy leadership had gone well. She told Jamie she was encouraged after being told recruiting would be difficult at an academy. She explained to Jamie their concerns about her understanding the constraints faced by cadets. A key factor in her perception of West Point and women's basketball was the support ODIA gave to the team. She emphasized how surprised she was to see the degree to which they backed the young women.

Then she stated the final result. "So, I accepted the offer."

Jamie, surprised and concerned, answered, "Whoa, wait a minute. Bob Knight and Mike Krzyzewski never made it to the NCAAs with Army."

Maggie replied, "But the passion and work ethic is unbeatable. They are wonderful women, and they are willing to work hard." Her tone of voice, and the zeal with which she spoke, pretty much said it all. Maggie Dixon was the USMA's seventh head coach of women's basketball.

As for Jamie, he later said, "I never thought she'd take the Army job."

On October 4, 2005, Kevin Anderson introduced Maggie as Army's new women's basketball coach. In his remarks, he emphasized her interpersonal skills in dealing with both the academy leadership and the team members, her understanding of the game, her understanding of the nature of the USMA, and her enthusiasm to join the West Point community. In his remarks, Anderson said, "She researched the team, each of the players, and the school . . . she had a plan, written out, regarding the layout of practices in the short amount of time we had to prepare for our first game, less than a month away."

Given the opportunity to make remarks, Maggie, although nervous, smiled like a kid in a candy store. She related,

> I am extremely honored to be given the opportunity to coach at West Point and to be able to work with the quality of individuals that are in our program. . . . I'm very excited about coming to a program having a foundation for success already in place, and I look forward to the challenges of bringing that success to another level.

Maggie praised Doug Bruno, a man she idolized almost as much as Jamie, adding,

> Being at DePaul, I've worked under one of the best head coaches in the country in Doug Bruno. He's taught me so much about the coaching profession and prepared me well for this opportunity. I feel that I'm ready to take over the reins of a program, and to be given this opportunity at Army is amazing.

Photographs were taken and congratulations given. Eleven days before opening practice, Margaret Mary "Maggie" Dixon took her first step as the new head coach for the West Point women's basketball team.

Game on!

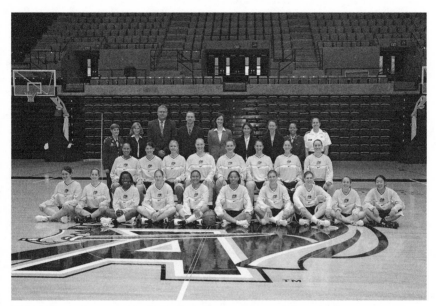

The 2005–2006 Army women's basketball team. *Army Athletics Communications*

Kevin Anderson with siblings Jamie and Maggie Dixon. *Army Athletics Communications*

The Dixon family, Julie, Marge, Maggie, Jim, and Jamie, at Maggie's introduction to the press. *Army Athletics Communications*

The GOLD team early in the season (Cara Enright, Erin Begonia, Megan Vrabel, Margaree King, Stefanie Stone. Missing: Jen Hansen). *Army Athletics Communications*

· 6 ·

First Win of the Season

$\mathscr{M}$aggie returned to West Point, her excitement obvious. Still, she knew time was not her ally. An immediate crisis confronted her in the hard, cold fact that she had not been able to bring in her own coaching staff. The timing was as bad as it could get, and she immediately faced a moral question: How honorable would it be to fire the current staff with little hope of any of them finding a new position in October? Maggie expressed her concerns early on to the leaders at ODIA.

In addition to Kevin Anderson and Gene Marshall, both of whom had been at West Point only months, there was another player in the game who had plenty of experience: Bob Beretta, the senior associate athletic director, born but a few miles north in Newburgh, New York. Being raised locally, Beretta was familiar with numerous basketball coaches, men's and women's, in New York, New Jersey, Connecticut, and surrounding areas. Among his first duties, Marshall, having been a successful women's basketball coach, had volunteered to oversee conditioning and individual workouts for the coachless team. Collectively, the women's team members knew all was not well without a formal coach at that time of the year and appreciated the efforts Marshall gave to their well-being. For his part, Beretta clearly understood the dilemma Maggie faced. It was not part of their job descriptions to personally help Maggie build a staff, but Marshall, with his women's basketball experience, vested interest in the Army women, and a seven-year tenure as director of athletics at Ramapo College in Mahwah, New Jersey, and Beretta, having been part of Division I athletics and a member of the West Point community for many years, joined forces to help find an assistant coach candidate with a strong track record.

The men entertained some interesting thoughts leading to a game plan for helping Maggie find the right person to join the team as an assistant coach. One name bubbled to the top of the list almost immediately—Dave Magarity, a former men's coach at Marist College. Unbeknownst to Magarity at the time, Gene Marshall and he had a mutual friend in Paul Lizzo, formerly the men's coach at Long Island University, who judged Magarity to be a perfect match for the needs of a young coach hired as the oncoming season loomed on the horizon. He made no bones about it, Dave Magarity needed to come to Army. Lizzo promoted Magarity to Marshall with no reservations whatsoever. The planning moved forward immediately.

A few days before the October 8 home football game between Army and Central Michigan University (CMU), the new assistant commissioner/director of men's basketball operations for the Mid-American Conference (MAC), Magarity made a call to Beretta concerning the upcoming game. In addition to standard logistics, their discussion covered a reception to be held the Friday night before the game. The reception was to be held at Eisenhower Hall. The building had a footprint of almost 193,000 square feet and served as the entertainment venue, with supporting office facilities, for the academy and the general public. Capable of holding more than 4,000 people for Broadway shows, symphonies, and various other entertainments, "Ike Hall" has additional facilities for hosting casual events. After discussing the specifics of the visit by the CMU leadership, notably the reception, Beretta mentioned that he needed to speak with Magarity but couldn't discuss the matter until they linked up at West Point. Obviously, something significant was in the wind. Magarity didn't push Beretta but was intrigued by his skirting the issue.

Magarity replied, "No problem. We can talk at the reception."

It started on Friday afternoon, October 7, during a short cruise on the Hudson River in the Supe's Boat.[1] Both Bob Beretta and Gene Marshall honed in on Dave Magarity during the cruise, letting him know West Point wanted him to join the young new coach and her staff; the recruiting effort continued at the Eisenhower Hall reception. During a lull in activities, Magarity and Beretta moved away from the gathering and found a private spot at the base of some large windows looking down on the Hudson River where it takes its sharp turn and heads directly north toward Albany. Lights from Newburgh pierced the darkness and small pockets of light shone from homes along both banks of the Hudson. The panorama spreading out in front of them, even in darkness, provided a strangely beautiful and comforting view. But they weren't there for sightseeing.

Beretta continued the discussion, stating unequivocally that Maggie Dixon was as good as they come, but she needed help from someone who had been "in the arena" of college basketball, albeit men's, for an extended period of time. He and Gene Marshall believed Dave Magarity was the final missing piece to the puzzle. The team had decent talent, wanted to be successful, and, with the right leadership, could do great things. Beretta ended the conversation with acknowledgment of Magarity having been out of coaching for a year, implying Magarity might be missing his time as a college coach. He asked if Magarity would at least be willing to speak with the new coach the following evening during dinner.

The entire experience with Beretta and Marshall was a stunning shot out of the blue. Dave, not expecting the question, processed what had been lobbed in his direction for a few seconds before responding, "Hey Bob, I've had 23 years of coaching, and every day of it has been with men." Beretta countered Magarity's statement with a repeat of his earlier statements; Magarity knew the game and had spent some two decades in Poughkeepsie, New York, with Marist. He did know a little more about West Point than other coaches, regardless of gender, in the country.

"Bob, you've caught me off guard," Magarity responded. "I don't really know what to say. Working as an assistant with a women's team was never on my radar screen. Plus, I'm now part of the MAC and have an obligation to them. Tough timing."

Beretta apologized for having kept the topic close-hold during their phone conversation. On the other hand, Magarity had already surmised the subject of basketball would eventually enter the picture.

Beretta returned to the question of having dinner with Maggie Dixon. They could meet at the Thayer Hotel. He added that her father, Jim Dixon, would be with her, and her brother was Jamie Dixon, the head coach at Pitt.

Dave Magarity stared at the trail of evening lights snaking along the Hudson, but his mind focused on women's basketball, not scenery. He saw vague visions of coaching women. He knew Jamie Dixon and respected him as both a player and coach. Dave's daughter Maureen played Division I basketball at Boston College and Marist, so he wasn't a total stranger to the coaching and nurturing of female players. But West Point cadets?

Something gnawed away inside of Magarity. It was small, but it felt good. He answered, "Sure. I'll be glad to. What time?"

Beretta recommended a meeting time of 7:00 p.m. at MacArthur's Restaurant inside the historic hotel.

"I'll be there," Magarity answered.

Saturday, October 8, unfolded poorly for the Army faithful. On an absolutely miserable, rain-drenched day, Central Michigan's 14–10 victory left Army football at 0–5. Save for the contingent of cadets suffering through a lackluster day, few fans even showed up. Misery did not visit the West Point football team in isolation; men's soccer stood at 3–8, and sprint football (player's weighing no more than 172 pounds)—a perennial powerhouse—showed a 2–2 record, featuring a 33–3 pounding at the hands of Navy. The only significant success was women's soccer, with an 8–4 record and a win over Navy. The excruciating thirst for success in athletics left the entire West Point community longing for a winner—a big winner—to rise from the ashes.

The timing of Beretta's invitation the night before proved right. Newly hired by the MAC, Dave Magarity had not moved his family to Cleveland, Ohio. They still lived in Poughkeepsie, a maximum commute of 45 minutes to and from the academy. During Magarity's 18-year tenure as head coach of Marist, the Red Foxes garnered a solid degree of success, including trips to the National Invitational Tournament and the NCAA Tournament—"March Madness." In 23 years as a head coach, he received numerous accolades and awards, including coach of the year in three different leagues. Magarity is an imposing figure, barrel-chested, standing 6-foot-5, and sporting a full head of salt-and-pepper hair. During the Vietnam War, he enlisted in the U.S. Navy and served with the Seabees. Importantly, he knew basketball as well as any coach in the business.

Growing up in Philadelphia, he played football and basketball in high school and at St. Francis University in Loretto, Pennsylvania, lettering in both sports. His basketball coaching career started at St. Francis, where, following an apprenticeship as an assistant coach, he was selected to lead the Red Flash as the youngest coach—at the age of 27—of a Division I team. Magarity coached the Marist men's team against Army fairly often. He did not know a great deal about West Point and its idiosyncrasies, but—other than Duke's Mike Krzyzewski (West Point class of 1969) and former Army coach Bobby Knight—he really did know more than most other coaches in the nation.

That night, Dave and Maggie, along with Maggie's father, Jim Dixon, had dinner at MacArthur's Restaurant in the Thayer Hotel. Not a wallflower by any means, Jim Dixon had plenty to say and contributed much to the evening. The meal turned from a quick "hello–goodbye" to a more than three-hour marathon during which time Dave and the Dixons developed a mutual understanding of the possibilities his joining the coaching staff could bring to the team. The evening started with a degree of understandable uneasiness, but once they settled in on a mutually agreeable topic, the night moved into a smooth, natural flow. The catalyst was former Iona coach Pat Kennedy. Maggie and Dave knew and had great respect for Kennedy. As an assistant coach, Dave learned much from head coach Kennedy at Iona. Kennedy later coached the DePaul University men's team while Maggie Dixon was an assistant for Bruno with the DePaul women's team. They saw Kennedy as an honorable man with a gifted knowledge of the game and respect for people of all walks of life. The conversation concerning Pat Kennedy provided the segue into Dave having a role with the Army women's basketball team.

They discussed many other topics, including mutual friends and her brother Jamie's success at the University of Pittsburgh. It was clear from the beginning that Maggie loved and respected Jamie.

Once the evening turned to the discussion of Magarity serving as an assistant coach to a 28-year-old first-year women's coach, both were crystal clear in their concerns for the relationship between the two of them and the process needed for them to work as a team within a team. For Maggie, she needed someone who had been around college coaching, regardless of gender, to keep her going in the right direction; Dave had concerns as to whether she was facing pressure to hire a "father figure."

He told her, "Look, I know we don't know each other that well and I feel a little awkward. If someone is trying to force you to hire me, just say it. I want you to know I have a very good job with the MAC. I don't want to be in a position where someone is shoving me down your throat." Magarity leaned forward just a bit and continued. "But, that being said, going back to coaching wouldn't be a problem for me since I had done that once before in my career. My background has been with men's teams, not women's."

Concerning Magarity's joining the coaching staff, Maggie had done her research. She told Dave, "Well, my sense is we could work together very well. I have talked to other people and studied your coaching history; quite honestly, your background tells me this could be a good fit."

At this crucial juncture, Dave's sense of well-being exploded. The embryonic sense of wellness was in full bloom. Deep down, Dave was excited. So was Maggie.

By dinner's conclusion, Maggie had tendered the position to Dave. She added a major incentive. "If you do decide to join the team, your position would be as associate head coach. I'm one, you're two, and everyone else is three."

Her "associate head coach" offer resonated well with him. With 23 years as a Division I coach and the only person being recruited by Maggie, he was pleased with her understanding of where people belonged in the coaching staff pecking order.

Years later, he reflected on their dinner conversation. "At dinner that night I had the feeling she felt very comfortable about me. I'm sure she had done some research. It was also clear someone had obviously approached her about my coaching with her as soon as she was selected head coach. When I left, I had a lot to think about."

As for the team, it had been a rough year. The players knew little of what was really going on until Maggie accepted West Point's offer. The only thing they had known was confusion.

So, there it was. Less than four hours after meeting Maggie Dixon, Dave Magarity looked squarely into the eyes of a change in life. It was his turn to step up to the plate. His decision involved the entire Magarity family—and the clock was ticking away.

Dave's first call was to his daughter, Maureen, then an assistant coach at Fairfield University. If he wanted an easy out, he called the wrong person. "I think it's great. It will be something you will really enjoy. You're a coach, not an administrator," she declared.

In his mind and in his heart, Dave Magarity completely agreed with Maureen. Reflecting on their discussion, he said,

> Quite frankly, I had been out of coaching long enough to know it was something I really missed. I was open to maybe getting back into it if the right situation presented itself. I had not ever thought seriously about coaching women until that weekend. My own daughter knew more about me than I did.

He talked to his wife Rita—a woman also knowing more about him than he did. Rita was a perfect sounding board. So were some others he called— who presented both pros and cons. He received the following comments: "Are you crazy?" "You gotta do what you gotta do." "You've got to do what's best for your family." Dave felt bad about resigning from his position with the MAC. He had been offered a fair financial package and liked the people, but he simply wasn't passionate about the job. He missed coaching.

The final impetus came from Rita. She asked, "So, instead of moving to Cleveland, you'll just have the short commute to West Point?" Rita knew exactly what was going on inside of Dave's head. He wanted to coach, regardless of gender. Rita loved the idea of staying in the Lower Hudson Valley. Rita's final question was straightforward, "Do you really want to do it?"

The answer? "Yes."

"Then enjoy saying 'yes,' and we'll stay in New York," Rita replied.

Dave Magarity found excitement in returning to coaching with a young woman exactly half his age; he called the next day with his decision.

"I'm all in."

With Magarity accepting the associate head coach position, Maggie Dixon, at the age of 28, scored her first win of the season. Dave had one last mission. On Sunday, he drove to Cleveland to inform his boss, Rick Chrystl, commissioner of the MAC, of his decision. He needed to do it face-to-face.

Of Carrots, Sticks, and Slates

$\mathcal{A}$nna Wilson lay in a bed at Keller Army Community Hospital (KACH), located at the northern end of the academy grounds, recovering from surgery to remove a cyst on her neck. The phone rang. Still groggy from medication and sleep, she answered with a slight slur. "Cadet Wilson."

"Hi Anna," said the voice on the other end of the line. "This is Maggie Dixon. I just wanted to let you know I'll be your coach. Let me know if there is anything I can do for you while you're in the hospital."

No differently than was the case with the other players, Maggie was Anna's first choice. The phone call confirmed choosing Maggie was a brilliant move by the team; without touching a basketball, Anna's season started out far above any positive expectations she may have harbored. She felt a surge of energy course through her body. She couldn't wait to get out of the hospital and on to the basketball court. Anna, far more alert than two minutes earlier, lay back in her bed and smiled at the ceiling. She could not go back to sleep or stop smiling.

The ink on Maggie's contract had barely dried when she gathered the team together and set the ground rules for how she and the other coaches would make decisions about playing time. In doing so, she gave each player a shot at the gold ring. Maggie told the team point-blank, "Whether you started every game or played very seldom does not matter. Whatever happened last year is ancient history." She went on to say, "I have not even looked at films of your games." The players zeroed in on every word the new coach offered. There would be no prima donnas on the team; playing time would be based on performance in practices and games, and each player had a fresh start at the beginning of practice every day. The coaches would determine the roster each week, and the team would be broken into three performance-related groups. She ended with the statement, "Each of you is starting with a clean slate."

In the earliest days of her tenure as coach, Maggie partitioned her time among learning more of the nuances of West Point and its leaders, getting to know the players, and building a coherent plan for the coaching staff and administrators. Collectively, Maggie did indeed represent a "huge breath of fresh air." She listened to the individual concerns, both on and off the court, of the 18 women she needed to coach, mentor, and inspire. She treated the managers—Tatiana Blanc, Alexys Myers, Juliana Regis, and Samantha Smay—with the same respect she gave to the players.

By the end of her first 10 days as coach of the West Point women's basketball team, Maggie had conversed with most of the players and dealt with many human concerns: Sarah Anderson was afraid she was going to fail physical education because of push-ups and sit-ups on the Army Physical Fitness Test (APFT) and the agility skills and upper-body strength required in a course known as "Military Movement"; Megan Evans had the same concerns; Jo-Jo Carelus wanted to know what it would take for her to get more playing time; and Stefanie Stone was thrilled at being told by Maggie that she would be a personal "project" for the season. Unbeknownst to Stone at the time, the "project" would end up paying huge dividends for the team and her. Firsties Adie Payne and Micky Mallette were told not to worry about previous injuries and that they were part and parcel of the team's future; Megan Vrabel's confusion about her role on the team melted with the knowledge she would be a key player—but she had to practice and play well. Smash Magnani appreciated the candor Maggie brought to the table. All four firsties received an uplifting message—Maggie would not throw any firstie under the bus even if they received limited playing time. Each player, from firstie to the lowly plebe, would be a participant in any successes or any failures during the next five months. Maggie Dixon knew if their successes were to outweigh their failures, she must inspire each player.

As for Adie Payne, prior to the first game of the season she had the opportunity to experience the inspirational nature of the new coach. Payne recalled a specific event remembered to this day. During a preseason one-on-one practice with Coach Dixon, Adie found herself frustrated with the fact that her coach was playing better than Adie. In Adie's eyes, her previous injuries, including three shoulder surgeries for tearing an AC joint, labrum, and subscapular muscle, had wreaked havoc on her basketball skills. The injuries had caused Adie to miss her entire cow year. Adie had no intention of giving up on basketball, but she knew she was in her last year at the academy, had lost more of her skill set than she wanted, and was a complete unknown to her new coach. She was prepared for the worst—being let go.

Maggie, who had not known of Adie's existence only 39 days earlier, would not let Adie feel sorry for herself. According to Adie,

> Coach was beating me like a drum, and I was getting very frustrated. I just didn't have my "A" game in terms of shooting and dribbling. Coach Dixon pulled me to the side of the court, looked me directly in the eyes, and told me, "I know you're a great player. Just keep at it. Don't put your head down." Coach Dixon's words—especially "I know you're a great player"—remain with me to this day. I'm so glad to carry that moment for the rest of my life.

Whether she knew it or not, Adie Payne was speaking to legacy.

By the time Maggie met one-on-one with Erin Begonia, she knew quite a bit about the possible starter at point guard. Erin certainly depicted the virtue of tenacity. Growing up in Bellflower, California, she loved the game as soon as she was big enough to pick up a basketball. She lettered all four years at Bishop Amat High School, receiving numerous honors, notably three tournament MVP picks during her senior year. At 5-foot-7, Erin was both tough and quick; she looked forward to the upcoming West Point challenge. Unfortunately, Beast Barracks wreaked havoc on her body.

As part of the physical fitness component of Beast Barracks and an escape from the unfamiliar military regimen, new cadets are given an opportunity to "blow off steam" in what is known as "Mass Athletics." Most of the new cadets engage in such sports as soccer, softball, and flag football. Those new cadets destined to play a Division I sport, and those who wanted to try walking on to a team, gathered in separate formations and were taken to a practice venue to play their particular sport. During a basketball scrimmage, Erin suffered a serious knee injury. The injury represented a harbinger of things to come; her journey at West Point would not be easy.

Erin reflected on the incident.

> I landed straight down on my right knee. I heard a loud pop and felt the immediate pain. Lying on the floor, I knew my knee was done. I also thought my career in the military was just as done. The doctors told me I would never play basketball again, let alone be able to stick it out the rest of my time at West Point. At that point, I was ready to pack my bags and go home, but I had already become close to those who would be my teammates, and they are the ones who convinced me to stay.

Erin's injury kept her off the court her plebe year and the first half of her yearling year. The team trainer, Sara Wiskow, worked at length with

Erin during her rehabilitation. It was a long haul, but the Wiskow–Begonia team succeeded in bringing Erin back to near-full strength. It took major efforts to convince the doctors to approve Erin's return, but she finally received the "go-ahead" to play. On January 21, 2005, Erin returned to the competitive court. She played six minutes in the game against American University, taking two 3-point shots, hitting one of them. For Erin, those six minutes were magical.

In Maggie's office, just two days before the official season started, Erin learned from her new coach that she would start as point guard. Maggie told her the decision was based on Erin's performance in the practices.

In response, all Erin could do was to suck in a huge breath, let it out, and answer, "Yes Ma'am. I'll be ready."

Said Maggie, "Please call me coach. Don't make me feel too old." Both coach and player smiled.

"How's everything else going?" Maggie asked.

"Fine coach," Erin replied. "All's under control."

But Erin's first grade in English composition was not fine at all. There's a fundamental canon for academic performance at the USMA: No cadet will graduate without the ability to communicate with others at every level of society. But Erin, who had performed well in mathematics and science—even well enough to select systems management as her major—did feel she would be able to overcome her shaky academic start.

Maggie reminded Erin that starting required performance in every facet of the game.

"Absolutely coach. I wouldn't have it any other way."

Maggie and Erin talked a little bit more about Erin's family back in California and the spirit of the basketball team. Erin's family was fine, the team's morale was growing every day, and Erin Begonia was the happiest person on the planet.

Erin's interaction with Maggie Dixon paralleled that of the other 17 players. Before the season started, a new Army team was being born.

Maggie had the wisdom to use the experience and immediate loyalty of Dave Magarity. She also knew she needed to trust the staff "as is." Her key assistants included Magarity, Kelly Flahive (BS in mathematics, College of Staten Island), Craig Madzinski (BS in marketing, Saint Leo University, Florida), Mary Kurnat (BS in English, Mount Saint Mary College, Newburgh, New York), and Jennifer Fleming (BSE from USMA, MS in software systems engineering from George Mason University, Virginia). Throughout the season, Fleming provided not only excellent basketball know-how, but also as a graduate of West Point, mentored Coach Dixon and the younger cadets from a "cadet/athlete" perspective. She had "been there, done that." As for the current coaching staff, Dave Magarity was the only coach brought on board by Maggie Dixon.

Maggie and Dave hit it off from the start. He remembered the early days of their coaching relationship, relating,

> I could tell immediately Maggie was going to be a fine coach. She had a presence, a feel for the game, and unvarnished enthusiasm for finding out just what the team could accomplish. I certainly planned to support her in any way I could, but I was not about to attempt to be her mentor. Jamie Dixon would always hold the title of "mentor and confidant."

Along with those qualities, Maggie Dixon held true to her word and made it clear to all the coaches that Dave Magarity would be the associate head coach; as such, he was second in command. She meant what she said, and, for his part, Dave never violated his most basic principle: Maggie Dixon would always be the head coach.

Immediately following her selection, Maggie held a coaches' meeting almost every day. The process for each daily meeting was pretty much set in concrete. Discussions included scouting reports (once the season was underway), the conduct of practice for each given day, observations related to the players and how they were progressing, and the structure of the day's practice. On some days, Dave Magarity felt he was scratching his fingernails on a blackboard. Still, he knew he made a vow of loyalty, and he planned to stick with it.

In 2005, West Point did not have the luxury of separate practice facilities for the men and women. Arvin Gymnasium, a massive athletic facility housing three swimming pools, boxing and wrestling rooms, a gymnastics facility, squash and handball courts, and multiple basketball courts, was scheduled for use every day by the main cadet population. Both the men and women's basketball teams had to share practice times in Christl Arena. From the start, Dave and Maggie understood practice on some days would not start until 6:00 p.m., not a good situation given the demands of the West Point academic program.

Before Maggie arrived on campus as the new coach, Mary Kurnat had settled into the position as director of women's basketball operations. She developed a strong working relationship with her counterpart on the men's side of the house. The team captain for two years at Mount Saint Mary College in Newburgh, Kurnat served as an assistant coach at her alma mater until being hired by Army in mid-2005. She wasted little time in mastering her duties related to team travel, academic progress of players, on-campus recruiting visits, and scheduling facilities. For as good as it already was, the relationship between both teams improved quickly as Maggie sought out the advice, support, and friendship of the men's coach, Jim Crews. Crews captained the undefeated Indiana University national championship team of 1976; he coached Evansville for 17 years before taking over the reins at Army in 2002. Crews and Magarity represented more than 40 years of basketball experience, albeit in the men's domain. The Magarity–Crews experience, coupled with her time under the tutelage of Doug Bruno at DePaul, represented a gold mine of potential for Maggie.

The practice schedule situation dictated the structure of daily practices. Unlike most schools in the American landscape, studying integral calculus following a grinding two-hour early evening practice can be an unclimbable mountain to a cadet struggling with academics. The rule "Every cadet an athlete, every athlete a cadet." Just as those cadets who do not play Division I sports must participate in some form of athletics, the players on a major sport team must take a minimum 40-course curriculum; most will end up taking as many as 43 courses. When Maggie Dixon and Dave Magarity walked in the door, majors being taken by their players in the upper three classes included Spanish (3), human and regional geography, the American legal system (3), systems management, French, life science, civil engineering (2), and human geography. The women of West Point basketball did not choose easy rows to hoe. The plebes had yet to choose a major.

Maggie conducted her normal meeting on the first day of practice. Most follow-on meetings were held after lunch. She initiated a system where each coach had the okay to state any opinion he or she might have, and recommend ideas about the conduct of practice or traits of any of the players. Before the meeting, Maggie would have a "straw" plan of each coach's responsibility for each of his or her segments of practice; specifics would be hammered out during the meeting. Beyond the sequence of practice events, several questions needed to be answered early on. Were the players in shape? Had they improved in various skills in the preseason? How would the newcomers meld with the team? Can we start looking for a starter at each position? Granted, the coaching staff had seen the players at Christl Arena a great deal as they stretched, practiced free throws and their most polished personal shots, and played some pickup ball; however, for the most part, they were still very much a work in progress. So now it started: During the early meetings, a plan for the conduct of practice was nailed down.

Dave Magarity had his problems with the meetings, but he never discarded his loyalty to the head coach. Of the meetings, he said,

> I was not used to the daily "do practice" meetings as an entire staff. I didn't do that. I would meet with assistants, but not like Maggie. She had a specific plan for each coach. We would meet and construct practice, and the

meeting could last from 30 minutes to two hours. We didn't have as much time once practice started.

He paused a moment before continuing. "I want to say this in the right way, but some of the meetings would be a little tedious because there were a lot of voices involved. I felt it wasn't for me, but, if this is what Maggie wanted, so be it. I wasn't confrontational, but some of the meetings were very painful."

As for practices, they ended up being exactly as advertised by Maggie. She had planning and organizational skills reaching far beyond the norm. Following stretching, the next 10 minutes involved the entire team in a drill with the purpose of getting everyone "into the zone." Next, the team was broken down into position work. A great deal of guard–forward work was assigned to Jen Fleming. Captain of the 1989–1990 basketball team (and the 1990 softball team), she was the recipient of the Army Athletic Association Award for leadership and achievement. She knew basketball fundamentals "to a T" and still "had game." Kelly Flahive and Craig Madzinski also had specific duties at specific times. Practices worked with military precision, certainly a positive situation given the institution where they coached. The assistant coaches were also tasked with scouting upcoming opponents. Throughout time, flare screens (used mostly to open up the floor for three-point shots) and back screens were emphasized. Practice also involved setting up (and getting used to) specific plays for coming out of a timeout.

At one of the first practices, Maggie gathered the team around her at midcourt.

She looked at the players one at a time and told them to go back to their lockers and return to positions along the midcourt line, "with your playbooks."

The dreaded playbook.

Courtney Wright, in her first year at the academy, thought negatively to herself, *I can't believe we're going to use a playbook this year. I can't keep up with my studies as it is.* Wright, once at the top of the pyramid in New Mexico high school sports, was disappointed and a little fearful that some of the negatives of recent seasons would still be wreaking havoc on the team.

The upperclass players winced but did as told.

Once the players reassembled on the line, Maggie walked to the side of the court and grabbed a trash barrel. She returned, saying, "Put the playbooks in here. We're going to be a different team."

Maggie, the eternal optimist, had an uncommon ability to make practices downright fun. From the first day, practices had a flow to them; the players sensed that Maggie's knowledge of the game and her ability to get more and more progress out of each practice were going to lead them where they had not been before. During stretching, the players would engage in light bantering, some of it basketball and some of it related to random topics. Next, the warmup drills relied on the competitive spirit of each player. One of the favorites was Knockout.

Simple in scope but intense in execution, Knockout is a case of each player competing against 17 opponents—the rest of the team. The players line up single file behind the three-point line, with the first two each holding a basketball. On the coach's whistle, the first player takes a three-point shot. If she makes the three-pointer, she's made it to the next round. She grabs the ball and passes it to player number three. After passing the ball to player number three, she runs to the end of the line for the start of round two. If she misses her three-point shot, things get competitive. Player number two, as the next shooter, puts up a three-pointer. If it goes in before player number one has rebounded her miss and made a basket, then player number one has been "knocked out." If player number two misses her shot, she is in jeopardy of being knocked out by player number three. And so it goes until only one player remains. The cheers rise in waves as the number of competitors dwindles. The game proved enlightening for the coaching staff in that the coaches saw firsthand who were the best shooters when facing pressure. The odds-on favorites were Cara Enright, Jen Hansen, Erin Begonia, Alex McGuire, and Anna Wilson, but there were occasions in which Adie Payne, Jo-Jo Carelus, Megan Evans, Megan Ennenga, or any of the other players would end up the winner. Maggie's enthusiasm during these types of drills was infectious to players, coaches, and bystanders alike. The team was working hard, extremely hard, and enjoying every minute of it.

Following the warmup drill, the team was broken into groups according to each player's dominant position. Anderson, Busch, Evans, Schmidt, Vrabel, and Wright spent plenty of time in the low post. Stone started out as a pure forward but, in short order, found herself playing in the low post as well. The pure guards were Begonia, Carelus, Ennenga, Hansen, King, Mallette, McGuire, Payne, and Wilson. Enright and Magnani could handle either the guard or forward position. Although easy to Maggie, the players had a hard time following the flow of a new offense. The players switched positions in response to Maggie's instructions for the offense she was bringing from De-Paul. Defensive practice included man-to-man and zone defenses, as well as working on the full-court press and defending out-of-bounds plays. Regardless of a player's size, blocking out for rebounds and defending against passes down low were emphasized.

Maggie also started working with the other coaches to design out-of-bounds plays. Her intention was to have a play for every timeout or out-of-bounds play. Once the different facets of a practice were completed, Coach Maggie let the team scrimmage for a good 20 to 25 minutes. Scrimmaging has always been the most enjoyable part of any practice. In a place like West Point, scrimmaging relieved personal stress more than anything else in the players' daily lives. The Army team was getting stronger and better. But, lest someone think it was all fun and games, each practice featured extensive physical demand. At the end of practice, the young women were ready to slow down and relax in their barracks. Of course, academics always loomed for the next day.

Life above the Hudson River was, indeed, changing. In her quest to inspire each player to reach her potential, Maggie Dixon, in her conduct of practices, had served up a huge carrot at the beginning of the new season. The slate really had been wiped clean.

Every Thursday before an Army football game, a sports buffet luncheon is held at the West Point Club, the perfect venue with a ballroom overlooking the Hudson River. Capable of holding several hundred people, it welcomes fans from the community, mostly the officers and civilians from the staff and faculty, along with their spouses, to join in on an enjoyable, spirited occasion. The superintendent, high-ranking officers, and the rank and file cheer in response to the cheerleaders and cadet pep band. The football coach, Bobby Ross in this instance, gives a few light comments, to be followed with a team update, a scouting report on the upcoming opponent, and, as a highlight of the event, words from one of the key players. The young cadet player usually speaks with enough comedic content to elicit an enthusiastic response from the crowd. It is a lot of fun.

With Army struggling through most of the 2005 football campaign, the "hope springs eternal" cohort was fired up. The possibility for a season-ending turnaround, including a victory against Navy, seemed possible. The week before, the Army football team had pulled off a colossal upset by defeating the Air Force Academy, 27–24, in Colorado Springs, Colorado. At the Army versus University of Massachusetts spirit luncheon of Thursday, November 10, one of the attendees was Brigadier General (ret.) Maureen LeBoeuf. For most of her career, LeBoeuf represented one-half of a "dual-military" couple. She and her husband, Colonel (ret.) Joe LeBoeuf, were ardent supporters of everything Army.

Joe graduated from the academy in 1974, and served as deputy head of the Department of Behavioral Sciences and Leadership. Like Micky Mallette, Joe had been a regimental commander during his firstie year. Maureen, a 1976 St. Bonaventure graduate, spent 28 years in the Army, a significant part of the time as a helicopter pilot in the United States and Europe. She had excelled in every assignment. A former Division I swimmer holding a doctorate from the University of Georgia, she was selected as the first female full professor and department head at the USMA; in her case, the relevant department was the Department of Physical Education. By virtue of her position, she was the 26th person since the academy's founding in 1802 and the first woman ever to wear the title "Master of the Sword." Recently retired, she returned to West Point on business and, almost by habit, attended the luncheon.

With a plate of buffet food in hand, Maureen found an empty chair at one of the tables. Next to it sat a young, well-dressed woman.

"Excuse me. Is this seat taken?" she asked, looking down at the vacant chair next to the young woman.

"No. Please join me."

Maureen sat down, and the two women smiled and shook hands.

"I'm Maggie Dixon." Maggie had a bright, genuine smile.

"I'm Maureen LeBoeuf."

Maureen asked, "So, Maggie Dixon, what do you do here at West Point?"

With genuine enthusiasm, Maggie answered, "I'm the new head women's basketball coach."

Maureen made the connection immediately. "I should have remembered. I've heard about you. Speaking of the women, while at the academy, I served several years as OR for the women's basketball team."

Maggie replied, "I know. I've read all about you."

Maggie's response caught Maureen a little off guard. It said something to Maureen about the thoroughness Maggie gave to learning the full nature of West Point.

For the next several minutes the two women settled into a comfortable discussion, focused on basketball and life at West Point. By the time the pep band and cheerleaders arrived, both knew a lot more about one another and Maggie had added to her knowledge base of what made West Point tick. Maureen gave Maggie an in-depth view of the responsibilities of an OR, both in-season and out-of-season. In Maureen LeBoeuf's words, "Used correctly, an OR can be a major 'value added' to any team at the academy."

At program's end, Maureen, more than satisfied West Point had made a solid selection for the new women's coach, pulled out a business card. "I enjoyed our talk immensely. If I can be of any help to you at all, give me a call. It can be challenging at West Point if you didn't graduate from here. If you want a safe person to talk to, I am that person. Call me anytime. I really mean it."

"I will. I appreciate your offer," Maggie responded.

They smiled, shook hands one more time, and went their separate ways. Maggie held on to the card, realizing she may have a need for it. What Maggie did not know was she would be making that call in less than two months.

Maggie and Dave spent hours alone discussing the strengths and weaknesses of the different players. From Dave's perspective, the team had a core of solid players, but he felt uneasy about how deep their bench would be. Cara Enright proved herself during plebe year and could handle either guard or small forward. Megan Vrabel, a 6-foot-1 senior, appeared to have more talent than her previous seasons indicated. Micky Mallette had solid skills but still suffered from major medical problems. Ranging from a kidney stone to a back injury, Mallette was in and out of KACH and Walter Reed Medical Center; practice always exacerbated her condition, mostly her back. Bottom line: Micky Mallette had problems galore.

Firstie Ashley "Smash" Magnani played in all 28 games the previous season, averaging a little more than seven minutes a game. She was not a major scorer but played defense with wild abandon. Rounding out the firsties was Adie Payne. She played well as a plebe but never fully recovered from her shoulder injuries. Cow Erin Begonia came off an injury to play in 12 contests during 2004–2005; the jury was out on her postinjury potential, but she had been penciled in as point guard. Cow Jen Hansen, a 5-foot-10 guard from Seminole, Florida, had plenty of talent and could be counted on for additional outside scoring. Cow Jo-Jo Carelus played for short periods in 22 games and had scored eight points; she was a defender, an assignment she clearly enjoyed. Cow Jillian Busch, a 6-foot-2 forward, performed well in 24 games during the 2004–2005 season.

Yearling Margaree "Redd" King played in 17 games as a plebe. Her scoring was sporadic, but Redd was very athletic and a hard-nosed defender. Not gifted in size, 5-foot-5 Anna Wilson played well during her plebe year, seeing playing time in 27 games, with 12 starts to her credit. A good shooter and afraid of no one, she could play either point or shooting guard. Yearlings Natalie Schmidt and Stefanie Stone were the two players who, during the previous year's campaign, were so far down the bench neither thought any of the coaches knew their names. Both women considered significant playing time an unreachable fantasy. The five plebes, Sarah Anderson, Megan Ennenga, Megan Evans, Alex McGuire, and Courtney Wright, had strong resumes coming out of high school but were unknowns to Maggie and Dave.

Essentially, deciding who would start was yet to be determined.

Maggie's intention from the beginning involved breaking the 18 players into three groups—the "Gold" team, the "Black" team, and the "White" team. The Gold team consisted of the basic starters; the Black team would move back and forth in terms of how much playing time each player would receive; and the White team would be the scout team, providing opposing team offense and defense schemes to both the Gold and Black teams. Given the amount of effort shown by the players on the White team, they would find themselves receiving some playing time throughout the year. The White team's firstie, Adie Payne, became known as "White-6." The number "6" on Adie's title comes from general military communications protocol in which the commander of a military organization is given the identifier of "6." In radio communications, if a unit has a call sign like "Bird Dog," the commander of the unit is called "Bird Dog-6." Initially, Payne was discouraged by being on the White team. Still, she accepted her role and remained upbeat. She didn't know it at the time, but she would play in 20 of the 31 games.

Dave Magarity had no major problems with Maggie's plan. He certainly knew she would approach coaching differently than he did. Each person— and, thus, each coach—is unique. She decided to bring the full coaching staff into the decision-making process in determining which players would be assigned to each of the three teams. At one of the early meetings at which the coaches were trying to rank the 18 players to select a starting five for the opening game of the season, Magarity read off his list—and Cara Enright was listed in the middle of the pack. The other coaches laughed in amazement.

"What? Are you out of your mind? She's the best player on the team." The retort was unanimous.

"Look," Magarity answered, "she didn't practice well this week. Until she is more consistent in both practice and in games, she'll be on my Black team list."

Maggie grasped his comment. Neither Maggie nor Dave wanted to select the teams based on history. They were interested in the present. Magarity explained it as, "All Maggie and I cared about was how the kids played *now*. And that's how Stefanie Stone and Megan Vrabel got their chance to show the coaches what they could bring to the team."

Although players would migrate up and down depending on performance, the form of the team became relatively stable. The general breakout for the beginning of the season was as follows:

GOLD: Begonia—Enright—Hansen—Stone—Vrabel
BLACK: Anderson—Evans—King—Mallette—Magnani—Mc-
    Guire—Wilson
WHITE: Busch—Carelus—Ennenga—Payne—Schmidt—Wright

As mentioned earlier, Maggie offered a huge carrot in the form of scrimmaging. The players enjoyed coming to practice because they enjoyed playing the game. Too many coaches don't understand the need for kids at all levels of sports to experience the "fun" in fundamentals. Offense, defense, rebounding, passing, dribbling, blocking out, running plays, free throws, out-of-bounds plays, steals, and on and on. All of those skills are needed. But, regardless of the level of play for any given sport, let the players also play the game. That means let them scrimmage. A major strength, almost a God-given strength Maggie possessed was her organizational and planning skills. Each practice ran like clockwork, with each player and each coach having a specific task to accomplish and place to be at any given time. Even Dave Magarity, who never could fully buy into the length of some of the daily meetings, confessed, "Talk about organizational skill, that's Maggie Dixon."

Maggie's relationship with her players turned out to be exactly what each player wanted. Humor was one of her unheralded trademarks. The ups and downs of the unfolding season did not outwardly bother Maggie. She knew the team was a matter of "work in progress." She and Dave both had concerns for progress on offense. Maggie was the optimist; Dave was the pessimist.

He mentioned early on, "Maggie, they're just not getting the inverted flex offense."

Maggie's response was positive but clearly in opposition. "But they will. They're smart kids and just need to run it enough times to be second nature to them. Hang in there with me."

So, he did.

For all the concern about offense, other facets of the game—man-to-man defense, rebounding, executing set plays, and free-throw shooting—were doing better than expected. With each practice the all-around confidence of the team would rise. Maggie's intention to play as many players as possible was certainly about as big a carrot as a nonstarter could ask for. She made no promises she did not intend to keep. Her interactions with both the team as a whole and each individual player signaled a "sisterhood" of the highest order. She firmly believed basketball should be fun when it's time to have fun and serious when it's time to get down to work. But for the players to experience both fun and seriousness at the same time requires a rare breed of coach. On the "funny" side of events, consider then-plebe Sarah Anderson.

The daughter of Dennis and Mary Anderson, Sarah Ella Anderson and her brother Jacob grew up in Honey Creek, Iowa. Anderson lettered in basketball all four years at Tri-Center High School. Her team was the 2005 Iowa State Class 2-A runner-up. She made the state tournament all-star team in 2005. At 6-foot-4, she played center and garnered third-team All-State honors in Class 2-A. Academically strong, she was selected to the All-State Academic Team every year in high school. She also lettered three times in both volleyball and track. Sarah topped it off by serving as president of the National Honor Society at Tri-Center High School. Finally, Sarah Anderson has a sense of humor.

The most basic drill in basketball, used in elementary schools, middle schools, high schools, and beyond throughout the country, is the "passing while moving" drill. It simply requires two players running downcourt passing the ball back and forth until reaching the far end of the court, then returning in the same manner, except, on the return, the passes are bounce passes. Army used the drill during game warmups and at the beginning of almost every practice. During one early season practice, Redd King and Sarah Anderson comprised the first pair on the baseline. Starting at the north end of the court, they moved down the eastern half of the court chest passing back and forth. They weren't trying to set any records, but Redd and Sarah's passes were leading one another significantly to improve their passing and catching skills. Redd was going down the court along an imaginary line halfway between the sideline and the imaginary line from basket to basket. Sarah was moving down the sideline. What no one seemed to notice was that Sarah had started to drift outside of the sideline—and was closing in on the ball cart with significant speed.

Wham!

Sarah's left leg hit the end of the ball cart like an 18-wheeler T-boning a Volkswagen. Following the laws of physics and the rule of conservation of momentum, the ball cart flipped and flew off toward the team benches; the balls were catapulted throughout the arena; two wheels were knocked off and slid partially across the floor; the rods that held the basketballs were no longer connected to the cart; and, last but not least, Sarah went headfirst into the floor. Her remembrance years later was, "I looked like I was sliding into home plate."

Sarah, slightly battered, bruised, and confused, slowly looked up from her sprawled position on the floor. She shook her head to remove cobwebs, gathered her faculties, and sheepishly looked around in an attempt to know what had just happened. She needed to know the reaction of Coach Dixon, the other coaches, and the players. Sarah recalled, "Still sprawled out on the floor, I looked directly at Coach Maggie. She was crouched down at about center court looking at me. She was laughing hysterically."

After a few seconds, Maggie composed herself enough to walk over to Sarah. She asked, "Are you okay?"

At that point, Sarah and her coach both started laughing—with Sarah still on the floor.

Then Sarah noticed Redd.

Her eyes were open wide, and she was holding our ball. Her expression looked to me like, "Oh, my!" We were all laughing, especially when we investigated the damage to the ball cart. My teammates helped pick up the balls from all over the gym. None of my teammates gave me a hard time for being a goofy plebe; we all had our moments, plebe or not. I guess the "cart incident" just so happened to be my time in the spotlight.

We laughed the whole practice. It was like we couldn't stop. Even Coach Dixon and the other coaches joined in laughing out loud at a 6-foot-4 player taking out a ball cart. From that time on, we never started that specific drill without moving the ball cart well to the side and ensuring there was plenty of room on the court.

One other plus for the entire women's team came in the form of the relationship between Maggie and Dave. Micky Mallette was the oldest player, at 22 years of age (only six years younger than Maggie), and Sarah Anderson was the youngest of the plebes, at 18 years. While many youngsters in this age bracket are still immature, each player could see that Maggie Dixon and Dave Magarity made an absolutely superb coaching team.

Jo-Jo Carelus said, "Coach Magarity had a big role in the team's success. They really worked well together."

Megan Evans saw the synergy between the two as, "She and Dave Magarity were a great team. They were on the same page 99 percent of the time. They were dynamic. It took very little time for me, even as a plebe, to feel part of the team."

Prior to the first game of the season, Maggie Dixon had given the team plenty of carrots, some very small sticks, and clean slates for everyone. For the expanded team—managers, players, and coaches—morale and expectations blew through the roof. The season could not begin soon enough.

· 8 ·

The Unfolding Season

$\mathcal{G}$ray granite exteriors of medieval-looking buildings, shortened daylight hours of the coming winter, the sea of gray uniforms, and looming academic requirements couple with the pale, barren winter landscape to produce what is cynically known among the Corps of Cadets as "Gloom Period." From early November to mid-April, bristling winds, cold rain, sleet, and eventually snow dominate cadet life. Dreams of spring float unceasing in the minds of the cadets as they perform their military, athletic, and academic duties. One of the few escapes is participating in or witnessing athletic events at the academy. Unfortunately, women's basketball games required a significant walk to Holleder Center (named after Donald Holleder, class of 1956, All-American football player, killed in Vietnam on October 17, 1967), the main facility holding both Christl Arena and the hockey venue, named in honor of brothers Joseph S. Tate, '41, and Frederic H. S. Tate, '42, who served as pilots in World War II and were killed when their planes were shot down.

For the Army women to draw larger than the historically small crowds— and using the word *crowd* might be an overstatement—required significant improvement by the team. The challenge seemed overwhelming. But, unbeknownst at the time, no one really knew Maggie Dixon.

Starting with the first game of the year, Maggie introduced the team to the "Ten Programmatic Keys to Success in every game we play." She had seen the success Doug Bruno achieved with them during the five years she coached at DePaul. Using a subheading of "THESE ARE ARMY'S PRO-GRAMMATIC UNIVERSALS," 10 principles for success were highlighted using "WE WILL" statements. Her intent was to focus the team on how they would approach each facet of each game, to build camaraderie and trust, and, as remembered by one of the players, "to pump us up." When the team returned to the locker room for the final pep talk/plan for the game, the list—either framed (at home) or in a document protector (on road trips)—was always placed randomly on some of the team chairs. The 10 UNIVERSALS (shown as written) were as follows:

1. WE WILL get off to a quick and efficient start through high-energy Army ball defense and running game.
2. WE WILL totally outdefend our opponent through clean, constant (every player, every trip), purposeful (every constantly changing function requires a different purpose), communicative, swarming, in your face Army ball defense!
3. WE WILL totally control our defensive glass! No shot, bad shot, and always one shot!
4. WE WILL execute our running game and finish!
5. WE WILL take care of our rock. Make the simple pass, measure twice, pass once, hit the open woman! Pass with your eyes! Strong with every touch.
6. WE WILL understand tempo and execute our offense in the half court. WE WILL have the smarts, the competitive WILL to win, the competitive hate to lose, and the TRUST in each other to FINISH each game. Every shot is a pass to an Army player!
7. WE WILL totally dominate the offensive glass! Every shot is a pass to an Army player!
8. WE WILL finish all close games! Every game has a life of its own. WE WILL have the smarts, the competitive WILL to win, the competitive hate to lose, and the TRUST in each other to FINISH each game.
9. WE WILL make adversity our best friend. WE WILL always strive to play the perfect game; but since we are not perfect WE WILL embrace any adversity that comes our way and turn adversity into a positive.
10. WE WILL, when we inadvertently, infrequently, and unintentionally mess up, forgive ourselves and forgive each other! GO ARMY!!!!!

At first, the players felt a little awkward with reading each statement. But, as time went on, the players became more comfortable with the notion of using the list as a springboard to winning. It did not take long for the players to get pumped up while reading a statement. Maggie's favorite was the first sentence of the ninth Universal, "WE WILL make adversity our best friend." She absolutely believed there were few limits to what her team could achieve. While a win against the UConn Huskies would be nearly impossible, she knew the team had far more potential than advertised. And the season had not even started.

On November 11, 2005, Army did play an exhibition game against Pace University. Cara Enright may not have impressed Dave Magarity in practices, but she certainly came to play during games. Against Pace she poured in 30 points, including 14 of 17 from the charity stripe. Erin Begonia also turned in a strong performance, going 6-for-7 from the field and hitting both of her three-point attempts. Just as important, the team outrebounded Pace by a 37–29 margin. One week later, Army would begin the official season against the Coast Guard Academy. Among the starters: Stefanie Stone.

In a form of serendipity, members of the sprint football team became available to help. Sprint football is the same as regular football, the main difference being the players cannot weigh more than 172 pounds. Players are weighed four days and two days before a game. The young men are all solid high school players who are either too small or do not quite have the talent of the members of the Army Division I team. Given that the 2005 sprint football season ended on November 4, the men were required to aggressively continue with weight training and conditioning throughout the remainder of the semester. For some who played basketball in high school, they jumped at Maggie Dixon's invitation to work with the White team.

The men, strong, quick, and talented, worked in tandem with the White team women to provide stiff competition to both the Black team and Gold team. As such, a strong bond developed between the sprint football team and the women's basketball team. Throughout the remainder of the season, the women could count on support from the men on the practice court and in the stands. Over time, some members of the Division I team joined in supporting the women. Conversely, the members of the women's team often sat in the front row of the stands at Army's home football games. It's the way college sports should be.

During the one-week interlude between the exhibition game on November 11 and the opening game of the season, Maggie devoted a majority of the time to the inverted flex offense she brought from DePaul University. Coach Doug Bruno had used the inverted flex and enjoyed great success with it. It only made sense to bring it with her to West Point. The flex offense requires each player to be capable of taking any position. The key components of the flex offense are an ability for continuous movement, good passing and screening, and the ability to shoot a soft jumper from around the "elbow" at either end of the free-throw line or take an inside shot beneath the basket. The inverted flex is a variation, albeit slightly more complicated, of the standard flex offense.

Dave Magarity saw problems with the inverted flex. The team simply did not have a sense of "flow" for it. They were too mechanical and somewhat timid in its execution. Again, the military requirements, scheduling of practice facilities, and academic load demanded of each cadet took a toll on a player's ability to absorb what she needed to know. It wasn't coming naturally for them. Maggie, the eternal optimist, was confident the team would be able to grasp the inverted flex early in the season. And so, the 2005–2006 Army women's basketball season began.

On November 18, 2005, Army opened the season at home against the Coast Guard Academy. At 103–51, it was a total blowout in favor of the Cadets. Army was taller, faster, stronger, and simply more talented than the determined Coast Guard team. If the game had the potential to gauge where the team stood in terms of both offense and defense, it was lost in the constant rotation of players in and out of the game. The Army staff did not want to run up the score, but it is difficult to tell the last player or two on the roster not to do her best. Nonstarters accounted for 63 points. By the end of the game, every player on the Army team, 18 in all, had logged at least quadruple the playing time Stefanie Stone played the entire previous year. As for Stefanie, she played for 10 minutes; it would have been more had the substitutions not been so plentiful. Things really were changing at West Point—especially for Stefanie Stone.

Less than 48 hours later, St. John's visited West Point. The coaches and players learned quickly that the team had a long way to go. St. John's won, 74–55. They outrebounded Army 36–26, shot 50 percent from the field, and took care of the ball. The cadets turned over the ball 21 times. Army's offense did not click, and the team paid for the loss of a high-functioning offense.

In the locker room following the game, Maggie remained upbeat. "What we just faced out there is known as adversity." Maggie told the team that they did have the makings of a good team and not to get down on themselves. She ended with a call to fixing some things the next day. "Bring it in." The team gathered in a tight circle, cheered "WE WILL!" and headed for the showers.

Dave had talked about the inverted flex for a good while. Maggie told him she would consider changing to the simpler motion offense if they had to.

Maggie had given her honest opinion of the team's potential if only given enough time. "They're smart, smart, players. I don't think the inverted flex is too much for them. Might take a few more practices," she said.

Dave answered directly, but not with rancor.

I think the inverted flex is beyond them. I agree they're smart, but they just don't have the basketball IQ as other teams. They may have been solid high school players, but they all had other activities in high school. They're all achievers in areas not basketball. Say what you want, but it's my opinion we need to scrap it. We don't have rhythm with it. The kids aren't playing instinctively. Instead, we're overthinking everything. Almost every possession ends with us confused as the shot clock is about to expire.

Maggie replied, "So, what's the solution? Can we change in midstream?"

Dave was clear in his answer. "Yes, we can. All we're doing is simplifying what we've already worked on. I think we should make the change to motion soon."

Maggie pondered his recommendation before replying. "Tell you what. We'll start the Manhattan game with the inverted flex and see how it goes. If we need to change, we'll make the change." For Maggie, moving away from the inverted flex was not much different than moving away from a close friend. But she did understand what Dave was saying.

The Northern Arizona Tournament in Flagstaff had some downs and ups. Against Manhattan College, Army struggled again with the inverted flex offense and found themselves down at halftime by nine points, at 30–39. Army's field-goal shooting came in at a woeful 30 percent in the first half, including 0–4 from three-point range. The team had 18 turnovers for the game and let Manhattan win the rebounding war. Cara Enright had a poor shooting night, going 6-for-19 from the field, 2-for-9 from behind the arc, and a subpar 5-for-10 from the charity stripe. The one bright spot came at halftime, with Maggie asking Dave if he felt they needed to move away from the inverted flex to the motion offense. Dave was clear. "Yes, we can."

She walked up in front of the team and told them the inverted flex did not work. When she told them to change to the standard motion offense, every player on the team was both relieved and encouraged. Said another way, the players were thrilled. They could start playing their game.

The second half of the game was not good enough to win the game, with Manhattan taking a 72–65 victory, but Army did outscore the Jaspers and felt much more comfortable with the motion offense.

The next morning, the Army team conducted a walk-through with the simpler motion offense and planned to take advantage of continual passing, screening, or cutting. They looked eagerly to a system of flare screens, back screens, and down screens. For better or worse, the results would speak volumes about the team's future.

Army met California State University, Fullerton, late in the afternoon. The Titans forged ahead on the shooting of Amber Pruitt and Charlee Underwood, much of it from inside. At halftime, the score stood at 44–37 in favor of Cal State. Despite the seven-point lag in the game, Army had played much better than the day before against Manhattan. Maggie kept enforcing the conviction that the motion offense was beginning to work. Good passing and proper screens were needed, but the requirement for each player to play all five positions was eliminated. The Army players felt comfortable playing a similar offense to what they had played in high school. She wanted them to run right at Cal State with the motion offense. She emphasized cross-screening with the post. Three out, two in was the recipe. Relax. The switch to a motion offense worked—and worked well in the second half. One basket at a time, Army began grinding its way back from a 10-point deficit at the 19:10 mark in the second half to a six-point lead with 2:20 left in the game. The final score: Army 80, Cal State Fullerton 79. The game proved a watershed event in West Point women's basketball history. The remainder of the season would find the Army women's team running the motion offense.

The Cal State game also told a story about Coach Maggie Dixon's loyalty to the team. In a game decided by one point, 12 players participated. Although talent did drop off after the first seven or eight players, she had enough confidence in her players to let them play.

In the Cal State game, nonstarting players came through with a collective 28 points and 16 rebounds. In only seven minutes, Jillian Busch went 3-for-3 from the field and pulled down four rebounds, including two at the offensive end of the court. Adding to Busch's effort, plebe Alex McGuire logged 23 minutes of playing time, scored eight points, handed out four assists, and added a steal. McGuire showed her potential to handle the point if needed. Seven weeks later, McGuire would be in a starting role.

Stefanie Stone remembered the transition to motion quite clearly. She almost had a double-double in the Cal State game, scoring 11 points (her first game with a double figure in scoring) and taking down nine rebounds, three of which were offensive. She remembered Coach Dixon switching the offense early in the season. As to how she perceived progress for the team, Stone put it in her own words:

> We didn't start off with a great record that year. We had ups and downs. You could tell by our wins and losses that early on we were still trying to figure each other out. It's hard when you had a certain rhythm from the year before and you're now working with different players and having a new coaching staff. I remember in one of the early games we had drawn up all these plays, and it was just not working. She told us, "This is not working—we're going to make it simpler." She drew up a simple play that high school teams would play. It's the motion offense. But it brought out more freedom for us to move comfortably. The fact that she could do that

on the spur of the moment was a turning point for our season. The new, simpler plays did allow for more freedom and movement on the court.

The ebb and flow of the unfolding season did not outwardly bother Maggie. It would have been nice to win the majority of their games, but Maggie and Dave both knew such an outcome would be miraculous. They saw that the team was a "work in progress." It would take a while, but they were absolutely certain the team to take the court in March would be a far better one than they were seeing now. As they worked with the rest of the coaching staff, progress was seen in the offense, the man-to-man defense, and the all-around confidence of the team. Her playing as many players as possible was certainly her goal in every game and further strengthened the camaraderie of the team. Maggie's decision to accept Dave Magarity's recommendation to abandon the inverted flex offense played well with the team.

Another aspect of her decision-making became obvious to the players. Beginning at the start of practice, they saw Coach Dixon and Coach Magarity working as a dynamic team. Any doubts that Maggie's willingness to listen to other points of view wilted away when Maggie went with Dave's recommendation to drop the inverted flex in favor of a motion offense.

In terms of pure leadership, Maggie Dixon had communication skills far superior to the average individual. Two stories, one fortunate and one not so fortunate, highlight her skill—and her ability to be responsible when problems occur.

First, consider the plight of Megan Vrabel. From Stafford, Virginia, Megan played for Stafford High School and had compiled a strong record. She lettered three years in both basketball and volleyball, was selected to the 2002 Virginia State All-Star Game, and, topping it all off, received all-academic awards each season. She had a decent plebe year, playing in 22 games, starting once, and scoring a total of 31 points. As a yearling, Megan played in 28 games, starting eight times and scoring 90 points. Her cow year, she played less than her plebe year and scored but 51 points. To put it in her own words, "I had a rocky three years. I just did not have the support I needed. Cow year was really bad. I worked so hard and did not get the playing time. I lost some heart for the game."

Initially, Micky Mallette was elected captain of the team. A few days later, both Maggie and Dave asked for Megan to come to the coach's office. Megan remembers thinking, "Why me? Why alone? What have I done?"

Megan was in for a surprise. She knocked on the office door and was invited in to join both coaches. She soon found out the discussion would not be about Megan's minuses, but her plusses. Both Maggie and Dave talked to her about how hard they had seen her work.

Maggie wanted to give her more responsibility. She said, "We want to make you a co-captain."

In Megan's own words, "What a grand shock to know they believed in me. I was totally motivated and invigorated about life on and off the court. It meant so much."

She continued, "Micky was a guard and I was a forward. Unfortunately, Micky had a back injury [along with other medical problems] and did not play as much as she wanted. We got along great."

As a side note, even though Megan and Micky were the official captains, the firsties worked together so well that Smash Magnani and Adie Payne were quickly brought into the fold as co-captains. The underclasses respected each of the firsties.

Megan started playing better, with one complication. When she had a subpar game, she would get down on herself—to the point that Maggie noticed. She brought Megan into her office and spoke about leadership. She told Megan, "Being a leader doesn't mean leading with points and rebounds. It means doing what needs to be done to benefit the team the most."

Maggie ended the conversation with a simple statement, certainly appropriate for the West Point team of 2005–2006. "There are no superstars."

Megan was mesmerized by their discussion.

The following not-so-fortunate story about communication says a lot about learning from a mistake.

Jo-Jo Carelus would never become a starter, but no one on the team outworked her on the basketball court. Although she remained on the White team, Jo-Jo thought she would be on the travel squad to Arizona based on her performance and work ethic. When she arrived at Christl Arena the day before the trip and found out she was not on the trip roster, Jo-Jo was devastated. When she asked Maggie why, her coach's response was, "Jo-Jo, not making the trip was based on performance."

Jo-Jo, in tears, replied, "But coach, you didn't tell me I was not on the trip section."

Maggie realized her communication had not been good.

"I'm sorry Jo-Jo, I simply was not clear in my messages. I apologize." It is rare for a college coach to apologize to a player. Coach Maggie Dixon did the right thing.

Jo-Jo did not make that trip, but the overall outcome of their interaction was terrific. Maggie vowed to communicate better to every player. She also took a hard look at how Jo-Jo was perceived by the team. She saw that the team viewed Jo-Jo as "bringing a lot to the table." On Jo-Jo's part came the realization that, for as hard as she thought she was working, she could actually leave more on the floor every day. It was, after all, up to Jo-Jo to make the travel roster.

Jo-Jo made every trip from that point onward.

By the time snow arrived in the Lower Hudson Valley, Maggie had endeared herself to each player and the team's support staff in different ways, but always with a strong bond between coach and player, coach and staff, and Coach Maggie and anyone else. Those in her immediate sphere of influence always seemed to feel better about life after spending some time with Maggie. Consider this story.

One winter evening, plebes Sarah Anderson, the Iowan, and Megan Ennenga, from Minnesota, decided to do what no respectable Southerner would ever consider—go for a run in the snow. They bundled themselves in as many layers of clothing as possible and headed out the door to run through, around, and over the piles of snow. The West Point campus is exceptionally beautiful when snow falls gently on the granite buildings, The Plain, and the statues of heroes from the Long Gray Line. Lampposts line the roads, and at night they highlight the patterns of vehicular and pedestrian travel, and, on a snowy night, give life to each falling snowflake. The blanket of snow quieted the evening sounds to a whisper.

As 18 years of age, the two young ladies were no strangers to snow; both were visual people and enjoyed themselves immensely while breathing in their surroundings. Having run farther than they originally planned, the two plebes found themselves looking at an on-post home with a small sign reading, "Coach Dixon." On a brash whim, that is, not following standard protocol, they rang the doorbell, their intention being to just say hello. Maggie answered the bell.

Looking at the two pink-cheeked, hard-breathing young ladies, she opened the door wide and asked them to please come in.

She told them to put their sweaters on a couch and continued, "How about a tour of the coach's home?" Both Megan and Sarah were thrilled by their coach's hospitality. Given Maggie's demanding schedule, she had not been able to complete her moving-in tasks. The house was neat in some places and a little disheveled in others. Sarah and Megan looked at each other and smiled when they noticed a basketball game playing on the television. Maggie stopped in the kitchen and put a pot of chicken noodle soup on the stove and then continued with her tour. In a spare room were several kids' tents and a toy Maggie explained were for her niece. Shannon Iwalani (Hawaiian for "Heavenly Bird") Dixon, almost two, captured Maggie's heart from the start. After all, Maggie was Shannon's godmother. Her nephew, Jack Connor Dixon, a little less than two years Shannon's senior, was also a pretty good stealer of hearts. Maggie was thrilled at even being asked to be Shannon's godmother. Shannon and Jack were magical, and Maggie wanted to make sure they would always want to return time and time again to visit Aunt Maggie.

With a big smile, Maggie turned back toward the kitchen. They could smell the chicken soup on the stove.

Maggie brought out some drinks and healthy snacks, and then made another trip to retrieve two bowls of the piping hot soup.

She began talking. Sarah and Megan were mesmerized at having this wonderful woman as their coach.

Maggie used her comments about Shannon and Jack as an introduction to talking about her entire family in general. She loved every one of them. Her stories of her niece and nephew, big brother Jamie, older sister Julie, and parents, Jim and Marge, along with aunts, uncles, cousins, and others, warmed both Sarah and Megan as much, if not more, than the bowls of hot soup. Other basketball and nonbasketball stories followed. Both Megan and Sarah asked themselves, "How can I possibly be so lucky?"

Sarah and Megan had expected a short visit to say hello to their coach; the visit lasted well beyond what they had intended, bringing them danger-ously close to the "witching hour." If a cadet is not back in his or her room by the time requirement, punishment of some sort will be waiting. And both Sarah and Erin still had homework looming on the horizon. Maggie solved the problem—she drove Sarah and Megan back to the barracks.

On occasion, Maggie enjoyed participating in the physical component of basketball. Rebounding was a point of emphasis and a source of physical fitness. At 5-foot-11, she was tough on the boards—but she did have one shortcoming. One of the rebounding drills called for a shot to be intention-ally missed to make the players fight for possession of the ball. Unfortunately, Maggie seemed to make more shots than she missed. It didn't take long for the introduction of a broom to make sure the ball would not go through the net. Finally, an investment was made to buy a basketball hoop cover. Made of plastic, the bottom portion was cone-shaped to easily fit into the hoop. The top of the cover was anything but flat. It angled in multiple directions, not only providing a covering over the basket, but also ensuring an unpredictable flight path of the ball as it bounced off of the hoop cover.

Speaking of Maggie's being "tough on the boards," it was during one of her early participatory events that the team realized another facet of their coach's makeup. By the time Maggie arrived on campus as the new coach, the coaching staff had taken the coaches' practice uniforms. She solved the short-term problem by just wearing sweats to the early practices. During one of the rebounding drills, Maggie leaped high in the air to grab the ball. Her leap pulled her shirt up just enough to reveal the symbol of her proud heritage—a small tattoo of a shamrock resting on her hip. Inside the shamrock were the letters "MD."

One of the players saw it and blurted out, "Coach, is that a tattoo?" The entire team buzzed with amazement. Their coach certainly was a modern-day woman. She responded with no embarrassment and a proclamation of being proud to be Irish—thus, the shamrock.

During short breaks in practice, players gossiped about their "hip lady with the hip tattoo."

Each player loved her just a little more.

The final game of November was played against the Great Danes of Albany. At two wins and two losses, Albany looked very much like Army on the stat sheets. But on this night, Army performed like a well-oiled machine, winning 72–60. Army allowed Tani Thrower a whopping 26 points but held the other players below double-digits. Offensively, scoring for the West Point women was balanced, with Cara Enright and Stefanie Stone scoring 14 and 13 points, respectively. Possibly the brightest spot came in having only 14 turnovers. Thirteen players got into the game, and 10 of those scored. That positive personal statistic paralleled the team's positive accuracy from the free-throw line, going 14-for-15. The atmosphere, having fed off of the team's solid performance, was festive to say the least. Maggie congratulated the team for its performance, particularly the small number of turnovers and superb free-throw shooting.

And so it started. The players looked forward to basketball practice every day. They did work hard, but each player had fun. Practice was an escape from the regimented life of a West Point cadet. Coach Maggie Dixon, with less than two months coaching a team of future military leaders, had forged a winning record. Step by step, and as recollected by Smash Magnani, Maggie Dixon was "teaching us how to fly."

· *9* ·

Adversity

The entire month of December and the first week in January saw a queue of uninvited guests joining the team, all in the form of adversity. If ever Maggie were to hang her hat on a single "WE WILL" statement, the odds-on favorite would be the one she thought most important—the first sentence of UNIVERSAL #9: "WE WILL make adversity our best friend." In addition to personal, academic, and military adversities hammering away at the individual players, the team's play roamed back and forth between hot and cold. Athletically, December turned out to be the definition of adversity.

The women visited Cornell University on December 2, 2005. Cornell, coming into the game at 1–4, handed the Army women an unexpected 64–61 setback. Army's woes came in a cascade of mediocre play. One could hardly smile at a field goal percentage of 39.4, miserable 3-for-17 shooting from three-point range, a subpar 6–11 mark from the free-throw line, and the embarrassment of losing the rebound war 49–43. Still, at the end of the game, Army had one final opportunity to tie the game. But, adversity reigned again—Jen Hansen, arguably the best long-range shooter on the team, lofted a soft shot from just behind the three-point line. The ball hit the rim and bounced off. They knew it was a badly played game. Maggie let the team know they had not played well and were capable of far better performances for the rest of the season. They just needed to get their act together on an everyday basis. They needed to hone in on the "WE WILL" statements.

Morale at that time was understandably low. The women gave a game away to Cornell, and the football team suffered a lopsided loss to Navy, 42–23. As she often did, Maggie called Gene Marshall the following day. She called him a lot; he was a sounding board for her to take away some of the pressure.

71

In telling the story, Marshall recalled their conversation. "I couldn't hear her very well because of the remaining noise in the bowels of Franklin Financial Field, so I moved outside. We must have talked for 40 minutes. By the time we ended, I was ice-cold, freezing in Philadelphia."

The following Monday afternoon, Marshall walked into Christl Arena just as the players were stretching. They respected him and were grateful to him for his support and individual mentoring during the chaotic days of September.

"Hi coach."

He responded with, "Team, I want your undivided attention." All eyes focused on Marshall as he chided them for playing so poorly. Then he added, "You know she's brand new here; you know how much respect you have for her. Well, let her see it firsthand. Since she's new to West Point, you need to protect her. And Friday night you did not protect her one bit."

He walked away.

A closer-than-expected game was played against the Central Connecticut University Blue Devils on December 6. For the second game in a row, Army shot poorly from beyond the arc (3-for-13), allowed the Blue Devils to win the rebound war, shot less than 40 percent from the field, and had a mediocre day from the free-throw line. The one positive was Cara Enright hitting a jump shot with a little more than seven seconds remaining in the game. The final stood at Army 65, Central Connecticut 63.

The next two games were losses against Princeton and Baylor. Princeton was a solid team, destined for a 21–7 record (12–2 for the Ivy League regular season) and a solid favorite to win. But Army's losing by 21 points did not sit well with any of the coaches—or, for that matter, the players. Twenty-five turnovers dictated the outcome of the 73–52 drubbing.

The defending national champion Baylor Bears visited West Point on December 19. The Army women played their hearts out against the Bears. An astounding statistic was Army's ability to more than hold their own on rebounding, losing the battle of the boards to the Bears by a slim 43–39 margin. But once again, field goal percentage fell below 40 percent, and three-pointers came in at an abysmal 3-for-19 (15.8 percent). The final score ended at 85–68, Baylor.

A 67–54 win against an overmatched Gardner-Webb Bulldog team provided a small breather for Army to lick its wounds. A key positive in the game came in the form of numbers: Fourteen players received playing time on the court, 12 of them ending up in the scoring column.

Someone, probably Sherri Abbey-Nowatzki, used great wisdom in scheduling the game against the Air Force Academy Falcons. The 10 days between Gardner-Webb and Air Force were precious. Gone was the intricate inverted flex offense. Flare and back screens were the order of the practice day. Additional time was given to set plays for coming out of timeouts. Maggie also added a small extra portion of time for scrimmaging. Best of all, although Maggie ran intense practices, she also displayed wisdom in giving the women the opportunity to catch up on some of their courses. Maggie understood term-end projects and papers piled up on cadets during the month of December. She gave them several days with no practice at all. Her purpose was to relieve the players from much of the stress caused by the juxtaposition of basketball and its demands with the academy and its demands. Little pockets of stress were ubiquitous.

With one exception, the break in her well-planned practices did pay handsome dividends on the academic front. It should have paid off athletically as well, but external factors diminished the team for the next, very important game. Almost to the same degree as the Navy games, Army wanted to take it to the Air Force. The 60–53 home victory in 2004 tasted mighty good; everyone felt the Army team would repeat as the winner again in 2005. But it was not to be. The flight to Colorado Springs was longer than anticipated. The team took up lodging at the United States Olympic Training Center. No basketballs were made available for pregame practice. Road trips tend to be fairly simple operations. The trip to Colorado was an exception—nothing seemed to go smoothly, most notably the game. It was decided in the first half when the Falcons went on a 19–2 run and eventually ended Army's agony with a final score of Air Force 73, Army 61. Of all the statistics from the disaster, rebounding was the most startling. Air Force pulled down 48 rebounds to Army's 25. Army suffered a total beatdown at the hands of another service academy.

Two days following the Air Force debacle, the University of Connecticut Huskies loomed on the horizon. To play against the Huskies, West Point needed to accommodate the UConn game schedule. With the schedule set before her arrival, Maggie made the decision to fly directly from Colorado Springs to Hartford, Connecticut. The team arrived on December 30, with the game set for noon on New Year's Eve. At that point, feelings among the players ran the gamut from "this is still better than last year," to "we can do better," to "we're letting our coaches down."

Not long after dinner, Maggie called a team meeting in her room. It turned out differently than the players expected. Maggie spoke little about the UConn team or, for that matter, basketball. Of UConn, she did say, "Get your heads up. We're going to have some fun tomorrow." With that, she opened up a huge banquet of ice cream with every fixing possible. She smiled and walked out the door.

One player, who certainly enjoyed sweets, held her bowl up and opined, "That coach, she's unbelievable. She always knows how to pick us up and point us in the right direction." With that, she dug her spoon into a small mound of chocolate ice cream. When everything settled and the players returned to their rooms, their last collective conscious thoughts centered on playing so well they would upset the mighty Huskies in the Hartford Civic Center. Could it happen? Maybe. Who knows?

On January 17, 1978, the University of Connecticut men's basketball team upset the University of Massachusetts men's basketball team, 56–49, in front of 4,746 exuberant fans at the Hartford Civic Center. Early the next morning, under the weight of a heavy, wet snow, the entire roof collapsed. Had the progressive structural failure, brought about by incorrect design, failure to build according to the drawings, and shoddy construction, occurred several hours earlier, several hundred, possibly thousands, of people would have been killed and injured. One thing was certain—it was a spectacular collapse.

In terms of basketball, the virtual roof of the new Hartford Civic Center collapsed again—but this time it collapsed on top of the Army team. The final score was a crushing 39-point loss. To be fair to the Army team, the story of the loss to UConn is hidden in the chronology of the game.

Following Maggie's guidance, the West Point women ran directly at the Huskies.

Cara Enright opened the scoring with a short jumper: Army 2, UConn 0. For the first five minutes, the Army women held their own at 8–8, until the Huskies' Renee Montgomery hit a three-pointer. The UConn team slowly built a lead. Ann Strother's three-pointer brought the score to 35–20 with 6:08 to go in the first half. The Army team did not fold. With Cara Enright leading the way, the West Point women fought their way to a single-digit deficit. A three-pointer by Barbara Turner with 13 seconds to go finished the scoring for the first half. Score: 42–30.

Emotions in the locker room were high. Maggie, Dave Magarity, and the assistant coaches went over the statistics from the first half and felt good about the rebounds (22) and a decent shooting percentage (46.4 percent). Another positive sign was Army's total lack of being intimidated by the UConn players. For that matter, the players were doing exactly what Coach Dixon instructed them to do—play hard and have fun. The Army team played a first half better than the score indicated. They decided to continue putting emphasis on man-to-man defense and the simpler motion offense they had been running since the end of November.

For a little more than four minutes of the second half, Army played UConn on even terms. When Cara Enright hit two free throws less than five minutes into the second half, the deficit stood at 46–37, less than double digits. Could a miracle be in the making?

No.

At the 16:36 mark of the second half, Megan Vrabel hit a short jumper. During the next 10 minutes and 30 seconds, Army scored exactly one field goal (by Cara Enright). At the end of the drought, the only mystery was the final score. The second half statistics were not good. Army shot 20 percent from the field and 1-for-6 from long distance, and pulled down an unsatisfactory 12 rebounds. Final score: UConn 85, Army 46.

It was not the time to berate the team. They gave it all they had—and that was all that Maggie wanted. She told them that the final score did not matter. UConn was a sure contender for the national championship. Maggie was pleased with the team's effort and the fact that Army played unafraid.

While Maggie was genuinely upbeat about the team, there weren't a whole lot of other believers. Kevin Anderson, speaking but a few words, let Dave Magarity know the final score was unacceptable. Anderson's comments irritated Magarity to no end. He thought to himself, "Do you even know who it was we were playing?" Fortunately for everyone concerned, Magarity bit his lip and let the subject fall away. He had to put his efforts into the next three days and Army's home game against the Gaels of Iona College.

New problems, far more important than a basketball game, came to the forefront.

The first bad news came from the English Department. Erin Begonia failed English composition. She would play her last game on January 7. Erin and Coach Dixon met before the next game against Holy Cross. Erin's staying at the academy was in jeopardy. During the previous three decades, the academic program had changed greatly in content but not in the rigid rules of survival. It remains unforgiving. Erin needed to pass the course or she would not graduate. In the past (pre-1976), if a cadet failed any course, the standing protocol allowed him (the academy was all-male at the time) to take a "turn out" examination. If he passed, he would continue as a cadet. If he failed, he was removed (known as being "found"). In rare circumstances (e.g., General George Patton, class of 1909), a cadet would be "turned back" and could join the class behind his original class. By 2006, a cadet had the opportunity to make up the course, either during the following semester or an intense, three-week summer period, always at the expense of his or her personal leave time. The three-week hiatus from enjoying freedom away from the academy was affectionately called "STAP," standing for "Summer Term Academic Program."

Maggie Dixon and Erin Begonia met in Maggie's office.

Maggie received word of Erin's failure prior to their meeting. She sat down in a chair next to a small couch where Erin sat. Erin remembers Maggie's concern for her as a student was her priority, not as a basketball player. Erin said Maggie was about as positive as one could be given the circumstances.

> She told me, "You've been a solid leader on the floor, and I appreciate the effort you have put into our team. But failing a course, especially in a subjective area such as English Composition, leaves me no choice but to pull you from the starting roster. You won't be able to make it for away games. I need you to graduate more than to lead the team. I'm not going to sacrifice your future for the sake of playing basketball."

Erin continued to speak of the meeting. She remembered the encounter clearly and recalled her words as well. "I told Coach Dixon, 'I'm sorry Coach. My professor didn't like my writing style. In his eyes, I just couldn't write to his satisfaction. He's not a bad guy, he just doesn't like my writing. And I'm sorry I let you down.'" At the time, Erin hoped somehow her troubles would go away. They didn't.

Erin will never forget the conversation.

> I remember her smiling first and then telling me, "First of all, you didn't let me down. You just misplaced your priorities a bit too much. But we can't take that back. It's adversity in a new form. But I have a plan—I always have a plan." Then Coach Dixon told me of my future with basketball. "I'm going to move you to the White team. Although you're on academic probation, you're still required to participate in physical fitness. You will still play every day we're practicing in Christl Arena. I expect you to spend the bulk of any free time on academics. On team White you'll play the role of the best guard of our next opponent. You won't be traveling, but you will drive the starters crazy."

Knowing the ruling of the Academic Board would not be official until the following week, Maggie gave Erin one last carrot. Maggie would start Erin against Colgate.

Erin knew she could still help the team get better and handled the academic demotion with class.

In an interview in 2016, Erin put her relationship with Maggie in perspective.

> Coach Dixon was so good with me during those days, making me forget my knee injury from the year before and priming me for the 2005–2006 season. Everything came naturally to me, and I loved just being on the court

with Coach Dixon. I loved working on all my skills, whether it be dribbling, passing, or shooting. Unfortunately, my major focus at the academy became basketball to the detriment of my studies. That's what caused me to slip on my academics. When I failed the English course, she did what she had to do, but she gave me all the reason I needed to stay on the team.

The other side of the coin was plebe Alex McGuire. Hailing from a military tradition, Alex might have been divinely tabbed to attend West Point. Her father Steve, class of 1981, and two uncles were graduates of the academy. Both of her grandfathers were military, one a World War II veteran and the other a retired air force master sergeant. Two great-grandfathers, Francis (Bud) McGuire and Charles McDermott, both served during World War I. By the time Alex could walk and talk, playing sports of any kind dominated her life. Glenn Graham of the *Baltimore Sun* wrote the following story:

> By the time she was four, Alex McGuire had already made clear her love for sports. She was perfectly content watching a football game with her father, Steve—at least until halftime. That's when the two would head for the backyard, where she would run the different pass plays she'd seen on TV.
> It was her mother, Mellanie, however, who took early note of what would become young McGuire's favorite sport—basketball. "Her brother is four years younger than her, and she wanted to name him Michael Jordan. I thought about that: How would she know who Michael Jordan was at 4?"[1]

Alex excelled in the high school girl's athletic program. As a kid, she played basketball, soccer, softball, and volleyball. By high school, Alex had pared it down to basketball and volleyball. It was basketball where she excelled, scoring 2,086 points in high school. The highlight of her high school athletic career rested with her taking the Arundel High School basketball team to the 2004 Maryland 4-A State Championship, featuring a final game in which she scored 34 points, including all 18 attempts from the free-throw line. She was selected as the Anne Arundel County Player of the Year for three straight years and the *Baltimore Sun*'s All-Metro Player of the Year once. She topped it off with also being selected as a member of the *Washington Post*'s "All-Met" team.

Alex is a private person, quiet by nature. But send her to an athletic venue of any type and you will encounter a tiger.

When she was 11 years old, Alex went for a drive with her parents somewhere in the Baltimore area. She saw a marquee advertising the Baltimore Ravens Regional Punt, Pass, and Kick (PPK) competition. Her parents noticed her focusing on the words; they asked her, "Want to give it a try?"

Her answer was a resounding "yes."

A natural athlete, she did not sit on her prior laurels; she practiced all three events as much as she could. She had a mother and father supportive of her dreams of success. The outcome of their support proved prophetic—Alex McGuire won the Baltimore Region PPK as an 11-year-old; she also won at the ages of 12, 13, and 14. As an 11-year-old, Alex competed at the American Football Conference (AFC) championship game between the New York Jets and the Jacksonville Jaguars, and, as a 13-year-old, at the Oakland Raiders–Miami Dolphins divisional round game. Alex ended up fourth in both events. During her competition as a 13-year-old, she did well in the punt and the pass. But, as she recalled the scene, "I shanked the kick."

As tough as it was losing Erin Begonia for the rest of the season, moving Alex McGuire up to a starting role would not hurt the team. Team White welcomed Begonia into the fold with open arms.

As an aside, McGuire would not be an academic risk, having accumulated a high school GPA of 4.1.

Adversity comes in many other forms as well. For Erin Begonia, it was a matter of the written word forcing her to step down from the starting guard position. For the women's basketball team, it was having more losses than wins early in the season. For some members of the team, adversity came in the form of injuries or medical conditions. But for Sarah Anderson and Megan Evans, it was the law of physics. Arriving for Beast Barracks at 6-foot-4, Sarah was not physically prepared for the APFT and the course in military movement. The basic requirements of the APFT are straightforward: A female soldier (a cadet in this case) whose age falls in the 17 to 21 bracket must be able to complete 19 correct push-ups and 53 correct sit-ups within two minutes for each event and run two miles in 18 minutes, 54 seconds or less. Sarah had no problem with the two-mile run, but the push-ups and sit-ups were a different story. Adding to her adversity, the word of emphasis is "correct." A correct push-up involves keeping the body straight, including the head, coming down to a position where the upper arms are parallel to the ground, lifting up, and locking the elbows. The sit-up requires the cadet to lie down, resting on the buttocks and back, hands locked behind the head and legs bent at the knees. With someone holding the cadet's ankles, the exercise requires movement to a position where the body moves up and forward to a position just beyond the vertical, then returning fully to the prone position.

Sarah worked as hard as she could during that first summer and was somewhat rewarded—she only failed the sit-ups by one. She passed the run with no problems and the push-ups by mucking out the required 19. Once into the academic year, Sarah ran headfirst into the physical education course PE117, Military Movement. A 19-lesson course, PE117 is designed to develop in all cadets the ability to move in many military and athletic situations. Skills required include rolling, hanging, climbing, crawling, jumping, vaulting, landing, mounting, supporting, and swinging. Actual events include mastering vertical rope climbing, the horizontal ropes, the Indoor Obstacle Course Test (IOCT), the horizontal bars, "ankles to the bar," pull-ups, rock climbing, and the trampoline. It is a tough course. Day after day, the only thing resonating with Sarah was the fear that she would fail the course and have to leave the academy. She needed help.

Maureen LeBoeuf answered the phone on the third ring. "Maureen LeBoeuf."

"Hi General LeBoeuf. This is Maggie Dixon. From Army."

"Hi Maggie. Great hearing from you. Other than UConn, how are things going up there?"

Maggie laughed. Maureen knew she was speaking with a friend. "Pretty well. We could use a few more wins, but all in all, the women have plenty of fight and we've started to come together." Maggie told Maureen a little about the games against UConn and Baylor. But, as she explained, "The team wanted to play against the best team in the nation." Maggie sounded upbeat about their competitive stature within the Patriot League. What she worried about was keeping the team healthy. With a couple of exceptions, the attitude was hanging in there at about 100 percent. Maggie hesitated for a second or two and then changed the subject. "I do have a problem though."

Maureen knew the problem and its solution. "Someone flunked a physical fitness test?" A rhetorical question, for sure. Maggie explained, emphasizing that both failed the APFT and one also failed PE117. The situation with Sarah Anderson and Megan Evans was nothing new. Maureen had seen it hundreds of times.

Maureen smiled just a bit when she heard "APFT," pleased with Maggie's ability to start using acronyms of the military. "Sure, I think I can be of help. Tell me about them."

Starting with Sarah Anderson, Maggie explained the situations of both young women. Sarah comes from Iowa. Her resume coming out of high school was outstanding, including volleyball and track. Academically, Sarah was strong and served as president of her high school National Honor Society. She stood at 6-foot-4 and was big-boned. She had no problems with running, basic movements, and flexibility. Her sole problem was upper body strength. She did not want to leave the academy and was committed to doing anything and everything to stay.

Maggie ended with, "We're willing to do anything you recommend. As a matter of fact, others have already been working with her."

Maureen and Maggie poured over Sarah's physical deficiencies, requirements of PE117 and the APFT, and what could be done for success. The basic solution came in the form of, "All hands on deck."

Maureen made it clear that, "The key to it all is for Sarah to make sure she has the correct form on each event and practice the event time after time." She continued,

> She should perform each repetition slowly and to the standard required. I would recommend whoever is working with her cuts her zero slack on the required standards. An improper push-up will not count on the APFT. A sit-up where the back does not reach or pass the vertical will not count. Once she has met the standard for a proper push-up or sit-up, she can start to speed things up.

LeBoeuf added some strong advice.

> Do not allow Sarah or Megan to only look at the minimum standard for repetitions. They must give everything they have to increasing the repetition count for each event. Once they have done that, then they simply need to pace themselves so neither works so hard on the first event, push-ups, that she wears out on the sit-ups.

The two women continued discussing strategies for a good while. Many of the strategies were already in progress; others could be implemented in short order.

Maureen ended the conversation by recommending Donna Brazil to help with the project to save Sarah Anderson from failure. "In addition to faculty in the Department of Physical Education, check with Colonel Brazil. She's a great asset, both physically and academically," LeBoeuf related.

Maggie answered that Donna Brazil had already helped both Sarah and Megan, and that Megan was making good progress, including passing PE117.

Sarah worked as hard as she could to increase her upper-body strength. Others refused to let her fail.

"I will never leave a fallen comrade." Taken from "The Soldier's Creed and the Warrior Ethos,"[2] this quote rang true for Sarah and, to a lesser degree, Megan. From every direction, help and encouragement was the order of the day—and night.

For starters, firsties Adie Payne and Megan Vrabel would get up early (5:00 a.m. during the week) to go on runs and do push-ups and sit-ups. Megan Ennenga, Courtney Wright, and Sarah conducted extra workouts before games, after shoot-arounds, in hotels, and in Arvin Gymnasium on weekends.

Sarah's tactical officer (a commissioned officer holding the rank of captain or major) had her log at least 50 push-ups a day—and she had to turn it in to him. Aside from the cadets involved with the basketball team, Sarah's team leader (a yearling), squad leader (a cow), and a male cadet known as "PT-stud" helped her as well. Megan received help from roommates, others in her company, and the strength coach. Although she flunked the sit-ups in the summer, Megan passed the events in September and never failed another test.

Both Maggie Dixon and Donna Brazil helped Sarah as often as possible. They would do push-ups and sit-ups with her. When the weather allowed, Maggie joined Sarah next to a softball field bordering the Hudson River. Maggie would hold Sarah's ankles for sit-ups and do push-ups with her. Moreover, from the Department of Physical Education people like Dr. Sue Tendy and Colonel Gregory Daniels, the department head (the current "Master of the Sword"), worked with her. The director of strength and conditioning, Mr. Scott Swanson, not only worked with her, but also put together a shelf apparatus with a climbing rope in the academy weight room for Sarah (and others needing help).

Sarah was required to retake PE117 in STAP. She passed. Although the struggle was always significant, during the next three years she never failed another APFT—or IOCT—or physical challenge of any type.

Maggie was on-site for the APFT. Although she passed with flying colors, at the end of the two-mile run Megan became nauseated and started throwing up.

In her words, "It was gross."

No sooner had Megan thrown up than Maggie Dixon, having watched the APFT from a safe distance, ran up to her wanting to give her a high five.

Megan backed away, saying, "Coach, I have puke all over me."

Her words were to no avail; Maggie grabbed Megan and gave her a huge hug, puke and all.

Micky Mallette and Adie Payne's medical issues also provided plenty of unwanted adversity. Adie was not concerned as much about her actual injuries as she was about her lost skill set caused by the injuries. In her mind, she had better skills coming out of high school. Micky had been in and out of the hospital numerous times for a multitude of medical problems. As mentioned, she graduated from USMAPS as the most valuable player, averaging 17 points and more than two steals per game. Although only 5-foot-8, Micky averaged 4.6 rebounds a game. Each of her first three years at West Point saw an improving quality of play paralleling her increasing strength. Her cow (junior) year, Micky played in 26 games, starting 11 times. She scored 152 points and planned to start every game at guard as a firstie—but, it was not to be.

With her torn ACL in high school, a back beginning to betray her, an eye infection she suffered just before the start of the season, and other maladies, Micky seemed to have been hanging around Joe Btfsplk, the once-famous cartoon character (*Li'l Abner*, by Al Capp). Joe was well-intentioned, but he was the world's worst jinx, bringing catastrophe to anyone and everyone, 24 hours a day. With her eye infection forcing her admittance to KACH, Micky was going to miss an early season "bowling night" with Maggie and the team. Micky was frustrated and down—until Maggie walked into her room. They talked about the adversity Micky was facing, life in the military, and Micky's place with the team. She would be the team captain. By the time Maggie left, Micky was very much back in sync.

Adversity of a personal nature is the toughest of all. Such was the case for yearlings Margaree "Redd" King and Anna Wilson. At such highly regimented institutions as West Point, virtually every cadet will experience feelings of "what am I doing here?" at some point in their 47-month journey from plebe to commissioned officer. There is another major factor in the decision-making process of whether a cadet will stay the course or leave the academy. By law, once a cadet steps into a classroom at the beginning of cow year, he or she is obligated to serve in the United States Army and/or pay back the expense the United States government invested in them.

In Redd's case, and putting it bluntly, she was depressed. Deeply depressed. Early in the season, Redd had played as hard as she could for someone in her condition, but she just wanted to leave. Her attitude deteriorated, and, unlike most of the others, she spent virtually no free time working on her game during the Christmas holidays. West Point was not where she wanted to be. At the same time, Redd wasn't sure where she did belong. Both of her brothers, Akili and Adisa, had gone to the academy and played football. Akili was a gifted athlete, but injuries and a degree of "antidiscipline" behavior led to his leaving West Point. Adisa graduated with the class of 2000 and was commissioned in the infantry. Still, Redd ran out of the psychological gas needed to succeed at West Point.

Following the 39-point blowout loss to UConn, the game in which Army suffered its abysmal 16-point second half and left her scoreless (shooting 0-for-5), Redd announced to the players in the locker room that she was going to quit—both basketball and the academy. Most of the players were stunned by her announcement and stood mute. In spite of UConn, everyone else believed the team was coming together. Megan Vrabel reacted differently—Redd ticked her off.

Megan let Redd have it. "Go ahead, quit. If you don't want to be part of this team, just quit. Everyone else is in for the whole ride. We're not quitting;

we care about each other, the team, and our coaches. Go ahead, quit. Just don't keep talking about it. You better go see Coach Dixon."

By the time word got to Maggie Dixon and Dave Magarity, Redd was ready to turn in her resignation. Maggie called Redd into her office to sort things out. The conversation lasted more than an hour—and changed Redd's life. After listening to all of Redd's reasons for leaving West Point, Maggie put everything in perspective. She got very personal with Redd.

"First of all, I want you to know that I love you," Maggie declared.

Redd did not know how to react to her coach's statement. The words "I love you" are seldom said by a collegiate basketball coach to one of their players.

Maggie continued. "Your teammates and classmates love you as well. I don't want you to make a mistake you will regret for the rest of your life."

More likely than not, Redd needed to know she was a far more valuable human being than she first believed.

Maggie added, "I don't think you really want to leave, but, if you do, you cannot leave West Point without a plan. Do you have a plan?"

Redd had no plan. She had zero idea of what a non-West Point future would hold. "No, coach. I guess not," she admitted.

Maggie bore in on the despondent Redd King. "If you make the final decision to leave, I will help you develop a plan to make you successful, but I don't really think you want to leave."

Redd was not prepared for Coach Dixon's attitude about her leaving the team. Maggie's words focused more on Redd as a person than what she could do for the team. Redd grasped the hurt she would experience by leaving Maggie Dixon, the basketball team, and the academy. She started to understand what could be possible by staying. She also began to understand the nature of Megan Vrabel's locker room challenge to either be with the team or against it. Maggie and Megan's coupled reaction to Redd's confusion turned out to be the perfect elixir of two different perspectives leading to a watershed event in her life.

To the relief of the entire team, Redd stayed the course. She was welcomed back to the fold without another word being said. Things turned around. Life got better. Basketball grew more enjoyable. No one knew the impact their discussion would have on the remainder of the season, the future of women's basketball, and her life.

The season was not a loser—neither was Margaree "Redd" King.

The story of Anna Wilson was similar in some ways—mostly personal confusion—and different in others. Just like Redd, Anna considered leaving West Point. Unlike Redd, Anna found basketball and her teammates the brightest part of the day. But she couldn't shield her emotions from her coach. And Maggie took action.

Anna remembers the encounters she had with Maggie. "At practice, I was positive and usually upbeat. But one day Coach Dixon could sense something was off and asked me what was going on. She realized that I was going through a tough decision when not many people knew that I was thinking about leaving."

Maggie affirmed Anna and told her just what she brought to the table. In addition, Maggie made sure Anna understood the value of a diploma from West Point. With her ability to communicate with Anna from a positive vantage point based on Anna's view of life, Maggie proved a great impetus for Anna to stay at the academy. Anna never forgot their interactions.

Anna remembered back to her playing days and the impact Maggie Dixon had on every player. She recalled, "Her ability to read the players and adjust how she communicated with each of us created a deep sense of trust among players and coaches, and translated to the success we had on the court."

In spite of adversity showing its ugly head during the first half of the season, the team began to thrive under Maggie's leadership. Teammates bonded and began playing as a single, productive unit. The players believed they could make a strong run in the Patriot League regular season. What they needed came in the form of following the challenge of UNIVERSAL #9: WE WILL make adversity our best friend.

· *10* ·

Big Mo

*W*ith the 39-point UConn loss in their rearview mirror, and with a simpler offense to work on, the Army women started the new year with a solid 67–54 victory against Iona. A 13-point victory seems an easy win; it was anything but easy. The halftime score stood at 35–33, Army. Continuing with her long-term strategy, Maggie made the conscious decision to get as many players into the game as possible. Fifteen players received playing time. The total number of player minutes in a game comes to 200; on this night, nonstarters accounted for 97 minutes played and 34 points scored. Everyone on the team felt part of the win—and part of the team. Although some of the adversity issues occurred in the first week in January, 2006 started out well. Spirits were high, the future of Army women's basketball looked a little bit brighter, and a touch of "we can beat anyone in our league" seeped into the minds of the players.

Several other positive realities occurred during the month of January. First and foremost, Army started the new year with three straight wins, including the 85–81 nail-biter against Colgate and a 59–56 stunner against perennial champion Holy Cross. The switchover between Erin Begonia and Alex McGuire went smoothly, and players from both the Black team and White team had shown significant improvement in the three months since Maggie Dixon walked into West Point. Smash Magnani and Micky Mallette still had limited minutes, but they played well in every game—well enough to ensure the team would not suffer on the scoreboard while they played.

Another bright spot was the continual improvement of the plebes, Megan Evans in particular. The 6-foot-2 forward/center arrived for Beast Barracks with a strong résumé. She received first-team All-New Hampshire honors, accrued both 1,000-plus points and 1,000-plus rebounds during high school, and led the Mascoma High School team to two Class-M state championships and two state runners-up trophies. Adding to her résumé, Megan also played field hockey and softball. Like many others on the team, she was a member of the National Honor Society. Just the opposite of Alex McGuire, Megan knew little about the USMA and had zero intention of ever serving in the military. When she received a letter from Maureen Morrisey of the Army coaching staff, Megan threw it away. Once her father Rick knew of the recruiting efforts coming from West Point, he told her, "No way will you throw that away. You're at least going to go through the process."

Megan talked a few times with the coaches, specifically with Morrisey, and agreed to visit the campus. Surprisingly, at least to her, the visit turned out just the opposite of what she expected.

> I really enjoyed myself. I met the players and liked them very much. The staff and faculty people I met, both civilian and military, were the kind of people I would like to associate with. I think my stereotype of military people was a little bit warped. The academy itself was absolutely beautiful. It turned out to be a pretty easy choice—I accepted the challenge.

The challenge she spoke of started out as a huge hurdle—Beast Barracks. Megan found the constant stress of the demands placed on her to be almost mentally and physically overwhelming. The toughest part was how much she missed her family.

She revealed, "I called my parents and told them, 'I want to come home.'" Megan added,

> My dad said to think about it. "Talk to some upperclassmen and certainly talk to Coach Morrissey. Then, if you want to be done with it, we can talk." Since Coach Morrissey was no longer at the academy, what kept me that summer were my teammates, classmates, the school, and the obvious opportunities. Ashley Magnani, a firstie, really talked it through with me. Finally, I made my own choice—I was staying.

As she had promised at the beginning of the season with Stefanie Stone, Maggie also made projects out of Courtney Wright, Megan Evans, and Sarah Anderson. In fact, through push-ups and sit-ups, Maggie played an important role in helping Sarah Anderson stay at the academy. Tall women tend to have trouble with push-ups; so do tall men. In Megan's case, the payoff was receiving more playing time as the season progressed. In January, momentum for the women of West Point grew significantly.

As expected, the Colgate game was tough and exciting. The first half ended 35–35, with neither team having held more than a four-point lead. An inside shot by Stefanie Stone put the cadets up 37–35 to start the second half. Unable to break loose during the first 20 minutes, Colgate took control early in the second half. Following Stone's basket, Colgate went on a 12–0 roll to lead Army by 10 points at the 14:44 mark. Gretchen Polinski and Melanie Cargle scored on layups; sandwiched in the middle of the run were three free throws by Cargle and Megan Ballard. Following another layup, this time by Devon Warwick, the run ended with a three-pointer by Meghan Curtin. Army's Megan Evans, on an assist by Erin Begonia, finally hit a short jumper to break Colgate's run.

In the next three and a half minutes, Colgate matched Army basket for basket, even adding to its lead. At the 11:05 mark, Colgate's Shervorne Martin scored on a jumper, giving Colgate its largest lead of the evening, at 58–44. Although many times Army would have its back to the wall, it was at this moment that a successful basketball season hung by a thread. Twelve seconds later, Megan Vrabel hit a jumper, with the assist coming from Begonia. Army trailed by 12, at 46–58. Only four seconds later, following a Colgate foul, Begonia hit a textbook three-pointer. It was a single-digit deficit, at 58–49. Finally, the cover on the basket unlocked.

A minute later, Colgate's Megan Ballard fouled Begonia. She calmly sank both free throws. Again, the deficit moved into single digits, 51–60. The Black Knights were back in the game. The last 10-point Colgate margin came at the 7:44 mark, when Cargle scored on a layup. Thirteen seconds later, Begonia launched another three-pointer—and scored. From that point onward, Army steamrolled its way back into the game. Uncharacteristically, following Begonia's three-point bomb, Colgate had three free throws during the remainder of the game. They missed all three. For Army's part, the Lady Knights hit three of four.

Given the new semester demands on the cadets, the crowd stood at a paltry 434. Mostly Army fans, the small number was not a major problem. Any lack of crowd size was lost in the intensity of the game. It was a great game—a game neither team deserved to lose. But basketball is a zero-sum game; only one team can win, always at the expense of the other. With less than two minutes remaining in regulation, Begonia scored her final layup of the season. The score stood at 69–70, with 1:59 remaining in regulation. A jump shot by Cargle gave Colgate a short-lived 72–69 lead. But a foul called on Polinski gave McGuire two free throws. She missed the first shot and made the second. The two-point deficit loomed large.

With Colgate holding onto the ball, McGuire fouled Ballard. To that point in the game, Ballard had had a mediocre day shooting from the floor, going 1-for-7. At the free-throw line, she had been a solid 4-for-4. Eleven seconds remained in regulation. Ballard took her time, inhaled, let it out—and missed the shot. Army rebounded the ball and took it down the court. It was time for Enright to do what she had done so many other times in her short year-and-a-half career. With no time remaining on the clock, her jumper fell through the basket. The scoreboard showed no time remaining and a score of 72–72. The momentum rested with Army.

Although close, the overtime belonged to the Cadets. Enright hit a jumper on an assist from—you guessed it—Erin Begonia. Colgate's Ballard missed two more free throws and fouled Enright. She made both shots. With the lead, the women of West Point were content to go to the free-throw line, making seven of eight. With nine seconds to go, Jen Hansen hit two free throws, giving Army the win at 85–81.

In the dressing room following the game, Maggie emphasized her previous comments about adversity to her exuberant team, telling them she knew they could finish in true "WE WILL" fashion. She spoke quickly, saying they could accomplish the same outcome in any game in which they trailed. "You did it one basket at a time. You can overcome adversity in any game you play." She ended with a big smile, stating, "I hope you had as much fun as I did." It was a great night of college basketball.

The Colgate game was Erin Begonia's last night as a competing player. Maggie, knowing Begonia was moving to the White team, decided to split time between the incoming and outgoing guards. Maggie gave Begonia 27 minutes and McGuire 32 minutes. McGuire's 15 points coupled with Begonia's 12 points for a "lights out" game from the point guard position.

Army won against a more-than-worthy opponent. The fear of a losing season began to fade from the minds of the Black Knights. Next up, a nail-biter with Holy Cross. The team almost welcomed adversity—almost.

With more wins coming in, momentum came in as well. Practices were high-energy affairs, and emphasis on individual skills continued. But at the same time, scrimmaging was part of everyday practice. The players loved it. For the White team, it was an opportunity to challenge the Gold and Black teams. With Erin Begonia at the point guard position, and Adie "White-6" Payne at the helm, team White gave as much as they received. Begonia, given her academic situation, could not move up, but the other players knew they had a chance for more playing time if the coaches noticed their strengths. "White-6" Payne and her marauding teammates did give the higher-rated players a run for their money. Life at a military academy is demanding and can drain cadets of energy; in the case of the women's team, scrimmaging was an escape from the smothering blanket of life at West Point.

Many other stories have been told and retold about the pure joy of playing basketball for Maggie Dixon.

On a snowy winter day during practice, Dave Magarity showed up a little late, wearing snow boots. One by one, the players began talking to one another about his boots looking eerily similar to those of Napoleon Dynamite, the main character in a low-budget movie of the same name. For those who have not seen the 2004 movie, Napoleon Dynamite was a 16-year-old kid living in Preston, Idaho, who always wore snow boots. The plot is not needed here, only that he was out to prove he had nothing to prove. Most of the players had seen the comedy (costing less than $400,000 to produce, it earned more than $46 million at the box office) and saw Napoleon as a sort of "doofus." A snicker here, a chuckle there, a . . . well, it's obvious Magarity's snow boots were a distraction.

Noticing the revelry of the players, Maggie stopped practice long enough to admonish the team—and Dave Magarity—in a lighthearted way.

"Okay, everyone. Let's get our laughs in about Coach Magarity's boots right now."

Everyone, except possibly Coach Magarity, laughed, some hysterically. Even he couldn't hide a small smile. Then it was back to practice.

The environment at almost every practice was extraordinary—healthy as one could imagine. Each time a set play was put into a practice, Maggie and Dave would come up with a question along the lines of "So, okay, what new name are you going to give this play?"

During one practice, free spirit Anna Wilson replied, "How about 'Liger'?" The entire team started laughing, knowing "Liger" came from the same movie, *Napoleon Dynamite*. A "Liger" is half lion and half tiger. According to the movie, a Liger is magical.

Stefanie Stone remembers Anna Wilson coming downcourt during one of the games. Suddenly, Anna raised an arm into the air, pointed toward the ceiling, and started calling out, "Liger, Liger." The Army bench cracked up at their teammate's having a little fun on the court. The coaches and players achieved an ability to balance pure fun with execution of a play exactly as drawn on Maggie's small whiteboard. Momentum continued its journey upward. And Maggie Dixon kept smearing whiteboard eraser on her hands.

On January 10, Holy Cross, the most dominating team in the league, came for a visit to Army. The game was important for obvious reasons. Among the most important was finding out how the team would play without Erin Begonia. It could not have gone better. In another absolute nail-biter, the West Point women came away with a 59–56 victory. There were three Army players who scored in double-digits: yearling Stefanie Stone (13); plebe Alex McGuire (12); and, coming off the bench, plebe Megan Evans (10). In 16 minutes of playing time, Evans shot 5-for-6 from the field and pulled down five rebounds, two of them offensive. By 9:30 p.m., Army's record stood at eight wins and seven losses. No need to worry about that kid, McGuire.

Aside from the physical success that night, Maggie, just as she did at DePaul, joined Dave and a couple of his buddies at a local restaurant and pub, the Park. One of his buddies was George Siegrist, a former player from Dave's tenure at Marist. The other was Steve Sauers, the associate head coach at Marist. Maggie was in a celebratory mood and asked to join them. It was one of those rare times where Dave Magarity wasn't sure how to react to Maggie Dixon. Was he happy with himself because Army had pulled off an upset, or was he happy because Maggie was happy? Probably both possibilities were pretty equally weighted. Maggie was as happy as one can be with a victory like Army's. The three men really fired her up, and she could not have been prouder than she was that night.

Four days later, the West Point women played at Lehigh. The Mountain Hawks gave Army a wake-up call, winning 60–53. Alex McGuire shot 9-for-12, ending with 18 points. Cara Enright shot 7-for-17 but missed four of five free throws. No one else scored more than six points.

After speaking with the other coaches, Maggie entered the locker room, a down atmosphere dominating the scene. She didn't smile. She let them know they had not played up to WE WILL standards, telling them, "We are a better team than Lehigh." But she did end on a positive note. "We'll play better at American. Bring it in."

Most of the players were disappointed with the Lehigh game. A few were not pleased with their individual performances. Others sensed they had let their coaches down. Everyone worked hard during practice before traveling to Washington, DC, to meet American University. Maggie looked at it differently. She knew the team played hard against Lehigh, and even had a 36–31 advantage in rebounds. But, giving up 20 turnovers, 17 of which came from steals, was unsatisfactory. Army also shot terribly in the first half (30 percent overall and 20 percent from three-point range). The Lehigh game was discussed at the next coaches' meeting with the outcome being simple: cut down on turnovers and take better shots.

Army did play better against American, the Naval Academy, and Lafayette, winning the games by 9, 14, and 15 points, respectively. In those three games, shooting percentage increased and turnovers were reduced.

The game against Navy was important for several reasons: Beating the Middies would put wins in double figures; the plebes would gain experience playing in a hostile environment; momentum within the Patriot League would continue building; and morale of graduates stationed at outposts as far away as Afghanistan and Iraq might just pick up a tad.

The game did not go as Maggie and Dave anticipated. Army never allowed the pro-Navy crowd of 2,010 to get into its collective mind. The cadets took charge from the start and never let the Navy team back into the game. The only concern came when Navy shut out the Cadets for almost four minutes of the first half, cutting Army's lead to 40–33. At that point, firstie Micky Mallette brought the drought to a halt with her only scoring attempt of the game, a beautiful shot from behind the three-point arc, touching nothing but net. With 1.7 seconds left in the half, plebe Megan Evans hit both ends of her free throws to move the halftime score to 45–33. Navy did cut the score to eight points (63–71) with a little more than four minutes to play, but the West Point women finished on a 12–6 run to put the game away.

High fives, hoots, hollers, and boisterous congratulations were shared by the entire team. It was a well-deserved win. The women had beaten a good team on their own floor. Every positive outcome hoped for by Maggie and Dave came to fruition. It was a great win for Army.

For most of the celebration, one could easily mistake Maggie for one of the players. She high-fived each one and hooted and hollered with the best of them. Once everyone settled down, Maggie took center stage. She told the team they had played an almost perfect game, even outrebounding Navy by 11. She knew Navy was a good team. Still, Army won every skirmish except, once again, turnovers (20–16). Army held the advantage in field-goal percentage (50 percent to 40 percent), three-point percentage (58 percent to 25 percent), foul shots (16-for-18 to 10-for-12), and the all-important rebounding category (42–31) in Maggie's first foray into battle against Navy.

Megan Evans kept it to herself, but she felt ecstatic about having hauled down a team-high 11 rebounds. But it wasn't just Megan; everyone felt good about how they performed as a team. With fellow plebe Alex McGuire playing well, the future of Army's women's basketball seemed limitless.

Maggie, her smile spreading from ear to ear, told the team what she saw for the future. "If we play this well the rest of the way, we will win the Patriot League."

The players erupted.

"Okay, bring it in."

Four days later, Army hosted Lafayette College, and the Army train kept rolling down the track. In a close game until midway through the first half, Army went on a 14–2 scoring spree to take a 36–28 lead at the half. In the second half, after a few minutes, Lafayette never got closer than 12 points. The game was remarkable in one manner. Stefanie Stone scored 22 points and pulled down 11 rebounds. Her performance would make almost anyone ponder, "How did she linger on the bench the entire previous season?" Some things just don't make sense.

And then came the game against Colgate in Hamilton, New York.

Playing their worst game of the year, the West Point team was outshot in field goals 23–19, was outrebounded 40–34, and turned over the ball a horrendous 27 times. From three-point distance, the team shot 1-for-10. The "limitless future" crashed in flames. Alex McGuire was the major exception, scoring 22 points on 8-of-13 shooting and hitting all six of her foul shots. Countering her good play, Alex also had no assists and turned over the ball seven times. The reality set in that the West Point women could be as bad as they could be good. The obvious result: Colgate romped to a 66–58 upset of the Army women.

Maggie Dixon let them know. In no uncertain terms, she told the team to either cut down on turnovers or be prepared to end up in the middle of the pack. Maggie was disappointed but not downtrodden about the season. She and Dave knew they were at a watershed point; either the team would respond or it could possibly fold. The team stood with a record of 11 wins, nine losses. Twenty games played and an unknown number of future games. The two coaches, as strong a pair as college basketball had to offer, spent many hours during the next week planning for a second encounter with the Navy team.

All things considered, Army started turning the ship around with the Iona game. Since the beginning of the new year, the team had won six games and lost two. In the Patriot League, the record stood at five and two. As for the team, every player judged herself better than she was on October 4—the day Maggie Dixon appeared in front of the press. Alex McGuire stepped up her game in the absence of Erin Begonia. All the players had seen action. In effect, the team was very solid. If the team could go no worse than 6–1 in the second half, it would have a great shot at the league title. If they could cut down on turnovers, the future looked good. How good was yet to be seen. One thing was certain: There was a bump here and a bump there, but Army still had momentum.

· *11* ·

A Season Ending Well

February 4, 2006
United States Military Academy
Midafternoon

$\mathcal{A}$rmy 63, Navy 63. Navy took possession to start the overtime. No one knew the effect Army's tying the game at the end of regulation had on Navy—or on Army. At the 4:36 mark of overtime, Navy's Betsy Burnett missed a layup, but Navy rebounded the ball. Nineteen seconds later, Burnett turned the ball over while committing an unnecessary foul. Army's ball. After working the ball around, Alex McGuire missed a short jumper. Fortunately for the cadets, the ball went out of bounds off a Navy player. It took Army eight seconds to get off another three-pointer by McGuire. She missed again. But this time Army took advantage of poor blocking out on Navy's part. As she had done most of the season, Stefanie Stone pried herself between two Navy players to rebound the ball; she was immediately fouled by Navy's center, Kate Hobbs. Stone sank both shots. Army 65, Navy 63. Maggie was not the type of coach to pull a player out because of a couple of missed shots; she just wanted to make sure Alex was not more wired up than necessary. She substituted Anna Wilson for Alex. To understand Anna Wilson's contribution to the team, one might want to go back a few years.

One of the special West Point players in the late 1980s was cadet Linda Schimminger. She exuded politeness and personality to such a degree that anyone meeting her on the street could believe Linda might be good on the debate team but probably not so good at playing basketball. In reality, Linda was as nice as advertised—until she stepped onto a basketball court: Ms. Jekyll meet Ms. Hyde. A tenacious defender, an excellent shooter, and a player who could "see the court" at all times, Schimminger was selected captain of the 1987–1988 team, which went 19–13. Linda was, in the words of her classmates, a "winner." She certainly was a winner, and she received the prestigious Army Athletic Association Award for "displaying the most valuable service to intercollegiate athletics during a career as a cadet." Her short biography brings us back to Anna Wilson.

Anna Wilson, coming to West Point from Somerset, New Jersey, might have been cloned from Linda Schimminger. The daughter of Teresa and Keith Wilson, a U.S. Navy veteran of the Vietnam War, Anna grew up in a home of four daughters, the others being Sarah, Emily, and Jessica. She loved volleyball (selected to third team all-state), softball, and basketball—but basketball reigned supreme. Her play in basketball brought her the title of MVP for the Rutgers Preparatory basketball team—state champions in 2001, 2003, and 2004. The only downside to Wilson came in the form of nagging injuries for much of her time at West Point. Anna, like every player at every level, wanted more playing time, but regardless of time on the court she would do anything asked of her to make Army a better team. She was dedicated to "bearing any burden." One of four members of the class of 2008 on the team, she operated somewhat in the shadow of her other three classmates—Cara Enright, Redd King, and Stefanie Stone. But she never slowed down, either playing as hard as she possibly could or cheering from the bench. Unknown to her at the time, Anna Wilson would be selected captain of the 2007–2008 team—by unanimous vote.

Wilson promptly fouled Lauren Skrel. Skrel sank both free throws to knot the game at 65–65. Navy fans comprised but a small portion of the almost 3,000 people attending the game. Still, they gave a more than satisfactory accounting of their ability to cheer their team on to victory.

At the 3:16 mark, Stefanie Stone scored from inside and was fouled by Margaret Knap. She missed the free throw. The Black Knights led by two points—only to have Burnett score on a layup and reset the score even at 67–67. The clock slowly dipped beneath the three-minute mark.

Army picked up two points on free throws by Enright, while Navy's Burnett added one point. Neither team was shooting well from the field, but Army increased its lead to three points on two more free throws by Enright. Following a missed three-pointer by Skrel, McGuire calmly sank a soft jumper to expand Army's lead to five points. Wilson hit one of two free throws to up the lead to 74–68. Navy had 27 ticks on the clock to catch the cadet team. Skrel caught a pass down low and barreled in to score with the clock showing 20 seconds to go. Navy's Coach, Tom Marryott, called a time-out. Maggie consulted with Dave Magarity and the coaching staff to decide on a winning strategy.

Dave opined, "They're going to foul. They've got no choice."

All agreed. Maggie turned to the bench. Every player wanted to go in. Maggie's decision was simple. "We need our free throw shooters in the game."

"Jen, Cara, Megan. You're in for Anna, Megan, and Redd"

As expected, as soon as Jen Hansen received the inbounds pass, she was fouled by Ali Currier. Hansen, an 87 percent free-throw shooter, stepped to the line. She hit both shots. Easy as can be.

Navy gave it all they had. Skrel hit a jumper with seven seconds to go, only to have Megan Vrabel take a long pass for an easy layup with one second on the clock.

The horn sounded; the fans and the Army team exploded at another win against Navy. The Army faithful, having roared throughout the game, were happy, drained, and mighty glad to have come to the game.

The Navy game was Army's 21st of the season. They stood at 12–9, a far cry from the 5–7 record coming out of the starting gate. In the locker room, Maggie made it clear that what she had said following the UConn 39-point New Year's Eve massacre ("We're coming together as a team. We're going to win a lot of games this year.") was coming true.

During the next three weeks, the women of West Point would win against Holy Cross, Lehigh, American, Bucknell, and Lafayette. Maggie had her team on a magical roll.

As commentary on the Navy game, Cara Enright and Alex McGuire each scored 18 points. In Enright's case, she seemed to find herself "in the zone" whenever she played against the Midshipmen. She would score in double figures in seven of her eight contests against Navy (scoring nine points in her only sub-double-figure game) during her career at Army. As a plebe, she once found herself in jeopardy with her civilian English professor two days before the Sunday Army–Navy game. When asked if she had finished a particular assignment, Cara, knowing she had to tell the truth, answered, "no sir." The professor could best be described as an academic "bull in a China shop" with a strong attachment to Russian history. He responded to her admission of guilt with, "Well, Comrade Enright, I'll tell you what I'm going to do. If you score 35 points against Navy this Sunday, I will extend your paper due date by one day. If you don't score 35, you will have it done by our next class. Are we agreed?"

"Yes sir!" was the reply.

Everyone in the class smirked and tried to muffle outright laughter; all assumed, as good as she was, 35 points was out of the question. But she had a chance to do the near-impossible. After all, she scored 23 points against Navy in her first game, including three 3-point shots, remarkable for a plebe.

The second game against Navy—the one her professor challenged her on—saw Army hang on for an 89–81 victory. In the second game, Cara hit 12 of 17 shots, including five from downtown. From the free-throw line, she went 5-for-6. Seven two-pointers makes 14 points; five three-pointers adds another 15 points, bringing the total to 29 points, and five of six from the charity stripe. The final total came to—wouldn't you know it—34 points. Cara Enright, in front of her amused classmates, turned in the assignment as ordered and on time. Such is the life of a West Point athlete.

The first Army–Bucknell game was played at Army. Both teams were in the thick of the fight to win the Patriot League regular-season title. Unless Army ended up as league winner and, thus, the host school for the postseason tournament, this would be the last home game of the season. Events in prelude to the game provided a view into the soul of the Army coach and the response to her leadership by two of the seniors. The story unfolded at the end of practice a couple of days before the Bucknell women came to West Point. Maggie called Smash Magnani and Adie Payne over to talk.

Maggie told them they were good ballplayers and that she knew they could more than hold their own against the strong Bison team. She offered them both a chance to start the game.

Both players perked up. Smash took half a second to respond, saying, "Thanks coach. I won't let you down."

Adie added, "It's an honor. Thank you. I'll play harder than I ever have before."

The two young women looked at one another and beamed. They were going to start. Following tradition at many institutions, seniors who are not starters are often given a chance to start and play for a couple of minutes in the last home game of the season. Both Magnani and Payne, as is often said, would "give their eye teeth to start." They were all-star high school players in Maryland and California, respectively. Ashley, physically strong and a solid player, still had been unable to crack the starting lineup. In the previous game against American University, Smash shot 6-for-7 and pulled down nine rebounds. The unending injuries denied Adie's quest to reach her full potential as a Division I player. She served as "White-6" out of loyalty to her coach and the team. She was the perfect leader for the White team, but she did not like it. She wanted to play—period. She did play in 20 games; however, only twice did she play more than 10 minutes. In a nutshell, Smash and Adie were used to starting in high school, and the urge to start never goes away. It had been tough on them not getting the playing time each wanted. Both felt confident they would do well and immediately accepted Maggie's invitation to start.

Megan Vrabel was pretty much a full-time starter, and Micky Mallette had started several games. If Smash and Adie started against Bucknell, all four seniors would be able to say, "I started for the league champions." As of that moment, however, the Army team had not captured the league regular-season title by a long shot.

The two excited teammates met in Adie's room that night.

"I can't believe we're actually going to start. I've waited so long for this to happen. I'm going to go nuts out there," Smash said, pacing back and forth. She was envisioning the upcoming events at Christl Arena and feeling excitement she would never forget.

Adie, sitting on her bed, back to the wall, answered, "Me too. It's been so long. Too long. I've wondered 'What if?' a thousand times. 'What if I didn't get injured? What if we had Coach Dixon for all four years? What if . . . what if . . . what if?'"

Smash looked at Adie and asked, "I wonder whose place we're going to take? And for how long?"

Adie replied, "Don't know. Funny though, I'd like to say 'Don't know and don't care.' But I do care."

"So do I," Smash related. "The starting five does have a special chemistry, and the team is clicking on all cylinders. We really don't need to fix something that isn't broken." Smash sat down on a chair next to a study desk. Again, they looked at one another and, to a degree, into one another's hearts.

The conversation morphed into a discussion of the opposite side of the "What if?" coin. In their eyes, it was not a matter of talent. Both felt they were either as good or nearly as good as any of the starters. But what began to bother them was the possibility that by their starting, they might foul up the chemistry of the team and disrupt the flow of the game. Against a team like Bucknell, the price paid by the Army team might be too much. For the next hour, Adie and Smash talked themselves out of starting.

Early the next day, they told Maggie, "In the best interest of the team, we need to turn down your offer to start us. We believe it's best for the team. We want to play, but we don't need to start." Emotionally, the maturing women succeeded in overcoming the ego of being able to say, "I started for Army."

A few years later, Smash recalled the event clearly.

I remember Adie and I had gotten together that evening after Maggie let us know that we could start our last regular-season home game. I remember the excitement I felt, as this was the moment I had been waiting for all year, but quickly after that I almost felt sorrow or even disappointment, for we both knew that this was not in the best interest of the team. I will not deny that it took much to put my pride and ego aside, but we were clicking on all cylinders and there was no point in fixing something that wasn't broken. This was the most important game of the season, as it would seal our fate atop the Patriot League for the regular-season title, as well as give us home court advantage throughout the tournament and inevitably for the championship game. A change in even something as simple as the starting lineup could affect the outcome, positively or negatively, of the game, and in that instance, setting aside our pride to start one game was much easier to accept than being semiresponsible for the loss of one of the most important games in our basketball history.

Given the stakes and the timing, the home game against Bucknell was a huge game; it was possibly the most important game since Army became a Division I team. A win would fortify Army's position atop the Patriot League for the regular-season title, giving Army, as written about by Smash Magnani, home court advantage throughout the Patriot League Tournament. If they played well, a tournament championship and a trip to the "Big Dance" would be theirs. In that instance, Smash and Adie did choose to set aside their desire to start and do the right thing for the team.

With a temperature failing to reach higher than the mid-20s, and a sizeable covering of snow remaining from the massive storm of the previous week, the day stood out as perfect for a near-perfect game. Some 800 fans showed up at Christl Arena anticipating a hard-fought, in your face basketball game. Given the weather, the crowd size was both surprising and pleasing. Maggie had certainly done as much as anyone to build a fan base. And, to her, it was only a start. For the fans, the trip on such a cold day turned out to be well worth the miserable weather. Army jumped out to a quick 7–0 lead on a tip-in by Megan Vrabel, a jumper by Cara Enright, and a beautiful three-pointer by Jen Hansen. As though a switch had turned off, Army's hot shooting went stone cold, and Bucknell picked up the slack. In the next five minutes, Bucknell went on a 13–0 run, with Jacquie Searight and Lindsey Hollobaugh leading the way. Finally, Vrabel hit one of two free throws to break the drought. The teams fought tooth and nail for the remainder of the first half. A layup by McGuire at the 3:17 mark returned Army to a one-point lead at 26–25. In the last minute of the half, a free throw by Lindsey Hollobaugh put Bucknell up by three; two free throws by Stone brought the halftime score to 32–31, Bucknell.

In the Army locker room, Maggie went over where the team had performed well and a couple of areas to improve upon. As she had done throughout the year, and to the specific amusement of Dave Magarity, she wiped her writing off the whiteboard with the palm of her hand. He remembered thinking often, "How can anyone so impeccably dressed, use her hand as an eraser?" Each time he had the thought, a thin smile would break across his face.

Looking at the players, Maggie reminded everyone that Bucknell was playing on Army's court. They needed to get after them immediately. No Bucknell shot in the second half would go uncontested. She ended her half-time strategy session with her famous words: "And have some fun."

All in all, Army had played a solid first half against a good Bison team. And, for that matter, Bucknell had played a solid first half against a very good and improving Army team.

The team gathered in a tight circle, yelling "WE WILL" before heading back into battle.

Bucknell's Hope Foster, with an assist down low from Hollobaugh, opened the second half with an inside shot. Army responded with eight straight points, including three-pointers by Hansen and Enright, and a uncomfortable 39–34 lead. Physically tough, the Bucknell squad forced its way back again, tying the score at 43–43 with 14 minutes left. Half a minute later, Lauren Schober hit a jump shot, giving Bucknell the lead. During the next five minutes, Bucknell maintained the lead, eventually growing it to 59–51. Cara Enright started the Army comeback with a short jump shot and, being fouled by Schober, a free throw. Bucknell maintained at least a five-point lead until Enright scored again with 5:54 remaining.

Maggie and Dave had gone over the strengths and weaknesses of each player hundreds of times during the season. Beginning at the 4:36 mark, Army substituted Jen Hansen for Alex McGuire. Bucknell responded with Lauren Schober coming in for Ashton Sprouse. While Bucknell's coach, Kathy Fedorjaka, made no more substitutions, Maggie made another six, rotating short periods of time among Enright, McGuire, and King. Her reasoning coincided with the changing needs for offense or defense, or both. In those four and a half minutes, the strategy paid huge dividends. Army shot 1-for-3 from the field and a solid 6-for-6 from the free-throw line; Bucknell shot 2-for-7 from the field and 0-for-1 from the line. Throughout the second half, Maggie Dixon displayed the degree of strategic savvy she had learned beginning with the first time she touched a basketball, through high school and college, and eventually under the tutelage of Doug Bruno.

King pulled down a rebound with 100 seconds to go. Fifteen seconds later, she hit a jump shot to bring the cadets within one point of the Bison. Following a layup by Schober as the clock went beneath the one-minute mark, Stone was fouled by Foster. Stefanie walked to the line and sank both shots—still a one-point game.

Trailing 65–64, Army's Megan Evans blocked a shot. Jen Hansen grabbed the rebound with 13 seconds to go. Army moved the ball around, hoping to hit a last-second shot to win the game. McGuire drove toward the basket and was fouled by Kesha Champion. Four seconds remained. She walked to the free-throw line, received the ball, and relaxed as best she could. Alex had faced his type of pressure before, especially the 34-point scoring spree in the Maryland AAAA State Championship game. As she had done thousands of times before, she dribbled the ball quickly, took a breath, and lofted the ball gently into the air. It was good—game tied at 65. Almost as a robot, her mechanics were the same for the second shot. Quick dribble, take a breath, relax, and shoot. Army 66, Bucknell 65. Bucknell's Corinne Keller missed a jump shot as time expired. The crowd exploded. What a game. Most important, Army stood by itself atop the Patriot League standings, with 10 wins and two losses. Army won against a very talented, physical team.

The only cog in the wheel came a week later; Bucknell returned the favor, beating Army, 60–47, in Lewisburg, Pennsylvania. Unfortunately for Bucknell, Army's 11–3 league record rendered Bucknell's victory irrelevant for the Patriot League regular-season championship. Army had its one-point victory over the Bison, Holy Cross had two wins (one in overtime), and, in a shocker, Lehigh orchestrated a 56–55 upset on Bucknell's home court.

Following the second Bucknell game, Maggie let the team know they could not afford to play in the tournament as they had against the Bison. If they did, she predicted the team could fall in the first game.

There are bad teams, average teams, and good teams; and then there are great teams stepping up to the plate when adversity shows its ugly head. In the case of the 2005–2006 Army women's basketball team, it was clearly a matter of the "18 Musketeers: all for one and one for all." That Army won the 66–65 thriller only adds to the question, "What would the outcome have been if Smash Magnani and Adie Payne had started the game?" No one will ever know. It is an interesting question—and also irrelevant.

At the end of 2005, Army's record stood at five wins, seven losses. At the end of the regular season, the record had improved to 17–10. The team had gone 12–3 in 2006. Should the women capture the tournament, they would have a 20-win season and a trip to the NCAA Tournament. Cautious optimism best described the attitude of everyone associated with the team. It was possible to run the table in the Patriot League Tournament if the women played up to their potential. It was up to them. The next five days would tell the story of the West Point women's basketball team and just how much it had cast off the shackles of adversity.

· 12 ·

March Madness

$\mathcal{M}$arch is a month defined by two extraordinary events. First, on March 20 or 21, our planet experiences the vernal equinox. As Earth orbits the Sun and rotates on an axis inclined some 23.5 degrees from the plane of the ecliptic, it finds itself with exactly 12 hours of sunlight and 12 hours of darkness. In the Northern Hemisphere, the next day will have more sunlight and less darkness. In the Southern Hemisphere, darkness overtakes the sunlight. For the United States, the long winter is coming to an end, and the trees, bushes, plants, and grass are pregnant and ready to bloom. Secondly, and certainly more important to basketball fans, it is the start of the annual NCAA Tournament. Large or small, Division 1 men and women's basketball teams fight it out to make the Big Dance. March Madness ends in April, with one team crowned as the best in the nation.

The format for the women's tournament is straightforward. A total of 64 teams play in the single-elimination tournament; approximately 32 arrive by winning a conference tournament championship, and another 32 are invited "at large." An "at large" team is one beaten in a league tournament but having a solid record against highly rated opponents. For the lower-ranked teams, unless they win their conference tournament, they have no chance to be invited to the Big Dance. Once the league tournaments are completed, the 32 "at large" teams are selected. The 64 teams are then seeded from one to 64 and broken into four groups of 16. In each group, number 1 will face number 16, number 2 will face number 15, and so on.

On the men's side, until 2018 no men's number 16 seed had ever beaten a number 1 seed, although 16th seeded Princeton a lost 50-49 heartbreaker to top-rated Georgetown in 1989. In the 2018 NCAA Tournament, number 16 University of Maryland Baltimore County (UMBC), bludgeoned the top-rated University of Virginia Cavaliers, 74–54. On the women's side, number 16 Harvard took down number 1 Stanford, 71–67, in 1998, at Stanford. To their credit, throughout the years, the loss of two key Stanford players to injury prior to the game has been little used as an alibi. Quoting Stanford coach Tara VanDerveer, "They were a very good team—they had a great player [Allison Feaster], an excellent coach [Kathy Delaney-Smith], and I think it was the perfect storm."

The fact that Army won the regular-season Patriot League title was a "good news–bad news" situation. The bad news stemmed from the fact that they were nowhere near being ranked a "high-powered team." The message was clear—unless Army won the Patriot League Tournament, the season would be over. As for the good news, Army would be seeded first and host the number-eight team in Christl Arena. On the downside, winning three straight games, of which at least two would be against strong conference teams, is a monumental task—a task never achieved in the history of the West Point women's basketball team . . . or men's basketball.

The 2006 Patriot League Tournament had a single-elimination format, with teams seeded by final regular-season standings. Quarterfinal and semifinal rounds were held at the venue of the top two seeds for both men and women. The highest remaining seed was to be the host of the championship game.

Since the women's tournament began in 1991, Holy Cross had been the dominant team, amassing a 30–5 tournament record, including 10 championships and 11 regular-season titles. As the number-two seed, the Crusaders would have the home advantage for the first two games of their bracket. Based on the season records, the final seedings were as follows:

1. Army
2. Holy Cross
3. Bucknell
4. Navy
5. Colgate
6. Lehigh
7. American
8. Lafayette

Following its loss to Bucknell at the end of the regular season, the women made maximum use of the five-day interlude prior to opening the tournament against the Leopards of Lafayette College. With two easy wins during the regular season, Maggie and the remainder of the coaching staff had major concerns of a possible letdown. They knew Lafayette had nothing to lose and would come to West Point loaded for bear.

Prior to practice the next day, the coaches assumed there would be no need to remind the cadets what was at stake. The players had talked among themselves about the upcoming tournament. They knew Holy Cross, Bucknell, and Navy were every bit as talented as they were. The three schools also had strong coaches. Navy worried Dave Magarity the most. He said, "Navy is a good team, with a great coach. We beat them twice, and winning three in a row is very tough." Maggie and Dave also knew the team was capable of playing poorly.

Bucknell wasn't the only Patriot League team to beat Army; both Colgate and Lehigh had done so. The second Navy game had gone down to the wire before Army pulled out the win in overtime. The women vowed to tackle every moment of practice with determined energy and absolute focus. But, the West Point women were not perfect—they were human. At one of the first pretournament practices, the team had an unusually poor showing, leaving Maggie upset, Dave angry, and the other coaches bewildered. Maggie made it clear the championship would go to the team who played tough and under control. She called an early end to practice and sat the team down. After admonishing the team for the bad practice, as much mentally as physically, she gave them the hard truth about their play in the tournament.

Maggie said,

It's here. We can win this tournament; we can also lose in the first round. That, ladies, is up to you. If you play the way you can, we will be the Patriot League Tournament champions. If not, we're in trouble. With 10 losses, if we don't win the tournament, we won't even be playing in the NIT [National Invitational Tournament]. Our season will be over. We've put too much into our mission.

Micky Mallette, speaking for the team, responded, "Coach, we don't want to even think about the NIT. We will win the tournament."

"Well, don't tell me. Show me. Think about it tonight and show me tomorrow," Maggie retorted.

After Maggie and the other coaches left, the women held a team meeting, and it focused on two subjects: how they would practice and why they would win the Patriot League Tournament. The following day, the team came ready to practice every facet of the game. They were crisp, aggressive, and determined to show the coaches just how ready they would be. As for the tournament, it remained to be determined.

No differently than the late September day Maggie interviewed with the team, Smash Magnani recalled everyone's enthusiasm for basketball and reaching their goal—the NCAA Tournament. "I remembered the fire in coach's eyes. It was the same as the day she interviewed with us, on the day she sat us down to read us the riot act, and on the next day at practice." Smash smiled. Win or lose in the tournament, the USMA had picked the right coach, and Maggie Dixon had picked the right institution for her head coaching debut.

Maggie and Dave needed a few additional practices. Coaches throughout the nation always feel the same way. There's never enough time to get everything done to perfection. Time had run out; it was time to go to war.

On March 2, 2006, the first hurdle arrived: Eighth-seeded Lafayette College.

At the noon meal in Washington Hall, the 4,000-person Corps of Cadets looked up at the poop deck, a balcony 15 feet above the floor of the giant dining facility in Washington Hall. Maggie spoke as strongly as she possibly could to urge the cadets to come to Christl Arena and support the Lady Black Knights. The game against Lafayette College needed cadet support. She exhorted the mass of cadets with the stakes of a first-ever NCAA bid.

"We need you. Thank you and go Army!"

She received a quasi-enthusiastic response. Some of the cadets hollered back; some waved white napkins in the air. Unfortunately, those cadets near the poop deck were the only ones to hear her clearly. Maggie had had some success throughout the season with increasing the fan base for home games, but, other than the overtime thriller against Navy, cadet attendance at women's games was not what she envisioned. Whether it was the climb up the large hill (or small mountain) to Holleder Center or the fact cadets have huge constraints on their time, the women had little expectation of filling Christl Arena. Beginning with an attendance of 147 fans—of which less than 30 were cadets—for the Iona game on January 3, Maggie and the team forged ahead with the season and the task of winning games. Disregarding the always packed Army–Navy games, attendance at other games in the Patriot League showed a steady rise to the 600 to 800 range.

That night the crowd stood at 1,217, of which probably 800 were cadets. It was a good number and a solid payoff for Maggie's time on the poop deck. Now it was time for the team to make the cadets' walk up to Holleder Center worth the effort. The coaching staff did not expect an easy game. Lafayette had wins over archrival Lehigh (the two schools being separated by 17 miles) and Holy Cross. Any team who could beat Holy Cross could beat Army. And Lafayette had the same goal as the other seven teams in the Patriot League.

But on this night, Lafayette was in for a rude awakening. From the opening tipoff, Army held all the cards. The women shot 16-for-26 (61.5 percent) in the first half and never let up. Only Alex McGuire had more than 25 minutes of playing time for the game. By halftime, the score was 47–31, in favor of Army. The Black and White teams, although not shooting as well, played relentlessly and with great passion, contributing 23 points to the offense. By game's end, Army had outrebounded Lafayette by a 38–27 margin, with 17 belonging to the Black and White teams. Final score: Army 74, Lafayette 55. Next up for Coach Dixon and the women's team: a trip to the poop deck, followed by a game against the winner of the Navy–Colgate matchup.

MARCH 4, 2006: FROM THE POOP DECK IN WASHINGTON HALL, WEST POINT, NEW YORK

Maggie looked down at the churning mass of cadets; the decibel count reached significantly higher than two days before. Almost everyone was cheering, and half of the Corps of Cadets was waving napkins. This time she made full use of the microphone. She held it close to her lips and spoke louder than before. After thanking the Corps for the support against Lafayette, Maggie asked for even more support for the Colgate game. She remembered all too well that Colgate had beaten the Lady Knights by eight points at the end of January. This time on the poop deck, a significantly larger cohort of cadets was paying attention. Her beaming smile could be seen from the far corners of the dining facility. A din rose to the ceiling and echoed off the walls. She continued. She ended her talk by stating, "I'm asking for your support again tonight. We need you badly. Thank you so much. Go Army, beat Colgate."

The Corps, via its reaction to the new women's coach, sent Maggie and the team a not-so-subtle message: The number might be unknown, but tonight there will be many more cadets at the game than two nights before.

Colgate was a worthy opponent. The Red Raiders had taken Army to the limit in the overtime game at West Point. They beat Army by eight in Hamilton, New York. They also had wins over Holy Cross; Lehigh; and, in the first round of the tournament, Navy. As much as he admired Tom Marryott, the Navy coach, Dave Magarity was glad to see the Midshipmen eliminated. He knew defeating a rival service academy three times in the same season was a mammoth task. It wasn't time to think about Navy; Colgate loomed as a major obstacle.

Colgate came in with a game plan to take the fight directly to the cadets. With more than a thousand cadets in the stands, the West Point women simply took care of business. They never trailed. Cara Enright shot 11-for-14 from the field and pulled down 10 rebounds, finishing the game with 27 points; Stefanie Stone shot 5-for-10 from the field and a perfect 8-for-8 from the line, ending the night with 18 points; and Alex McGuire rounded out the double-figure scorers with 13 points. The turnover albatross never showed its ugly head, as the women committed a tolerable 15 turnovers. An especially significant indicator of fan support came in the form of cadets staying for the entire game. The pro-Army crowd cheered raucously throughout the contest. A final good omen for the women was not lost on Maggie or Dave—there had to be several hundred cadets in attendance who had never seen a women's game since arriving at the academy. Final score: Army 73, Colgate 55.

During the next three days, a basketball buzz roamed the barracks, the academic hallways and classrooms, the dining facility, and generally any other locations housing cadets. Each player experienced the exulting sense of pride as other cadets wished them well. Some signs began to show up on doors and hallways—"Go Army, beat Holy Cross" and "We're goin' dancin'." It was exhilarating.

There was one more hurdle to jump: the Holy Cross Crusaders.

Championship Day at West Point

March 8, 2006

Patriot League championship game or not, life on a Wednesday at West Point is carved in stone. A huge exception was Kevin Anderson supporting, and, General Lennox approving, the team's spending the night of March 7 at the Doubletree Hotel in Mahwah, New Jersey, as far from the madding crowd as possible. Maggie and Dave did not attend, leaving the oversight to Donna Brazil and the assistant coaches. For their part, the players relaxed, ate cookies, and watched *Brokeback Mountain* on television. As Smash Magnani remembers it, little was spoken about basketball. But, as much as they tried, thoughts of the upcoming battle with Holy Cross were difficult, if not impossible, to erase—after all, the most important event in their athletic lives was less than 24 hours away. Most of the players did not stay up late, although sleep reigned elusive. Plus, the life of a West Point cadet still existed.

The regimented schedule of formations, meals, classes, academic projects, athletics, and myriad other activities remains the same week in and week out. Regardless of the pecking order for expected playing time during the game that night, each player attended class as usual. No special exemptions were given. Classes in civil engineering, the American legal system, Spanish, French, human geography, systems management, life sciences, mathematics, and many of the dreaded distribution courses occupied each player's morning. The only exception was that inside many of the classrooms, professors reserved a small amount of time for some discourse concerning the upcoming game. After all, it was a big deal. Classmates joined the professors in wishing the team well. For the most part, the message was simple: "Good luck. We'll see you at the game."

At the noon meal, Maggie once again marched up to the poop deck and appealed to the Corps for support to bring home one final, historic victory. Once the orders of the day were announced by the cadet-in-charge, the microphone was turned over to Coach Dixon. Before she could speak, the Corps cheered, with many waving napkins in the air. She spoke with confidence that her message would be taken to heart. She told them how much the cheering cadets affected the team and could help in the championship game. "You made a huge difference against Lafayette and Colgate. Tonight, we need you to bring us the championship. We will do all we can, but we can't do it alone. We need you tonight. Thank you—and . . ." Her voice rose to the 4,000 young men and women below. "Beat Holy Cross!"

The cadets erupted in another cheer. But something was different. It was deafening, it was long-lived, and it clearly sent the message that, indeed, the Corps of Cadets would be at the game en masse.

Typical late-winter weather hovered over the Academy. Low stratus clouds blanketed the Lower Hudson Valley, but by midafternoon the temperature made it to a cool but tolerable 46 degrees. On a normal day such as this, "Gloom Period" would still have its stranglehold on the entire West Point community; cadets, officers, families, and people of the neighboring towns pined for the arrival of spring. The best medicine for this was a full bottle of women's basketball.

Well before the 7:00 p.m. tipoff of the championship game, fans from both schools began arriving for the game. Cadets, most wearing "ready for combat" BDUs (battle dress uniforms), filled in the north, south, and western sections of Christl Arena, while most of the Army and Holy Cross civilian supporters packed the eastern section. Army's bench was located on the southeast end of the court, and Holy Cross occupied the northeast section. Stereotypes are hard to break, but on this night, the cadets who packed into Christl Arena were little different from the "Cameron Crazies" of Duke or the rabid football fans in either Clemson's or Louisiana State University's "Death Valley" stadiums.

Wearing black jerseys with white numbers, almost the entire Army sprint football team came to support their sisters in arms. Each sprint football team member felt a small sense of pride that he had contributed to the women's toughness throughout the season. A large number of players from the Division I football team also arrived to spur the women on to victory. Representing many of the 36 companies (approximately 110 to 120 cadets per company), mascots in the form of a cadet wearing some outrageous outfit, signifying the company mascot, frolicked around the edges of the court. By 6:30 p.m., the Army pep band was blaring away, while cheerleaders fired up the crowd. Rock songs of the previous three decades comingled with the likes of "On Brave Old Army Team."[1] Although smaller in numbers, but with their own pep band, the Holy Cross faithful held their own with music and cheers. The cacophony of music and cheering reverberated off the flat cinderblock walls like hail on a tin roof. It wasn't just another basketball game; it was a happening.

On the court, both teams stretched, finished warm-up drills, and reached into their personal space to contemplate what was to come. For Holy Cross, the driving thought centered on an 11th Patriot League championship and another trip to the NCAA Tournament. For Army, the question was, "Can we win our first championship?" No differently from the case with Navy, the coaches and the players were well aware of the adage, "It's exceptionally tough to win three in a row against a similarly skilled team in a single season." It applies to all teams. That thought pried its way into to the minds of both teams and coaches. For Holy Cross, the adage bolstered their confidence. The Army players tried to dismiss the thought altogether. Army's two close victories against Holy Cross certainly could have gone the other way. But the fact remained—Army won both games, not Holy Cross. For Holy Cross players, the superstition baggage came from the color of their uniforms—they had yet to win a Patriot League championship game wearing purple. For the 2006 championship game, as the visiting team, Holy Cross was wearing purple; the home team Cadets were wearing white.

About an hour before the game started, Micky's father, Jim Mallette, walked out onto a large concrete deck outside of Holleder Center for a smoke (today he is a dyed-in-the-wool nonsmoker). Jim and Kathy Mallette had been close to the team the entire time Micky played basketball at the academy. Whenever the team stayed overnight in proximity to the Mallettes, they could count on being invited for some great family cooking. During the preceding two years, Jim Mallette often entertained thoughts about what he might say if ever asked to give a motivational speech to the team. By this time, maybe the last game his daughter would ever play at the college level, he had grabbed at selected words bouncing around in his mind. No sooner had he tossed the cigarette butt into a trash can than Maggie Dixon walked up the concrete steps at the entrance to Holleder. She stopped long enough to say hello to him.

"Hi Mr. Mallette. Big night for us. It's going to be tough." She smiled and leaned forward to shake his hand.

Jim Mallette agreed. Sensing serendipity, Mallette reasoned Maggie's coincidental arrival was a sign for him to speak to the team.

"Maggie, I've had a speech rolling around in my head. I don't suppose you'd let me talk to the women?" he questioned.

Maggie's smile grew larger. She answered with, "No problem at all. Just wait outside the locker room and I'll come and get you."

Word gets around quickly, and so it was with Jim Mallette. At that time, Micky was in the training room receiving heat treatment for her ailing back. When she walked out to do some warming up, her dad walked by and said, "Micky, I'm giving the pep talk before the game." Micky, focused on the upcoming game, smiled, shrugged her shoulders, and headed onto the court as though she had no concern. She had never heard her father give a formal speech, so she really did not know what to expect. Few minutes remained before the opening tipoff.

Inside the Army locker room, 18 players, 15 of them in uniform, sat on small folding chairs. The nonuniformed players did not like it, but they understood and accepted the league rule allowing no more than 15 players to be in uniform. A couple of days earlier, Maggie promised Natalie Schmidt that she would dress for the game. For each game, common team protocol called for two to three members of the White team to dress.

Schmidt recalled the event. "Coach Maggie promised me that I would dress for the championship game, but when the final roster was put up, my name was missing." Maggie noticed Natalie was not suiting up for the game, and her nonverbal was screaming. She realized a big mistake had been made. Without pointing to others, Maggie took full possession of the mistake and took time, when time was a scarce resource, before the game to console an upset 19-year-old. It came out later that an assistant coach made the mistake.

Behind them and along one of the walls, a large contingent of coaches, officers, and staff squeezed together for the final words of strategy and inspiration from their youthful coach. Among the group was Jim Mallette, waiting to fire up the West Point team. Each young woman had experienced the surge of adrenaline in high school championships and playing Navy; none had experienced a surge to this degree. The WE WILL messages were read and used to gather and maintain momentum from start to finish. Collectively, the atmosphere in the locker room was electric, fortified by an absolute belief—WE WILL win this game!

They tried to focus on the words of Maggie and the other coaches, but it was impossible not to hear the noise from the pep band or the pregame stomping of combat boots worn by the cadets.

Private thoughts, personal pledges, determined attitudes, and a little bit of sheer terror danced their way through the minds and bodies of the players. Many small prayers were given. Above all was the excitement of knowing, "This is it—this is really it." Win or lose, each player knew Wednesday, March 8, 2006, was the night she had been waiting for since the first day a mother, father, schoolyard friend, or friendly youth coach placed a basketball in her hands. Time spent on the hardwood, be it in youth basketball, junior high, Amateur Athletic Union (AAU), or senior high school, was finally demanding a payoff. None of the women on the Army women's basketball team would go on to play in the professional ranks. No, their future opponents would be far tougher than those in the WNBA. Their opponents awaited them in such places as the mountains of Afghanistan or the deserts of Iraq.

The whiteboard displayed the names and numbers of the top seven players for Holy Cross: Laura Aloisi—a tough, 5-foot-9 sophomore point guard known for her defense and who poured in 21 points the night before in their pulsating 64–60 victory against third-seeded Bucknell; Ashley McLaughlin—a 6-foot-1 sophomore forward; Brittany Keil—a 6-foot-2 junior forward capable of playing inside or outside and possessing a beautiful three-point shot, and who had put up 20 and 19 points, respectively, in the previous tournament games; Kaitlin Foley—a gifted athlete with a soft shot and quickness not expected of a 6-foot-4 center; Jessica Conte—a 5-foot-7 heady guard who complemented Aloisi to near perfection; Shannon Bush—at 5-foot-11, capable of playing either guard or forward; and Sarah Placek—a 5-foot-3 guard whose grasp of the use of space made up for any perceived height disadvantage.

Magarity made it clear to the Army team that Holy Cross was far better than the team they had beaten in two close games during the regular season. With solid wins over nonconference foes Boston University, Northeastern, and Memphis, and a 10–4 record in the Patriot League, the Crusaders would be hunting for Army.

Maggie returned to the team. She looked deeply into the eyes of young women who wanted to win not only for themselves, but also for the coach who had changed their lives. Only six or seven years older than the firsties, Maggie was, in so many respects, the person they wanted to be. She related, "I can't say this is just another game. But you need to play like it is. I want you to enjoy every minute of this experience. Play hard and play smart. If you do, things will work out."

Maggie looked toward the side of the locker room where Jim Mallette stood and continued.

"As you all know, Micky's mom and dad have always supported our team. Sir, we would be honored to have you share your thoughts with the team."

Micky was not sure what his message would be, she only wanted her father to do well in the eyes of her teammates.

Without hesitation, Jim Mallette stepped forward. He looked around the room and began to speak.

"There's a team on the other side of the wall. And there is a brass ring at West Point. They want to walk in here tonight and take that brass ring from you. You will not let that happen in your house." He stopped for just a second to let his words sink in, before continuing. "Tonight, you must follow the words of the famous Green Bay Packers head coach, Vince Lombardi, 'Winning isn't everything; it's the only thing.' And think of former Army men's basketball coach, Bob Knight, 'Never step on the court unless you plan to give 100 percent.'"

He added, "Be Army strong and do the very best you can."

The players stared intently at half of the parent couple who had supported the team unconditionally for almost four years.

His final words resonated dead-on with the team.

"Kick their asses! Let's go."

The women loved it. They jumped up and got in a circle and cheered. Then they ran out onto the court to do battle. It would be a team effort.

Of course, the ending of the pep talk story was the fact that, other than Micky and Alex McGuire, none of the other players had a clue as to who Vince Lombardi was. Still, the team was ready. And, as for Vince Lombardi, although credited with the proclamation, he really wasn't the originator of, "Winning isn't everything; it's the only thing." Most people chalk it up to Red Sanders, who coached the UCLA Bruins football team to a national championship in 1954.

At the sight of the first West Point player emerging from the locker room, the crowd roared in support of the Army team. This game was somehow different than playing Navy; it could possibly lead them to a place no other Army basketball player, man or woman, had ever been. A few layups and passing drills were followed by small groups loosening up; the centers and forwards moved to the basket, while the guards practiced skip and bounce passes. The same choreography unfolded at the Holy Cross end of the court.

At the sound of the buzzer, the court announcer, Joe Beckerle, addressed the growing crowd:

> Good evening ladies and gentlemen. Welcome to Christl Arena, the home of Army basketball on the campus of the United States Military Academy at West Point. At this time, we ask that you please rise as we honor America with the singing of our national anthem, performed by Cadet David Lindsey, class of 2009.

The West Point players, along with every cadet and most of the fans, stood at attention; Maggie Dixon, her light green eyes sparkling beneath bright lights, stared intently at the American flag hung high above the arena. The Holy Cross players paid similar respects to the nation. The game officials, Denise Brooks Clauser, Bryan Brunette, and Bonita Spence, stood at a modified parade rest. They were about to call a fine game; they would not affect the outcome.

At the conclusion of the final note of Lindsey's beautiful rendition of the national anthem, both teams broke to their benches and huddled. Position by position, the starters from each team, first Holy Cross and then Army, were announced. They ran through a team cordon, met their opposing team's player at center court, shook hands, and ran back to their end of the court. The handshakes and direct eye contact were both sincere and an attempt to send a message: "I'm going to dominate you." After introductions, each team met for a final few seconds. The Holy Cross players shook hands and huddled; the cadets formed a team circle, arms reaching across adjacent players' backs, and swayed back and forth. With a final pointing in the air and touching of hands, the team cheered and broke away. Game time.

Cadets and other fans of both teams cheered from the stands.

• *14* •

Women in the Arena

It is not the critic who counts; not the [woman] who points out how the strong [woman] stumbles, or where the doer of deeds could have done them better. The credit belongs to the [woman] who is actually in the arena, whose face is marred by dust and sweat and blood; who strives valiantly; who errs, who comes short again and again, because there is no effort without error and shortcoming; but who does actually strive to do the deeds; who knows great enthusiasms, the great devotions; who spends [herself] in a worthy cause; who at the best knows in the end the triumph of high achievement, and who at the worst, if [she] fails, at least fails while daring greatly, so that [her] place shall never be with those cold and timid souls who neither know victory nor defeat.—Theodore Roosevelt, adapted from "Citizenship in a Republic," Sorbonne, Paris, France, April 23, 1910

*H*oly Cross controlled the opening tip, with Kaitlin Foley tipping the ball to Jessica Conte. Once across half court, Conte passed to Laura Aloisi. It was Aloisi's job to control the tempo against a relentless man-to-man defense they knew they would face. Holy Cross had good shooters, but coach Bill Gibbons knew it was crucial to get the ball down low to Foley and Brittany Keil. Much to Gibbons's surprise, Army, although smaller in size, had dominated the boards in both league games. The player who had done the most damage was "one-minute wonder" Stefanie Stone. Someone needed to do something about her.

Holy Cross worked the ball around the perimeter until Foley was able to establish herself down low. A crisp pass from Ashley McLaughlin was followed by an inside shot by Foley. She missed. Megan Vrabel grabbed the rebound and passed to Alex McGuire, who took it down the left side. Holy Cross moved into a zone defense as McGuire moved to the right and passed off to Cara Enright. The Holy Cross defenders blocked her from driving the baseline. She passed to Stone, driving the lane. Aloisi reached in and made contact with the ball. Stone lost control, and Keil corralled it. The Holy Cross fans made their presence felt. At the other end, a blind pass from Aloisi gave McLaughlin an open shot from the three-point line. Her shot hit the rim, bounced high, and dropped into the net. Shooter's roll. But she stepped on the line, and the payoff was two points, not three. Twenty seconds later, Vrabel drove across the key, turned, and fired a short jumper. Swish. Nothing but net. The cadets and West Point fans roared. A little more than a minute into the game and the two teams were knotted at 2–2.

If Holy Cross was bothered by the Army man-to-man defense, they did not show it. They moved the ball quickly around the perimeter. Aloisi made a quick move from near the basket to the three-point line. Taking a pass from Keil, Aloisi put up a long shot; it dropped cleanly into the net. Her foot was clearly behind the arc; three points. Now it was Army's time again. The Black Knights moved the ball around the perimeter until McGuire saw Jen Hansen wide open on the right, well beyond the three-point arc. Exactly as taught by coaches for a hundred years, Hansen caught McGuire's pass in perfect rhythm and glided into her shot. The ball arced high and smooth, finally touching nothing but net chords. The score stood at 5–5.

On Holy Cross's next possession, Conte missed an inside shot; Aloisi rebounded. But no one on the team realized that the ball did not hit the rim. The shot clock reached zero, and Holy Cross turned over the ball. It was costly. On Army's possession, a beautiful skip pass from Hansen to McGuire resulted in an almost uncontested three. With a friendly roll of its own, the ball bounced once and fell into the net. For the first time, Army held the lead in a game that would see the lead change 17 times.

Holy Cross responded with an inside move and easy basket by Kaitlin Foley, Aloisi on the assist. Next, Army's Stone, struggling against the height of Foley, McLaughlin, and Keil, was tied up in the lane. The possession arrow rested in Army's favor. During the stoppage in play, Coach Gibbons made his first substitution: Shannon Bush replaced McLaughlin. Misses by Enright of Army and Aloisi of Holy Cross were followed by a foul on Shannon Bush and a media timeout. Once play resumed, Army had to inbound the ball with a throw into Army's end of the court. Enright took the ball and dribbled first to the middle of the court and then to the left corner. She faked to her right, moved left, and put up a soft jumper for another Army basket. Army's lead stood at 10–7.

At the 14:17 mark, with a stoppage in play after Holy Cross was out of bounds on a fight for a rebound, Bill Gibbons substituted McLaughlin and Sarah Placek for Jessica Conte and Keil; Maggie Dixon made her first substitution, with Redd King coming in for Hansen. As she had been for each of the previous 29 games, King was a stopper. She was quick, strong, and generally singled-minded as a defensive player. Offensively, her field goal percentage hovered slightly above .300, and her free-throw percentage was an anemic .465. She was not in the game to score points; she was in to keep Holy Cross from scoring. Maggie put King in to defend Aloisi. Speed versus speed; strength versus strength.

Army inbounded the ball, with McGuire taking it down the right side. She passed to Enright in the right corner as King moved just inside the three-point line on the left side. Enright's skip pass sailed over both teams to the waiting hands of the nonshooter King. But King was wide open and took a shot. Her form was textbook—and accurate. Swish; Army's lead grew to 12–7.

Army had the opportunity to take control of the game, but only if Holy Cross would allow that to happen. The Crusaders were not about to fold. While Army missed shots by King, Enright, and McGuire, Holy Cross scored on two baskets, one by Placek and a three-pointer by Bush off a pass from Placek. In three minutes and 13 seconds, led by Placek, Holy Cross turned a five-point deficit into a two-point lead. At this stage of the game, fans, players, coaches, and commentators sensed the 2006 Patriot League championship would be a game to remember. At the 11:28 mark, Holy Cross led, 14–12.

On Army's next possession, Enright missed a three-pointer, not even touching the rim. Although smaller in number, the Holy Cross faithful roared as loudly as possible, "Air ball, air ball." Bush grabbed the ball, but her long pass sailed off of Placek's hands at the baseline. Conte returned, and Placek, having contributed mightily to the Holy Cross cause, took a seat. McGuire took the inbounds pass down the middle of the court and dribbled to the right side. She made a fast, strong move toward Foley. Foley backed up to prevent a drive; when she did, McGuire backed across the three-point line and launched a mortar round. Three points. Army 15, Holy Cross 14. Christl Arena shook with seismic fury.

Holy Cross and Army traded turnovers, one by Army's Stone on a steal by Aloisi and one by Bush of Holy Cross. Stone fouled and was replaced by Megan Vrabel. On the bench, Maggie told Stefanie that she was doing fine. The wise coach emphasized Stefanie's need to simply continue playing "your game." Stefanie looked up at her coach and nodded. Until that point, Stone had brought down one rebound, turned over the ball twice, and scored zero points. Maggie's final comment to Stefanie was "enjoy yourself."

While Army missed shots by Enright, Evans, and McGuire, Holy Cross missed a three-pointer by Keil, committed a foul by Aloisi, and turned over the ball. With a stoppage in play, Coach Gibbons substituted McLaughlin back in for Keil. Army's ball.

McGuire drove into the left side of the lane, putting up a running shot that barely touched the rim. Fortunately for Army, she rebounded her own shot, but her pass into the middle, intended for Megan Evans, was deflected, and a scrum resulted. Evans moved toward the basket as the teams fought for the ball. It bounced away from two Holy Cross players and into the hands of Army's Hansen. In a split second, she fired a pass to Evans inside. Easy basket. Army 17, Holy Cross 14. Holy Cross responded 18 seconds later on an Aloisi pass inside to Foley. She put up a soft, but difficult, modified hook shot from the right side of the basket. It was as pretty a shot as Kareem Abdul-Jabbar ever took. With less than nine minutes remaining in the first half, it was once again a one-point game.

At the 8:32 mark, Keil and Bush replaced Conte and McLaughlin for Holy Cross. At Army's end of the court, Micky Mallette replaced Cara Enright. It had been five years since Micky's high school injury kept her from entering West Point with the class of 2005. Aside from a torn ACL, Micky's severe medical issues, both on and off the court, had the possibility of leading to her disqualification from being commissioned. She would graduate and receive her diploma but never serve in the United States Army. Given her love for basketball, and athletics in general, her sporadic participation in practices hurt. She wanted to practice, she wanted to play, and she certainly wanted to be a good team captain. She had scored 152 points the previous year and looked to this year with great hope. That she would score a total of 42 points this season did not mean she was not playing well; it meant she had overcome immense obstacles to still be playing at all. She was an inspiration to the team. She jogged onto the court to the cheers of her teammates and the boisterous cadets jamming the bleachers.

Barely into the game, Micky grabbed a rebound; she turned it over 14 seconds later. On the next possession by Holy Cross, Evans stole the ball from Foley and saw Mallette breaking downcourt on the left side. Evans threw what was almost a full-court pass to her. Mallette protected the ball with her body and, at full speed, put the ball up and off the glass. She did not know it then, but she had just scored her last basket as a college basketball player.

Once again, Holy Cross answered the challenge. Keil followed Mallette's basket with a soft shot from inside the three-point line. Her basket was followed by her steal against Vrabel. The clock stopped on an Evans foul, and a media timeout was called. King and Enright returned in place of McGuire and Hansen. Two seconds later, Holy Cross scored again on a basket by Keil. Holy Cross had taken a one-point lead at 20–19.

Basketball is one of those sports where someone can unexpectedly step forward and change the flow of a game. Following her basket at one end of the court, Keil blocked a shot by Vrabel at the other end. The ball went out of bounds off Holy Cross. Possession belonged to the Army Black Knights. The inbounds pass came to Vrabel out front. Vrabel basically handed the ball off to King moving to her left. Unexpectedly, King drove into the paint, executed a 180-degree turnaround, and put up a soft jumper just inside the free-throw line. A pretty shot worth two points. If Maggie and Dave did not want King taking shots, someone forgot to tell Redd.

King's basket was followed by a turnover by Aloisi; Army substituted Stone for Evans. To that point, Stone had been nearly invisible. Following missed shots at both ends, Micky Mallette was called for a charge driving to the basket. Here was a West Point cadet leader, bogged down with serious health issues, charging into enemy territory with almost reckless abandon. She defined the toughest of the tough. It's the type of toughness that identifies the American soldier. Holy Cross worked the ball around until Keil, coming off a screen, had an open shot from long range. It dropped cleanly into the net, and Holy Cross held a two-point lead. On Army's next trip, McGuire was fouled on a shot in the paint. She hit both free throws. Once again, the score was tied. Since the 13:23 mark, the largest lead by either team had been three points.

With Holy Cross in possession, the Crusaders again moved the ball around the perimeter. Keil took a pass on the left side and made a move to the inside of Stone. As she went up for the shot, Stone made a clean block from behind and took the ball. Keil tried to get the ball back, only to be thrown to the floor and called for a foul. It was a clean play by both women. Coach Gibbons brought Placek, Kathy Gruzynski, and McLaughlin into the game, giving Keil, Foley, and Conte a brief respite. Army's next possession was crucial. McGuire brought the ball down the right side. Holy Cross extended its defense, forcing McGuire to her left around the zone defense. She passed to Enright on the left side as Vrabel ran along the baseline to the left corner. Enright passed to Vrabel. The clock became a factor. Blocked from moving to the basket, Vrabel passed to Stone, who had moved to the top of the key. Stone drove toward the basket and then stopped and turned. King moved to the spot Stone had just vacated. With the clock winding down, Stone passed to King. She, in turn, made a stutter step to her right, drove to her left, and put up a jump shot from just inside the arc. Swish. The "nonshooter" had become the "hot shooter."

Absolute bedlam rang to the rafters. Holy Cross responded immediately. Enright tried to go around a solid Holy Cross screen but lost a step in the fight to keep up; Bush took a step back and launched an on-target three.

With 3:40 remaining in the half, Holy Cross led, 26–25. A couple of misses by each side ensued before Redd King committed a turnover. Foley returned to the game for Gruzynski. It took her exactly 15 seconds to score from inside off a rebound. Army returned the favor with a turnaround shot by Enright off a King assist.

The back-and-forth nature of the game continued. Foley hit another jumper off a feed from Aloisi, giving Holy Cross another three-point lead. At the 1:52 mark, Army called a timeout. Maggie gave King a rest and replaced her with Hansen; Coach Gibbons made an analogous substitution for the Crusaders, replacing Placek with Conte. King would sit for a total of 43 seconds before returning to the game. Maggie called the timeout to give the players both mental and physical rest. She wanted to keep their minds from running out of control. She told them they were playing well and to keep it up.

Reminding them they had beaten Holy Cross twice during the regular season, she ended with, "You'll remember this for the rest of your lives. Have fun out there." The words steeled in their minds.

On Army's next possession, McGuire lobbed a pass in to Stone. She was fouled by Bush. Stone missed the first free throw but sank the second. Army had a two-point deficit to overcome. "Let's go Army! Let's go Army!" The Army faithful just would not stop with the cheering.

Bush missed a short jumper off the dribble, Vrabel taking down the rebound. At the offensive end, a beautiful pass from Enright to Vrabel ended up with a foul call against Holy Cross's McLaughlin. Vrabel sank the first shot, cutting the deficit to one point. Her second shot hit the back rim and bounced off; fortunately for Army, Enright hauled down the rebound. No points resulted as McGuire missed a jumper and McLaughlin rebounded for Holy Cross. A missed three-pointer by Laura Aloisi was rebounded by King at the 41-second mark. Army worked the ball around again; this time King's jumper looked good but teetered on the rim and rolled off. By all reasoning, Holy Cross should have walked off the court with a one-point lead. But teams need to block out or trouble will come calling. Stone moved inside of the taller Crusader defenders, hauled in the rebound, and put it back up in heavy traffic; the ball touched the glass and fell into the net. Halftime. She had atoned for a subpar performance in the first 15 minutes of the game. Army led, 31–30.

Players retired from the court while the coaches on both sides gathered just outside of the doors leading to the team rooms. After a short wait, they received stat sheets with the highs and lows of each team. The statistics mirrored what had taken place on the court. Army was shooting at a little more than 44 percent, while Holy Cross came in at a little more than 43 percent.

Both teams shot 50 percent from three-point range, with Army going 3-for-6 and Holy Cross going 4-for-8. The biggest difference came in the form of free throws, where Army went 4-for-6. Holy Cross did not take a single free throw in the first half.

At the Army conclave, Maggie asked for observations and suggestions as to how to approach the second half.

"Okay," she said, "What is our approach to the second half?"

Dave Magarity responded, "We've got to stop the easy three-point shots. They're eating us alive. Guard them closer, and don't give them easy 'catch and shoot' opportunities."

One of the assistant coaches mentioned the need to keep focusing on rebounds, saying, "We've matched them so far, but we just can't let them beat us with their height."

Another added, "So far, we're hanging on to the ball better than normal."

One by one, the coaches gave their opinions as to what needed to be done to keep the pressure on the Crusaders. Maggie took it all in, made a few notes, and led the coaches into the team room. Everyone settled down, the players sitting in their metal folding chairs and others standing in the back.

Maggie told the team that the game itself was going great. She added that each player would remember the game for the rest of her life. Then, with a smile, she added a comment that struck close to their hearts, relating, "You need to make it a fond memory."

As the Army team ran back onto the court, the crowd was ready to rumble. The Army pep band struck up "On Brave Old Army Team." In the huddle, a sight normally unseen in college basketball took place. Anyone looking in could see Maggie smiling, almost kidding around with the players. It was an example of the rapport that had been seeded in her first meeting with the players the previous September. But, regardless of the lightheartedness on the Army bench, everyone knew the next 20 minutes would be the most crucial in the history of Army women's basketball.

Possession starting the second half belonged to the Crusaders, and they wasted little time taking advantage. Off an assist from Laura Aloisi, Ashley McLaughlin scored on an easy layup from the left side. Eleven seconds later, Army regained the lead on a Cara Enright spin move and layup from the right side of the lane. Another roar went up from the Army rooters. A soft jumper by Brittany Keil put Holy Cross back in the lead and quieted the home crowd just enough to enable the Holy Cross faithful to be heard. Just like Army fans, Holy Cross fans were almost fanatic in cheering for their team. Their ability to be heard had a positive effect on the team.

Alex McGuire missed on a three-point shot, but Stefanie Stone out-rebounded the Holy Cross defenders once again. She passed the ball outside, eventually getting it back to McGuire. Her short-range jumper missed, and Brittany Keil rebounded the ball. Ten seconds later, Kaitlin Foley was fouled by Jen Hansen in the act of shooting. With absolute calm, Foley sank both free throws. Army, now down by three points, worked the ball around Holy Cross's zone until McGuire was open enough for another outside shot—she missed again. Fortunately for Army, Holy Cross also suffered a mini-slump. With 17:15 left, Megan Vrabel stole the ball from Aloisi; seven seconds later, Enright fired a rocket skip pass to Evans just in front of the basket. Evans was fouled by Shannon Bush, who had replaced McLaughlin. For Army, Redd King replaced Hansen.

A 59 percent free-throw shooter, Evans sank the first shot and missed the second. Crucially for Army, Stone found herself early in the second half; she ripped down her second offensive rebound in less than two minutes; while still in the air and just before landing out of bounds, Stone threw the ball into the backcourt and the waiting hands of Enright. Enright passed to Vrabel, but Jessica Conte stole the ball from Vrabel as she drove the right side of the lane. Still, while Army failed to take advantage of Stone's rebound, her quality of play for the remainder of the game had been established. Holy Cross brought the ball down the right side. Keil, receiving a pass near the free-throw line, drove to her left for an easy layup. Holy Cross led, 38–34. McGuire brought the ball downcourt and passed to King on the right side. Two quick passes from King to Vrabel to Stone led to a shot from six feet away. Good. Holy Cross's lead had been cut to two points.

Next, Holy Cross missed a jumper by Keil and a layup by Foley. An offensive rebound by Keil went for naught as Stone knocked the ball loose. In the ensuing fight for the ball, Foley was out of bounds. Ball Army. During the stoppage in play, Placek and McLaughlin replaced Bush and Keil. Army worked the ball from right to left and back to the right. McGuire spotted King wide open and fed her. King responded with her fourth basket of the night. The teams had battled for a little more than 24 minutes, and the score was knotted at 38. Back and forth—Conte, on a perfect feed from Aloisi, sank a soft jumper. Then it happened again; King hit from the outside. The defensive specialist was in double digits. She pounded her fist into thin air, fully realizing she was in the throes of her finest night as a college basketball player. She had just tied the biggest game of her life at 40–40.

Holy Cross had been relatively successful in ball movement in spite of the tight guarding. Aloisi was quick; Army defenders gave her just enough space to be able to react to her moves. But, giving her too much space constituted a mistake. At the 14:40 mark, Foley saw Aloisi move beyond the arc;

she passed to Aloisi and watched her teammate nail another three-pointer. Army committed a turnover by Megan Vrabel, and officials called a shooting foul on McGuire against Placek. Following a media timeout, Placek made both free throws, giving the Crusaders an uncomfortable five-point lead. Maggie looked down the bench and called, "Ashley, Anna, you're up." For Smash Magnani and Anna Wilson, they were the words they had been waiting for. They were both ready and planned to leave everything on the court. Enright and Stone sat down for a breather.

Momentum moved to Holy Cross, and they took full advantage of it. Right out of the chute, Foley blocked a shot by Vrabel and grabbed the rebound. She missed a shot. Barely into the game, Magnani rebounded for Army. The Holy Cross zone defense paid off. After trying to work the ball around for an easy shot, Army began to run out of clock. McGuire put up another jumper—off target again. McLaughlin rebounded. At the 12:49 mark, Aloisi passed the ball in to Foley in the paint, and she scored. The seven-point Holy Cross lead was the largest of the night. Maggie called a timeout. She brought Enright and Stone in for Vrabel and McGuire. In the huddle, Maggie spoke to the players about keeping steady. She emphasized that they were taking good shots and should continue to play the same way they had been playing.

But, alas, the normally consistent shot belonging to Cara Enright seemed to be taking the night off. She missed another jumper, and the ball was rebounded by McLaughlin, who was immediately fouled by Magnani. Keil replaced McLaughlin for Holy Cross—and the Crusader momentum continued. Bush passed the ball inside to Foley for an easy short jumper. Holy Cross fans raised their hands in the air, pumped their fists, and screamed at the top of their lungs. In their eyes, it was time to "seal the deal." A media timeout was called with less than 12 minutes to go and Army trailing 49–40.

Army's shooting and general play told Maggie that the players were allowing Holy Cross to dominate. She needed to give them her own version of a significant emotional event, taking the team from its current deficient level of play and returning it to the strong, efficient team that had started the game. With Hansen, Stone, King, Enright, and Magnani sitting on the chairs at the edge of the court, and the rest of the team surrounding the two senior coaches, Maggie told a story of an elderly woman coming up to her and asking Maggie to find her seat. "She thought I was an usher," Maggie stated. Maggie looked at the team, expecting some sort of laughing response. Nothing. One by one, the players reacted with faint smiles. Finally, one of them said, "Coach, that's lame." Maggie's funny story was a lame joke. At that point, Redd King came up with a joke of her own.

"What do you call a deer with no eyes?" Redd asked, looking around the group. No one answered. She waited a few seconds and then gave the answer: "I have no eye deer." It took a few seconds before the joke touched base with the players, but eventually the entire team was laughing. Years later, they still laugh when thinking about it.

The bottom line was obvious—a sense of needed calmness returned.

Maggie returned to the game. It was time to "fish or cut bait."

With Dave Magarity leaning in to hear, Maggie told her young players with conviction, "We're going to overcome this adversity, count on it. We've got plenty of time. Let's cut the lead one basket at a time. You've done it before, and you can do it tonight. One small chunk at a time. Let's go." Years later, Smash remembered thinking, "We can win this game. We can win it."

On the next possession, however, Army's shooting woes continued with a missed three-pointer by Hansen. Foley and King ended up in a jump-ball situation—the possession arrow pointing in favor of Holy Cross. On the inbounds play, Army put some pressure on Holy Cross in the backcourt—to no avail. Aloisi received the ball in the left corner and simply waited for a driving Bush. Aloisi's pinpoint pass landed in Bush's hands for an easy layup. Holy Cross 51, Army 40.

In the upper stands, Jim and Kathy Mallette were sitting with a close friend and their two sons, Chris and Brandon, both former collegiate basketball players. Kathy leaned over and said to Jim, "We might not win this game."

He answered, "You may be right, but as long as they play Army ball I may be disappointed but I won't be angry."

Courtside, the game was on the verge of getting out of hand. Army was in trouble. Deep trouble. Someone needed to step up and take the lid off the basket.

One Basket at a Time

$\mathcal{A}$s a small sidebar to the Patriot League championship game, it is worth making a mental return to the final home game against Bucknell. The incident related to Maggie Dixon's asking firsties Ashley "Smash" Magnani and Adrienne "Adie" Payne if they wanted to start West Point's last regular-season home game against the Bisons, and their final response to the invitation, said a lot about not only the coach, but also the firsties and the entire team. The coach was willing to risk defeat to be loyal to two young women who had given all a person can give to a team. By declining their coach's offer, both firsties showed class above and beyond in their loyalty to Maggie and every player on the team. In return, although the game was a one-point cliffhanger, Smash and Adie both played in the game. The entire team knew of the offer and would have been fine with either decision. Team camaraderie at its best. They would never give up on winning the Patriot League championship game. Never.

Army still had one major advantage—the Corps of Cadets. It didn't matter that Army was temporarily behind by double digits, every cadet in the stands was, in his or her own way, supporting the team with an almost uncontrollable fervor. They were going to war.

On the next trip downcourt, Army moved the ball to the left side of the court. Smash Magnani received a pass just outside the free-throw lane. She took one right-handed dribble, taking her almost to the free-throw line, and then picked up her dribble; it appeared she had been stopped and had no options other than passing the ball beyond the three-point arc. Instead, with her left foot as pivot, she made a fake, turned, and took a huge step with her right foot, putting up a running left-handed shot from at least seven feet away. Good! The shot was not just good, it was magnificent. The Army faithful screamed as loudly as they could. After four minutes and two seconds of missed shots, Magnani had finally slowed the hemorrhaging. On Holy Cross's next possession, a three-point attempt by Shannon Bush was rebounded by none other than Smash Magnani.

Both teams traded missed opportunities from three-point range. Stefanie Stone helped the Army cause when she tied up Jessica Conte after Jen Hansen's missed three-pointer. Stone and Redd King retired to the bench while Megan Evans and Alex McGuire returned to action. With Army in control of the ball, Laura Aloisi fouled McGuire on a drive to the left side of the basket. McGuire made both free throws, the first hanging on the rim for a second or two until dropping through the net. In the stands, the cadets raised both arms in the air and, as the ball fell through the net, responded by bringing both arms down swiftly and yelling a loud, "Hoooh." The Crusader lead stood at seven points.

Colonel Donna Brazil, wearing her BDUs, focused on the Army bench. At the far end of the bench was one of the assistant ORs, dressed, as always, in her neat dress uniform. The medals on the young woman's chest signified she had served in either Iraq or Afghanistan—or both. Women served in most of the same branches as the men—over time all branches would open to women. Sadly, female graduates of the USMA, and through other sources of commissioning, have died in combat. So have enlisted women.

Realizing each of the young officers had experienced some pretty tough assignments, Brazil had a policy of offering the assistant ORs the opportunity to sit on the bench on a rotating basis. When Brazil's schedule demanded, the assistant ORs were afforded the opportunity to take trips with the team. Doing so was a small perk for the junior officers, who the players saw as mentors to go to when times weren't so good. Like Maggie and Dave, the ORs were a team inside a team. Brazil looked around and saw a delirious crowd of officers and cadets. It was a churning sea of humanity. It was what collegiate sports should be—real scholar-athletes on opposing teams who were as comfortable with macroeconomics as a 10-foot jump shot.

Years later, Brazil reminisced, "It was a magical week. It was like we were transported to a different location."

The games against Navy usually serve as the benchmark for rabid competition. But, truth be told, this one game rose above all others, including Navy, in intensity, determination, and excitement. Brazil explained. "You could feel the support of the Corps." The scene was unreal. Football players jumping up and down have the ability to damage stands, and that is exactly what happened to the pullout bleachers behind the north basket. The cadets did not break the bleachers on purpose; the bleachers were simply not constructed to handle a full load of West Point cadets, quite a few weighing 250 pounds or more, going nuts. More than 2,000 other cadets were also going crazy in other parts of the arena.

On the Crusaders' next possession, Army's man-to-man defense forced the ball outside. Aloisi roamed the court, first to the left, and then, with a between-the-legs move, to the right. But, try as she might, Aloisi could not find an open teammate down low. Conte came outside and took a pass near the left side of the three-point line. She dribbled left, hoping to break free of Army's Hansen. Hansen was ready. Conte attempted a pass down low, but Hansen deflected the ball out of bounds. Inbounding the ball required a long pass beyond the arc to Aloisi. She held the ball out front to set up for an easy basket. In a beautifully executed play, Aloisi moved left, two players moved toward the basket, and Brittany Keil ran from the far side along the baseline to a spot-up position on the left side of the court. Aloisi's perfect pass left Keil wide open for the shot. Keil was a great shooter—once again, the ball hit nothing but net.

On Army's next possession, the ball did make it down low. McGuire brought the ball to the forecourt and bounce-passed to Cara Enright. Enright drove the baseline, but Holy Cross blocked her path. She passed out to McGuire and remained near the backboard, just outside the lane. McGuire, near the free-throw line, spotted Enright and fired a return pass needing to be dead on-target. It was. Enright caught the ball, turned to her right, and powered her way past Kaitlin Foley to the glass.

In the next minute and seven seconds, a lot of basketball was played, but the score did not change. The teams traded missed three-pointers; Enright turned over the ball; and McGuire blocked a shot by Aloisi, the ball going out on Army. On the inbounds play, it took Holy Cross four seconds to get the ball to Foley for another basket, increasing the Crusader lead back to nine points. Megan Evans cut the lead to seven points with a short jumper from the left side. But no sooner had Army cut the lead than Holy Cross put it back into double digits at 58–48, on a beautiful three-pointer by Conte. Since Magnani had scored to end the shooting drought at the 11:09 mark, Army had reduced the lead by exactly one point. Less than eight minutes remained.

Evans, this time on an assist from McGuire, scored again with a soft jumper. Following a turnover by the Crusaders' Sarah Placek, a media time-out brought both teams to the sideline. Instead of an 11-point deficit, Army trailed by eight.

In the huddle, Maggie was calm and upbeat. She and the other coaches were happy with the team's play since the previous timeout. She told the players they were playing smart and to do what she had always told them—get back in the game one basket at a time. Her demeanor was nectar from the gods for the Army team. She looked around the group and told them, "We will win this game." The players returned to the court with fire in their blood.

Dave Magarity remembered thinking, "She's a kid. Only a kid. But isn't she great?"

The crowd continued its constant roar. Along the baseline a group of energetic cadets began leapfrogging in front of the stands. Their comrades loved it. Even the Holy Cross cheerleaders watched in amazement as cadets, soon-to-be army officers in some distant land, were playing games as though they were first graders.

Once play resumed, Murphy's Law took over. McGuire, going down the right side of the court, found herself out of control; she crashed into Bush. Foul against Army. Not a particularly smart play by McGuire.

The sign of a solid basketball player is to be able to make a mistake on one play and not think about it on the next. It's also the sign of a good coach not to pull a player for making a mistake. Both McGuire and her coach were good at letting the past stay in the past. On the next Holy Cross possession, Evans intercepted a pass intended for Foley and passed to McGuire. This time McGuire tried the left side, found a small opening, and drove to the basket. Taking a small hop-step, she put in a beautiful right-handed layup from the left side of the basket. The deficit dropped to six points.

The Holy Cross women had been "in the arena" many times and were not about to roll over and play dead. The Crusaders moved the ball around; it eventually ended up in the hands of Aloisi. She, as McGuire had done seconds before, drove the left side of the lane. Just as the Army defense closed in on her, she dished off to Conte. Conte took two dribbles and lofted a soft jump shot—good. The lead stood at eight points with 6:23 remaining.

Again, McGuire brought the ball downcourt, this time passing to a teammate rather than driving the lane. Receiving the ball, Megan Evans took a shot from beneath the right edge of the backboard but missed. Stone once again positioned herself in front of Bush. She grabbed the offensive rebound and instantly put it off the glass and into the basket, turning a great defensive play into an offensive highlight.

It was clear that Army's defense had stepped up the tempo. The tide ever so slowly began to turn against Holy Cross. On the next Crusader possession, Aloisi drove the right side only to have her shot blocked by Evans. Stone grabbed the rebound, and Army moved downcourt again. By focusing on McGuire, the Crusaders failed to track Hansen's move just beyond the three-point mark on the left side. McGuire passed. Hansen was in the perfect catch-and-shoot spot. "Whoosh!"—the sound was that of a basketball touching only the cords of the net. For a basketball player at any level of competition, the sound is one of the sweetest in existence. The ball barely cleared the bottom of the net before the next crowd explosion. Everyone could feel the vibrations from the roar of the crowd and the stomping of feet. The Army bench had nothing but empty seats; the team members were jumping and hugging one another. "One basket at a time. One small chunk at a time. We will win the game . . ." was playing out in front of them. Army now trailed by three. Coach Gibbons called timeout. Running to the Army bench, Cara Enright said to herself, "We're going to win this game. We're going to win."

No sooner had play resumed than King stole the ball from Foley. McGuire became the beneficiary of a pass from King and nailed a jumper. A one-point game.

Bush then missed a three-point shot, which was rebounded by Enright. Army continued its march against Holy Cross as McGuire hit another jumper off an assist by Enright. The 11-point lead had evaporated in a span of six and a half minutes. At 61–60, in Army's favor, Holy Cross knew they had left money on the table. Adding to their misery, Foley missed a short shot, and the ball was rebounded again by Enright. Another soft jumper by King brought the score to 63–60, Army. The pro-Army crowd went berserk, as King, the defender, had become a scoring machine.

Holy Cross historically fields tough teams, and this year's model was no different—a solid team unwilling to wilt. Allowing a one-point lead to turn into a three-point deficit was foreign to them, and, to the last player, they were going to turn things around. The jumper by King was intolerable. Foley rebounded a missed shot by teammate Conte; a subsequent basket by Bush cut the Army lead to one point. Coach Gibbons called another timeout. In a span of 39 seconds, three timeouts were called, two by Holy Cross and one by the media.

Coming out of the third timeout, Holy Cross wasted precious little time getting its act back together. With Aloisi at the controls, the Crusaders took advantage of a McGuire turnover. While the team passed the ball around the perimeter, Keil, normally a post player, moved to the top of the key and waited for an Aloisi pass. It came special delivery. Aloisi penetrated into the lane, stopped, turned around, and fired a pass to the waiting Keil. Her shot was perfect, and Aloisi notched her 12th assist. The lead returned to Holy Cross, 65–63.

Next came Army's turn to drive the crowd to near collapse. A short jumper by Evans was off to the side. Once again, Stone continued driving the Crusader team absolutely berserk. She moved inside the taller Holy Cross players, muscled her way to the ball, and put it back up before anyone could negate her quickness. Keil fouled her on the shot—one minute and 49 seconds remained. With the score now at 65–65, Stone hit the free throw, Army retaking the lead. On Holy Cross's next possession, Keil missed a three-pointer, rebounded by Enright. But, a few seconds later, Aloisi stole the ball from King. It took exactly 13 seconds for the Crusaders to retake the lead, as Conte's baseline jump shot, off a feed from Keil, fell gently through the net, leaving the score at Holy Cross 67, Army 66. The clock slipped beneath the one-minute mark.

The stakes were sky-high for players on both sides. Given the immense pressure, the two teams played with uncommon control. The clock ticked away. The West Point women were within reach of their first trip to the NCAA Tournament; the Holy Cross women were on the verge of their 11th championship. At this point in the game, the past had been forgotten; it was this moment and only this moment that counted. Army moved the ball around, and with 45 seconds left, Crusader Aloisi fouled Cadet McGuire. A plebe, Alex McGuire could be forgiven for cracking under the pressure. But, at crunch time, some players love to step up and make the big play. McGuire was one of those players. She seemed undisturbed. She had her thoughts under control: It was no different than the Maryland state championship or the first Bucknell game. Swoosh; swoosh. Both free throws were dead on. Army 68, Holy Cross 67. By game's end, McGuire would shoot 6-for-6 from the foul line. As a quick aside, for the games Army won by two points or less—or in overtime—Alex McGuire shot 25-for-26. Not to be outdone, Jen Hansen went 19-for-20.

Nine seconds later, Bush moved inside but missed a layup. Holy Cross's Foley was in the right place at the right time. Taking advantage of her height, she grabbed the rebound and put it back up. She missed the shot, but only because Stone had no alternative but to foul. Stone did not like fouling, but she knew it was better to make her opponent score from the free-throw line than by hitting an easy dunk from directly beneath the basket. Stone was playing both smart and physical.

Similarly to McGuire only seconds earlier, Foley appeared calm. Her first shot was all net. Score tied at 68. Her form for her second shot seemed perfect—but her mechanics were off ever so slightly. The ball hit the left side of the basket and bounced away. In the mad scramble, the ball was tipped out of bounds by Stone. Possession belonged to Holy Cross. Coach Gibbons called his last timeout with exactly 34.9 seconds to go in regulation.

With the exception of children younger than the age of three, everyone in Christl Arena knew the Holy Cross game plan: Hold the ball, move it around, score, and then cut the nets down. At worst, the game would go into overtime.

"Supe's Rocket—Supe's Rocket—Supe's Rocket!" It started as a murmur but became ever growing as the cadets in the stands called for their senior leader, Lieutenant General Lennox, to lead them to victory with the highly motivating "Supe's Rocket." As Army's favorite cheer, it had never been more appropriate and needed than at this moment. The chant reverberated throughout the arena—"Supe's Rocket—Supe's Rocket—Supe's Rocket." General Lennox signaled for the commandant and dean, both brigadier generals, and the post sergeant major (the senior enlisted soldier on post), to join him.

Lieutenant General William J. Lennox Jr. assumed the responsibility of superintendent of the USMA in the summer of 2001. He was a strong leader, highly respected by the Corps of Cadets. In football at Cardinal Hayes High School in the Bronx, Lennox played pulling guard on offense and linebacker on defense. At the academy, he gained fame as a boxer, once reaching the championship bout of the Brigade Open boxing tournament. He was also noted for being very intelligent and a solid leader. As a cadet, he was selected to serve on the brigade staff as brigade activities officer— much like Micky Mallette, his position placed him very high among the class of 1971, graduating 59th in a class of 729. He was commissioned into the field artillery.

Lennox received both a master's and a doctoral degree in literature from Princeton University. His doctoral dissertation was entitled "American War Poetry." His military record was as solid as his cadet record. He progressed from service as an artillery forward observer to positions of increasing responsibility, including a battery commander, battalion commander, brigade commander, and deputy commanding general of the Eighth United States Army in South Korea. He served in several crucial staff positions, including White House fellow and Chief of Staff, III Corps at Fort Hood, Texas.

In most circles, it would be acceptable for a university president to decline such a request from the students. But West Point isn't just any institution, and General Lennox wasn't just any school president. He arrived at the game wearing his BDUs and a face full of camouflage (dark green and black camouflage sticks being the source); he had every intention of leading the Supe's Rocket. All he needed was for the Corps of Cadets to request it—and request it they did.

Watching the contingent of senior leaders taking the floor, the cadets went wild. On General Lennox's signal, each cadet and some of the West Point fans started in a crouching position with both arms down. With true military precision, the superintendent crouched with both hands down. He started to stand up with a low whistle that rose in pitch as he brought both hands high into the air while moving to a standing position. More than 2,000 additional whistles sounded in unison as the Corps of Cadets joined their commander. In semirapid movements, the remainder of the Supe's Rocket followed:

BOOM (simultaneous with both arms down)

AHH (simultaneous with both arms up)

YOOS (right arm down) MAY (left arm down), RAH (right arm up) RAH (left arm up)

YOOS-MAY, RAH-RAH (repeat arm movements)

HOO-RAH (right arm down)

HOO-RAH (left arm down)

ARMY (lower and then raise both arms)-RAH! (lower both arms rapidly)

TEAM! (right arm up) TEAM!! (left arm up) TEAM!!! (both arms down)

BEAT NAVY!!

Whether the Supe's Rocket would do the trick would play out in the next 34.9 seconds.

Thirteen Seconds to Euphoria

$\mathcal{A}$rmy 68, Holy Cross 68. Two fighters slugging it out. Take your pick—Muhammad Ali versus Smokin' Joe Frazier, Joe Louis versus Max Schmeling, or Rocky Marciano versus Jersey Joe Walcott. The boxers may have been bigger and stronger, but they fought with no more intensity than these two women's basketball teams. Laura Aloisi and Redd King fought one another tooth and nail from the inbounds pass with 34.9 seconds left in the game. Aloisi protected the ball well as she dribbled down the right side of the court; King hounded her on every step. The frenzied crowd from both Holy Cross and Army rocked Christl Arena. It was pure, unadulterated bedlam. Thus far, Holy Cross had executed the game plan exactly as Bill Gibbons designed, a road map to scoring as the clock ran out, or, at worst, sending the game into overtime. The heady Crusader guard had played an outstanding game, particularly her passing. Her 13th assist of the game played out in her mind. It would win the game.

At the 18-second mark, Holy Cross's Brittany Keil moved toward the baseline with Stefanie Stone guarding as close as she could get. As Aloisi began to dribble toward the left side of the court, Keil reversed and moved back toward the top of the key. Wisely, she tried to rub Stone off on a screen by Kaitlin Foley. The screen slowed but did not stop Stone. She fought her way through it and, at the 14-second mark, was closing the distance separating her from Keil. Keil stopped at the top of the key and waited for a pass; Stone was still moving toward her. In the same time span, Aloisi dribbled from the right side of the court to the left. Again, King never let her have any free space. Aloisi finally made a mistake—she picked up her dribble with her back partly toward her teammates. She turned and threw a pass toward Keil at the top of the circle. Uncharacteristically of an Aloisi pass, it was soft. Too soft. The clock showed 13 seconds.

For reasons she never fully remembered—maybe intuition or maybe folly—something in her core told Stone she had a shot at the ball. Stone accelerated around Keil, tipping the ball toward the Holy Cross basket. An almost guttural noise from the pro-Army crowd rose to a deafening crescendo. Already running, Stone had the advantage and corralled the ball for what almost everyone in the arena hoped would take the team to a place only dreamed of as a kid. Keil did not give up; she recovered and bolted in pursuit of Stone. Had Stone simply gone off of her left foot for an easy right-handed layup, the basket would have been a lock. It wasn't a lock.

From the first time a youngster plays basketball, the layup should be the easiest of all shots. It is the easiest; it is also the most difficult. Stone came to a complete stop and started to make a little hop beneath the basket. Keil leaped toward her foe and caught a piece of the ball and a lot of Stone, knocking her to the floor. A shooting foul with 8.8 seconds to go. Cadets and West Point fans went berserk, jumping up and down, some screaming "intentional foul," waving their arms, and hugging one another. Could it finally happen? Stone wouldn't—make that couldn't—look at her teammates; she tugged at her shirt, seeming to concentrate partly on the floor and partly on some unknown space where she sought out calm, and quietly took her position at the foul line. She was experiencing the most stress-filled, and exciting, moment of her young life.

Stefanie Stone has a unique foul shot. She moves into a squatting position, takes three or four quick dribbles, holds the ball for a split second, and then hops straight up into her shooting movement. But, whatever works, works; she shot almost 75 percent for the season (and would shoot well above 80 percent during her firstie year). She did exactly as she had as a kid; the ball arced up, reached its apogee, and came down. Clunk. It hit the front rim and bounced off. A collective mixture of groan and total silence filled the air. The more than 2,000 cadets had to lower their arms slowly, hoping they could follow her next shot with a "Hooh!!" signifying success. She tapped the ball back toward the referee as Megan Evans came up, shook Stone's hand, and swatted her on the butt. Again, thousands of arms raised throughout the stands. For her second shot, Stone went through the same mechanics; on her hop, the ball arced up, reached its apogee, and arced down. Swish—the most endearing sound in basketball. The crisp, rousing "Hooh!!!" filled the arena simultaneously with arms coming down in unison. The cadets were delirious. White towels rippled through the sea of cadet battle dress uniforms, brown t-shirts and bare chests—and a ripe aroma of sweaty armpits. At several locations in the stands, a cadet, thrown by fellow classmates, would suddenly catapult from the teeming mass some five to six feet into the air. As for Stone, she was light years away from the one minute she had played the previous season. But the game was far from over. Maggie called timeout. The 8.8 seconds showing on the arena clock seemed an infinitely long time. Army 69, Holy Cross 68. Timeout.

The Army team formed an arc around Maggie. Whether in the game or not, each player—with the possible exception of the overcharged Redd King—stood riveted, focused solely on this remarkable 28-year-old coach, waiting on her wisdom to take the team to its "impossible dream." Maggie's first action was to give Stefanie an attagirl. She then immediately turned to Enright with defensive instructions. Had there been any doubt, at any level, as to who the head coach of Army was, it vanished in front of 2,500 screaming fans.

Maggie looked toward the scorer's table and raised one finger in the air. Her up-and-down nod signified Army had one foul to give. Dave Magarity spoke not to the huddled team, but to Maggie, with his perspective on how to handle the clock. Just as he had promised her at their first meeting five months earlier, Magarity settled into the background.

Kneeling, Maggie looked at the team. She spoke directly to the players. "We have one foul to give. If you need to, foul the ball handler, but if you do, do it before she's in the shooting motion."

Standing almost between Maggie and Dave, Redd King was psyched up to the point of allowing her coach's comment, "We have one foul to give," to float away meaningless into space. At that time, Magarity knew King was clearly wired tighter than a golf ball core—after all, it was her job to guard the Crusaders' quickest, and possibly toughest, player. Either way, to settle her down, he simply placed his hand gently on King's shoulder. To this point, King had played the game of her life. She needed less than nine seconds to finish well.

Since the opening tip there had been 17 lead changes. Basketball, men's or women's, doesn't get better than the 2006 Patriot League championship. An absolute barn burner.

Holy Cross ball. The Army–Holy Cross matchups for the final 8.8 seconds were Enright–Bush, Evans–Foley, King–Aloisi, McGuire–Conte, and Stone–Keil. Army was putting two plebes and three yearlings on the court to hold off the Crusader women. Conte's inbounds pass from the baseline came to Bush, not Aloisi. Bush drove hard to her left, with Enright defending. To keep from being hemmed in, Bush attempted a crossover dribble to her right, but the ball hit Enright's foot and bounced back toward the Holy Cross basket. Bush turned and ran to the ball. McGuire saw the ball and reacted in a split second. Faster than Bush, McGuire looked like she was shot out of a cannon. She flew to the ball and, with both players hitting the floor, split possession with Bush.

The crowd noise reached the roar of an EF-5 tornado. The arena seemed to vibrate. Unfortunately for Army, the possession arrow favored the visitors. Holy Cross still had the ball, with exactly five seconds to go. A final timeout brought both teams to the sidelines. For Holy Cross, it was do or die—get the ball to Aloisi for an attack on the basket, either a layup or a pass off underneath for a game-ending chip shot. The safety valve would be a three-point shot by Keil. For Army, hound Aloisi for five seconds and block any passing lanes—and remember, "We have a foul to give."

Back on the court, Keil and Foley broke immediately toward the free-throw lane, Keil peeling off toward the right three-point line; Bush moved partway down the left side of the court in case the inbounds pass to Aloisi couldn't be made. Stone guarded Keil tight, forcing her almost to the sideline, well beyond normal three-point range, while also making it tough for Keil to receive the ball unchallenged.

As expected, Conte's inbounds pass went directly to Aloisi in the Holy Cross backcourt. She took a quick stutter-step, then bolted to her right, guarded tightly by King. Supercharged as any player could be, King was in-credible in sidestepping, holding her hands in the air, and still giving Aloisi no more than six inches of breathing room.

Maggie, Dave, and the other coaches screamed at King, "Foul her, foul her!" At the three-point line, Aloisi drove toward the basket. Two seconds remained. That Army had a foul to give was long forgotten—or, for King, maybe never remembered—in the heat of battle. With Aloisi nearing the basket, Evans stopped guarding Foley and moved toward the low post to at-tempt blocking the shot if needed. Her move gave a small amount of open space to Foley. Enright moved toward Foley but could not prevent an Aloisi pass for an easy layup; Enright's position also left her with the possibility of fouling a shot attempt around the basket. But King was doing her job. She blanketed Aloisi, making a pass splitting King and Evans almost impossible. Aloisi made the decision to finish the drive.

In the end, both King and Aloisi knew they were the two players who would decide the game. Aloisi, holding the slimmest of advantages, took a final dribble and went into her shooting motion. A total of 1.3 seconds remained. King raised her arms as high as possible, trying to distract the coming shot without fouling. The extra dribble put Aloisi slightly nearer to the basket than she wanted. She moved the ball to her right hand as she went into her shooting motion. King defended with everything she had. The ball left Aloisi's hand and—in a moment of suspense—hit the underside of the backboard and bounced out of bounds as Aloisi hit the floor.

For a split second, fans and players searched for a referee's whistle. There was neither whistle nor foul—only an explosion. The roar of a thousand trains rang down on Christl Arena. The young women broke for the middle of the court. Simultaneously, the sea of brown t-shirts, camouflaged uniforms, black jerseys of the sprint football team, painted faces, and bare chests swallowed the players at the Army logo. On the Army sideline, three large cadets, most likely from the football team, ran to and grabbed Maggie; they placed her on their shoulders and plowed their way into the maelstrom. In the stands, the Army pep band immediately went into the rousing Army fight song:

> On brave old Army team
> On to the fray
> Fight on to victory
> For that's the fearless army way

Just like Maggie, the Army players were hoisted onto the shoulders of cadets and carried around the court. At first, Redd King went to the scorer's desk and simply bent over to grasp what had just happened. She was also hunting for the rosary she kept at the scorer's desk. Redd was not Catholic, but on this night a rosary might just be nondenominational. Maybe she was giving a small prayer of thanks—but whatever she was doing, it was short-lived. She, too, soon found herself hoisted above the throng. Redd was delirious—she smiled, hugged, and pounded her fist into her palm. She had done her job in spectacular fashion. For Redd, she had finished the game of a lifetime—a game never to be forgotten. Lifted onto the shoulders of celebrating cadets, Redd, never more excited than at this very moment, could hardly breathe. This night, this utter shining moment, would never have occurred without her discussions with and mentoring by her inspirational coach less than three months before; thoughts of leaving the basketball team and the academy were gone forever. Next to her, still riding on cadet shoulders, was that person Redd had learned to love—Margaret Mary Dixon, Coach Maggie.

One year earlier, Stefanie Stone, with the exception of the one minute in a game Army won by 30 points, had watched from the bench as her teammates played the game she loved so much. This night erased the crushing hurt of working so hard and playing so little. In this championship game, she had played for 33 minutes (33 times what she played the year before), gone 4-for-4 from the field, pulled down a team-high eight rebounds (five of them offensive), shot 3-for-5 from the free-throw line, and made three steals (the last leading to the final, winning point). As with the other players being carried on the shoulders of their comrades in arms, tonight would remain with Stone for the rest of her life. She could not wrap her mind around the scene. She was loving every second and did not want the evening to end.

The celebration on the court and in the stands continued. Baseball caps with "Patriot League Champions" written on the front were passed out among the players. When asked what was one of the highlights of the entire event, Cara Enright answered,

> We were being carried on the shoulders of other cadets, and everyone was celebrating like I've never seen in my life. I felt a tap on my shoulder and turned around. It was Coach Dixon. She, still being carried by the football players, placed a "Patriot League Champions" cap on my head. We both leaned toward each other and hugged. What a memory.

The Army pep band continued its mission. The next song up was none other than "Hey Baby (I Wanna Know If You'll Be My Girl)":[1]

> Hey, hey baby
> (ooh—aah)
> I wanna know-oh-oh
> (oh-ooh)
> If you'll be my girl

In between fist pumping and arms pointing in the air, many Army fans joined in the singing. Exactly as Colonel Donna Brazil had sensed a few minutes earlier, the scene was surreal.

The noise slowly abated, providing an opening to a long-standing tradition. The Army cohort stood at attention while the Holy Cross pep band played their alma mater.

Leah Secondo of College Sports Television, unaware of Army game etiquette, corralled Maggie for a quick postgame interview. Maggie, politely and quietly, knowing she was moments away from hearing the Army alma mater, spoke of her five-month journey, relating, "Standing in silence and hearing our alma mater being played . . . is so amazing. This team has been wonderful all year. They fought through so much. I'm so proud of them. They did this themselves. I'm just along here for the ride." Her comments were heartfelt, humble, and much too modest.

Following the Holy Cross alma mater, the cadets and fans faced the American flag and stood at attention for the playing of the beautiful, almost haunting Army alma mater. Maggie stood at attention, proud of her team and thoroughly satisfied at being part and parcel of West Point and everything for which it stands. Her use of the word *our* in the postgame interview was cathartic. Maggie Dixon had gone from coaching candidate, to Army basketball coach, and, in five months, to full-fledged member of the West

Point community. Everyone loved her. Although not much older than her players, Maggie personified the words inscribed on the West Point logo and sung in the alma mater[2]—duty, honor, country:

> Hail alma mater dear
> To us be ever near
> Help us thy motto bear
> Through all the years
> May *duty* be well performed
> *Honor* be 'ere untarned
> *Country* be ever armed
> West Point by thee

Cadets and graduates of West Point know the words of the alma mater by heart. The beautiful hymn was sung in a manner giving respect to those of the "Long Gray Line"—graduates who had served, were serving, or had died in service to their country. And, of course, two words always followed the ending of the alma mater—BEAT NAVY!

Jim Mallette worked his way down from the upper deck and found Maggie, still among happy cadets and other fans. He hugged her and exclaimed, "Maggie, we never would have won this game without you as our coach." He was almost in tears.

Without hesitation, Maggie responded, "No, Mr. Mallette. This would not be possible without your speech."

She reached out and gave the game ball to Jim Mallette. She was smiling; he was dumbfounded. He thought to himself, "What a woman! What a coach!"

A sizeable crowd of cadets and community members stayed for the trophy presentation and cutting down of the nets. It did not matter whether a member of the team had played most of the game, some of the game, or not at all—this victory belonged to every player, every coach, the ORs, the managers, and anyone else associated with the team. One by one, each player took her turn to cut one link of the net. It was an act they had all seen before on television and wished for since elementary school. The last one to cut the net was Maggie Dixon. She snipped the final cord, turned with another huge smile, and held the net in the air as the players raised their arms in victory.

For the first time in history, the Army women's basketball team was number one—in the Patriot League and the hearts of those at West Point. In their excitement and happiness, they knew they had completed a journey taking them from chaos to euphoria.

Maggie Dixon with Army team captains Megan Vrabel (L) and Micky Mallette (R). *Army Athletics Communications*

Maggie briefs players during a timeout. *Army Athletics Communications*

Megan Vrabel moves to the basket against Navy. *Army Athletics Communications*

Margaree "Redd" King drives against Navy. *Army Athletics Communications*

Alex McGuire drives against Holy Cross in the Patriot League championship game. *Army Athletics Communications*

Maggie Dixon coaching during an overtime win against Navy. *Army Athletics Communications*

Cara Enright on the move. *Army Athletics Communications*

Stefanie Stone blocks out Bucknell's Sarah Latham in an Army 66–65 victory. *Army Athletics Communications*

The Corps of Cadets and fans give support from the stands during the championship game. *Army Athletics Communications*

Maggie Dixon on the shoulders of celebrating cadets. *Army Athletics Communications*

Wild celebration takes place at West Point following Army's razor-thin win against Holy Cross. *Army Athletics Communications*

The Army women celebrate their Patriot League championship victory. *Army Athletics Communications*

Ashley "Smash" Magnani with the Patriot League Tournament trophy. *Army Athletics Communications*

Adrienne Payne with the Patriot League Tournament trophy. *Army Athletics Communications*

Lieutenant General William J. Lennox Jr., superintendent, United States Military Academy with the Patriot League Tournament trophy. Note his battle uniform and camouflage. *Army Athletics Communications*

Maggie Dixon and the Army team pose with the Patriot League championship trophy. *Army Athletics Communications*

Team photograph in the locker room following the game with Holy Cross. *Army Athletics Communications*

The Army team waiting to learn its opponent in the NCAA Tournament. They were matched against the Tennessee Volunteers. *Courtesy of Sarah Anderson*

The 2005–2006 team waiting for transportation to the NCAA Tournament in Norfolk, Virginia. *Courtesy of Micky Mallette*

· *17* ·

The Volunteers

*W*ord of the West Point victory spread throughout the country via television and from Army fan to Army fan. Before the women could change out of their uniforms, the last five seconds of the game, the mad rush of cadets onto the court, and the ensuing carrying of Maggie Dixon and her players on the shoulders of joyous cadets filled television screens with the message, "This is what college sports should be about." The announcers at ESPN's *SportsCenter* gave the celebration top billing. The team came right out of the casting room for such epic sports movies as *Hoosiers, Rudy, Miracle,* and *McFarland.* The night of March 8, 2006, belonged to the Lady Black Knights and the Corps of Cadets at the USMA. Since early October, every player, Maggie Dixon, Dave Magarity, the entire coaching staff, and others had worked together to create this magic moment in college sports.

Speaking to the reporters, the opposing head coaches and players remarked about the incredible basketball game they had just played on Army's home court. Army won—Holy Cross lost. Tears flowed from players on both teams. The height of Army's exuberance was matched by the depth of the dejection felt by Holy Cross. Both teams played magnificently. But, as mentioned before, basketball is a zero-sum game.

Coach Bill Gibbons captured the nature of the game, along with its consequences, succinctly and accurately. He said, "This was a heartbreaking game for us but a great game to be a part of. The environment provided by the cadets was one of the best I've ever been in." Of the Army comeback from 11 points down, he lamented, "The crowd won the game for them. We were up by 11, and the crowd kept them up and helped them back into the game. I'm a very big proponent of the highest seed hosting, and Army earned the right to host with their play throughout the season."

When asked at what point the season had turned around, Maggie answered, "I think it was the Baylor game. The (players) had a different feeling about them. That was the big turnaround for me. Also, at Navy. That was a big game, and we went down there and won."

Maggie, given the opportunity to speak of her team, added, "This is a special group. To give them a chance to play in the NCAAs is just a great feeling. When I came here, I wanted to help change the perceptions of this place and show people what we can accomplish here."

Players from each team showed great respect for their opponent. Of Stefanie Stone's stealing the ball with 13 seconds to go, Crusader Jessica Conte said, "It was a great defensive play on her part."

Of the same play, Stefanie Stone said, "Megan Vrabel tipped it a little, and I just went after the loose ball." She could not have been more wrong. Just as Jessica Conte posited, it was a great play by Stone. Video replays clearly show her coming from behind, swatting the ball toward the Holy Cross basket, and being fouled by Keil.

The coaches, players, and fans on both sides believed the game to be one of the most exciting ever played by either school. Before leaving Christl Arena, even the Holy Cross team began thinking ahead to the next season.

Holy Cross's Jessica Conte put the game in proper perspective. She hated losing, but the game itself was as good as it gets. She said, "It was a great atmosphere for a championship game. This is the type of crowd you want to play in front of for a conference title."

A short while later, family and close friends waited for their victors. Either alone or with one or two other players, each young woman walked out of the locker room and into the arms of her loved ones. It was then that the first inkling of a major question began to bloom: Who will we play in the Big Dance?

In many ways, Maggie seemed ubiquitous, appearing at different places out of nowhere. On that night, the night of the Patriot League championship game, Maggie had two missions juxtaposed with one another. Both were to be in New York City. Since Nicci Hays Fort would be staying at Maggie's following the Patriot League championship—or so she thought—she was invited to go along. Maggie's first mission was to attend Jamie's 9:00 p.m. game at Madison Square Garden against the Louisville Cardinals. Following the game, a nail-biter in which Pittsburgh gave up a 39–16 halftime lead to eke out a 61–56 victory, and a short visit with Jamie, Maggie and Nicci accomplished the second mission by attending a bachelorette party for Jackie Liautaud.

At the get-together Jackie asked, "What are you doing here? I can't believe you're here. You didn't have to drive all the way from West Point."

Maggie was still shaking from excitement. "Oh, my gosh. The cadets, they carried us on their shoulders. Oh, my gosh."

She could only stay a short while, so they shared the good news about the championship game, the upcoming wedding, and other topics that seem to come up at a bachelorette party.

As Nicci explained earlier, she and Maggie spent the night crashing in Jamie's hotel room. They watched the sports clip of the Army celebration several times, laughing each time it appeared. Maggie had several interviews the next morning and an important lunchtime date with the Corps of Cadets. Neither managed much sleep.

A short while after the game, Joe and Maureen LeBoeuf were relaxing at home in Cary, North Carolina, quietly going over notes for classes they were giving the next day. The phone rang. It was their son, Jay, a cow at West Point. Maureen answered the phone. She barely had a chance to say hello. "Maureen LeBoeuf."

Said Jay,

Mom. Wish you and Dad had been here tonight. Our women just beat Holy Cross in women's basketball for the Patriot League championship. The game was unbelievable. We beat them 69–68. At the end of the game it seemed like the whole Corps rushed the team and Coach Dixon, and hoisted them onto their shoulders. I've never seen anything like it. Army–Navy football never came close. The whole scene was surreal. It was unbelievable pandemonium.

Maureen LeBoeuf broke into a wry smile. Instantly, she remembered her interactions with Maggie at the West Point football luncheon several months earlier. She responded, "Great news, Jay. I met their coach a few months back and talked to her on the phone on occasion. You have an outstanding coach."

Jay, his voice as excited as it had ever been, continued,

You're right. We do. You and Dad teach leadership. She ought to be one of your guest speakers. You just don't know how good she is. There's something about her different than any other coach I've ever seen. She mixes it up with the Corps. Earlier today, and a couple of times before, she came to the mess hall to ask us to support the women's team. She's not afraid to ask the Corps to help the team. And I'll tell you what, I'm sure she would help anyone who asks. There's just something about her. Each night more and more cadets showed up for the games. The Corps loves her. They just plain love her. The players would run through a brick wall for her.

Maureen thought more of her chance meeting with Maggie Dixon and Maggie's responding to her offer to provide advice and counsel. She kept on smiling. In Maureen's mind, Maggie turned out to be exactly the type of coach West Point needed. The conversation lasted a good 10 minutes—most of it about the women's basketball team and their transformational coach.

The next day at the noontime meal, Maggie made another trip to the poop deck. A firstie, almost always holding a senior position within the Corps of Cadets, spoke into the microphone. "Attention to orders." Everyone in the dining hall quieted down to hear what official announcements needed to be passed on to the cadets. After a couple of items were mentioned, he announced, "Will the women's basketball team please stand up?" The Corps went wild. As the team waded through the sea of cadets toward the poop deck, continued cheering, whistles, and high fives surrounded the players. It was a genuine display of pride for the team. Once the entire team was present, Maggie raised the Patriot League championship trophy over her head. The Corps exploded. Other players took short turns holding the trophy while basking in the light of something held only in dreams. They were going to the NCAA Tournament—the first time in history that either the men or women had made their way to the Big Dance.

Considering the previous 15 hours, Maggie's close friend, Nicci Hays Fort, remembered what had taken place. She recalled,

> I was in the stands, and you could see how Maggie had electrified West Point. All the top officers were at the game, and the cadets had painted their faces. I got goose bumps. How many schools rush the court for women's basketball? I felt so good and happy for Maggie. It was a great moment in sports. I stayed over that night at her brother's hotel in New York City with Maggie, and we watched reruns of ESPN's video of the game's end. We laughed and laughed. It was absolutely a joyous time.

Hays Fort continued, a wistful smile on her face. "The next day, the team was formally presented the Patriot League trophy. When Maggie got up to receive the trophy, 4,000 cadets gave her a standing ovation. I was fortunate to be standing behind the team on the poop deck. It was an incredible sight. Absolutely incredible."

The explosion in Washington Hall was not a quickly forgotten event. Throughout the remainder of the week, fellow cadets, officers, and civilian professors not only continued to congratulate each player, but also ask questions about the bubbling coach.

Adding to the festive atmosphere at West Point, Spring Break started on Friday, March 10. Cancun, South Padre Island, Fort Lauderdale, and uncountable other venues were bracing for the annual collegiate migration. West Point was no exception. The upperclass cadets were allowed to depart on March 10. The in-season Division I team players remained on campus or were traveling for a competition. Depending on the coach and the existing schedule, players were given varying periods of time away from the academy. Plebes not playing an in-season sport were required to stay from March 10 until Sunday afternoon, March 12, for Plebe–Parent Weekend. Members of the West Point women's basketball team, plebes and upperclass players alike, needed to be at West Point on March 13. They had a date with ESPN and the NCAA Selection Committee.

As for Plebe–Parent Weekend, the entire class of 2009 and parents were provided many activities to enjoy. Although having a hard time not interfering with the events scheduled for the weekend, Maggie, as always, had a plan for the young plebes. She found a time frame during which she could squeeze in a boat ride. She rented the superintendent's boat for an afternoon cruise on the Hudson River. Cold, rainy weather spread throughout the Lower Hudson Valley but did not ruin the day. The landscape still had a beauty of its own. Plebes Megan Ennenga, Alex McGuire, and Sarah Anderson, along with their parents, had a wonderful time. The parents were thrilled to be able to speak to their daughters' coach.

Sarah Anderson remembered, "Maggie's chatting with my parents meant the world to them. Despite the weather, it is still one of my favorite memories from playing on the 2005–2006 team." The topics on the boat ride ran the gamut from personal histories, family, and life at West Point. Finally came the question, "How well are we going to play in the tournament? Who will we play in the opener?" It wouldn't take long to find out.

Monday night, March 13, 2006

Throughout the nation, women's college basketball teams were waiting to learn whether they would be seeded high in the NCAA Tournament; other teams just wanted to know if they had made the tournament at all. Year after year, such household names as UConn, Tennessee, Duke, Stanford, and Notre Dame knew they were going to the Big Dance and only needed to know how close they were to being seeded number one in their bracket. At the other end of the spectrum were those teams who won a small conference tournament or had some incredible wins against more highly respected teams. The second case was always very rare.

On the third floor of Kimsey Athletic Center, just above the basketball coaches' offices, an assemblage of players, coaches, support staff, family, and friends gathered in a well-decorated conference room. The upperclass players had returned early from their mini Spring Break and were on fire to find out who they would be playing in the tournament. Among others were General Lennox, Kevin Anderson, Gene Marshall, Bob Beretta, Donna Brazil, Kim Kawamoto, and the coaching staff. Some of the players squatted cross-legged on the floor; some sat on a large, comfortable couch, squeezing their coach in the middle of the pack; and others close to the program stood behind and around the couch. Everyone was looking at the television screen, knowing they were being televised by an ESPN camera placed to their front.

The players had never experienced moments like those they were now inhaling. Some of the players had experienced the thrill of a high school state championship, but those events paled in comparison to this speck of time in their lives. Delicious anticipation enticed each person in the room to plead for time to move faster. The gathering was peppered with excitement. The scene and the emotions were magical. As with all the other players, Sarah Anderson, sitting side by side with Maggie on the couch, could hardly contain herself. "I can't believe we're here. I just can't believe it," she stated.

Cara Enright thought to herself, "We've come so far. We can beat good teams. We can do it."

The bracket pairings started.

"And seeded number two in the Cleveland Regional, the Tennessee Volunteers will play the 15th-seeded Black Knights of West Point." The room erupted with excitement. Here they were, the small, underrated women of West Point, about to do battle with the mighty Volunteers of Tennessee. The cadets and everyone else in the room pump-fisted in the air, yelled at the top of their lungs, and gave bear hugs to anyone within arm's reach. The dance was about to begin. It was a well-earned celebration. If there is such a term, the mood expanded to "hypermagical."

Maggie was realistic about the selection of their opponent. She knew Army would be seeded low. She had hoped for a number-14 seed but was glad they weren't seeded number 16. Tennessee, a powerhouse ever since their coach, Pat Summitt, walked onto the Knoxville campus in 1974, won national championships in 1987, 1989, 1991, 1996, 1997, and 1998. With All-American Candace Parker leading the team, the Volunteers wanted another title in 2006. All in all, Maggie was satisfied with the selection. She declared, "Okay, we're not a number-16 seed. That's a good start."

As for Tennessee, the Volunteers were irritated with not being a number-one seed. After all, they stood at 28–4, with wins against number three LSU, number 12 Georgia (twice), number nine Michigan State, and number seven Connecticut. They certainly had an argument. On the downside of the ledger, their four losses hurt them badly. After starting the season at 18–0, the Volunteers fell to number two Duke by 22 points, lost 66–63 to unranked

Kentucky, lost 72–69 against LSU, and finally suffered a crushing overtime loss to unranked Florida in late February. Tennessee did win its last game of the regular season against LSU, avenging its earlier loss and leaving Tennessee with a valid hope for a number-one seed. But the Selection Committee picked LSU over Tennessee based on the entire season and the fact LSU had gone 13–1 in conference during the regular season and the Volunteers 11–3. An argument could always be made that the Big Ten did not have the power rankings of the SEC, and Ohio State clearly had an easier schedule. No one knew it at the time, but history proved the argument correct. Ohio State would lose to Boston College, 79–69, in the second round. The other number-one seeds would all make it to the Final Four.

Maggie and the West Point women's team had less than six days between the announcement of pairings and the team's game against Tennessee. Practices were no different than before, but players focused intensely on the task of upsetting Tennessee—better known as the Vols. Concentration on academics took a predicted hit. Since the rest of the academy was enjoying Spring Break, no academics existed, and time was available for both practice and study. It was hard for the players to study; their mindset focused on one thing and one thing only—upsetting Tennessee.

Maggie and Dave, along with the other coaches, studied the Tennessee team at length. Candace Parker would be almost unstoppable. Shanna Zolman needed to be shadowed lest she put up three-pointers throughout the game. The average height of Tennessee was more than 6-foot-2 for the entire team and 6-foot-3 for the starters. A formidable task for sure—but the women of West Point would be ready. The entire experience seemed surreal. Did they really win the championship? Could they win against the best teams in the United States? Could they beat Tennessee? Thoughts, mostly in the form of replaying the championship game, and visions of what might possibly be floated in and out of their minds. As difficult as it was to study, everyone would pass their courses. One final question resided in most of the players' minds. How did they get a coach as good as Maggie Dixon?

All Army needed to do to win the game was play the absolute best game in the team's history, while the Tennessee Volunteers needed to turn in a subpar performance. Number 16 Harvard's upset of number-one seed Stanford was proof it could be done. If a number-16 seed could pull it off, Army, as a number-15 seed, could take down Tennessee. At one point or another, each West Point player had enough optimism to ponder the possibility of winning. Even the "WE WILL" cards would take on a life of their own.

One of the most optimistic players was Cara Enright. She was not only thrilled to play in the tournament, but her mind also sorted through the many possibilities for winning the game. She thought to herself, "What if we play really well? What if Tennessee plays poorly? It's been done before. We can win." Dreams of a historic upset settled into a realistic possibility for her. Sure, the team had been blown out by Connecticut, but they played Baylor to a 17-point decision and were a much better team than the one greeting their new coach back in October.

The practices were well-planned, efficient, and tough. Every player, from Cara Enright on the Gold team, to Micky Mallette and Smash Magnani on the Black team, to Adie Payne (White-6), Jo-Jo Carelus, and Natalie Schmidt on the White team, left everything on the floor. They were not perfect by any means, but the practices paid off; the coaches were satisfied that the Army team was as ready as could be hoped for. Six days after learning of their opponent, the West Point women were ready to slay a dragon.

Shortly before noon, March 19, 2006
Norfolk, Virginia

Inside Norfolk's Ted Constant Convocation Center, most often called "The Ted," the Army women looked intently at their coach. Outside, almost 7,000 fans were on hand, many of them for Tennessee. Army had fewer die-hard fans, but the team believed the fans from George Washington University and Old Dominion University would cheer for the underdog Army team. Once again, "WE WILL" messages were read with conviction. The pregame coach's talk wasn't much different than for any other game. A few minutes earlier, the teams had stretched and run their warm-up drills. It was impossible for an Army player not to take a glance at the size of the Volunteers. Of the starters, only Shanna Zolman stood less than six feet in height. Sidney Spencer and Candace Parker were both at least 6-foot-3, Niki Anosike was 6-foot-4, and Tye'sha Fluker was 6-foot-5.

"I know they're good, but they're not that good," Maggie said, her words ringing true to some, but not all, of the players. Cara Enright did believe her. The same question commentator Al Michaels offered the nation in the stunning 1980 Olympic ice hockey win against the Soviets rang in her head: "Do you believe in miracles?"

"We can beat them. We can," she thought. She was ready to play.

The game officials—Sue Blauch, Norma Jones, Tom Danaher, and Kathy Lynch (alternate)—would have no bearing on the game. They were very professional. Game time.

Tennessee grabbed the tip-off and came downcourt. Shanna Zolman missed a jump shot 13 seconds into the game. Cara Enright rebounded. The Army team worked the ball around and got it inside to Stefanie Stone. Stone missed from inside, the ball rebounded by Zolman. Tennessee's Nicky Anosike committed a charging foul. Back and forth, the game's first minute was scoreless. At the 18:56 mark it was Army who drew first blood. Jen Hansen hit a beautiful shot from behind the arc. Army took an early lead at 3–0, and the crowd, as hoped for, lustily cheered on the outmanned cadets. The cheering clearly indicated one fact: Those fans at the game who would cheer for their own particular team later in the day definitely did support the underdog Black Knights. They would love to play Army rather than Tennessee. They also knew an Army win would be the greatest upset in collegiate women's basketball history.

Tennessee's Tye'sha Fluker missed a jumper but grabbed the rebound and scored. Army 3, Tennessee 2. On Army's next possession, Enright's pass to Megan Vrabel cleared the way for a short jumper. Good! The Cadets increased the early lead to 5–2. They were holding their own. The majority of fans continued to cheer for Army. Almost two minutes had passed, and Army still had the lead. Just a little more than 38 minutes to go. Candace Parker hit a jumper for two points, followed by another jumper by Fluker, who was fouled by Hansen on the play. She made the free throw. Parker added to the damage by scoring on another jumper, moving the score to 9–5 in favor of the Lady Vols. On Army's next possession, Enright missed a layup.

Fighting the height and athleticism factor, Stone grabbed the offensive rebound. While trying to get in position to score over the much taller Tennessee team, she was stripped of the ball by Zolman. Tennessee quickly moved the ball around and got it to Fluker for an easy layup. She missed the shot but was fouled by Vrabel. Fluker missed both free throws, and the score remained at 9–5. Next up was Parker; she stole the ball from Army's McGuire and was fouled by Stone moving to the basket. She hit both free throws, and the score moved to 11–5, Tennessee. The teams traded baskets, one each by Sidney Spencer and Enright, leaving the score at 13–7, in favor of the Vols, with 15:56 left in the first half.

At that point, Tennessee turned the ball over twice, and Enright made them pay for the miscues. She hit a three-pointer, closing the score to 13–10; a jump shot, bringing the score to 13–12; and a layup, which brought the crowd to its feet. After almost six minutes of play, the Black Knights of Army held a 14–13 lead over the powerful Volunteers of the University of Tennessee. Only 34 minutes to go. Pat Summitt was more than unhappy; she was furious. The pro-Army fans were loving every minute of it. To this point the play by Army had been magnificent.

And then—Candace Parker.

Spencer blocked a jump-shot attempt by McGuire and fired a perfect outlet pass to Parker racing well ahead of Army's Redd King. Parker's lead gave her a wide-open path to the basket. Wham! For the first time in women's NCAA Tournament play, a female player dunked the ball. She *dunked* the ball. With Parker's basket, Tennessee took the lead at 15–14.

The Army players hung on as much as possible. Alex McGuire scored on a layup, closing the score to 20–16, with 11:11 to go in the first half. At that point, Army had reached its high-water mark. For almost a quarter of the game, the Army team had more than held its own against the Volunteers. Unfortunately for the Lady Knights, during a span of almost five and a half minutes, Tennessee scored the next 17 points. The game was out of reach.

At halftime, Tennessee led the West Point team 50–26. Parker would go on to dunk the ball a second time, and nonstarters would see plenty of playing time. Each of Tennessee's 10 players logged at least 14 minutes, with each player scoring, and all of Army's 15 players would get into the game, with 11 players scoring, including Ashley "Smash" Magnani and Adrienne "Adie" Payne. As foretold by every aficionado of the game except those from Army, the game would end with a very large point difference. Parker finished the game with 26 points in 26 minutes, Shanna Zolman shot 5-for-8 on three-pointers, and Tye'sha Fluker shot 5-for-7 both from the field and the free-throw line. For Army's Cara Enright, her 21 points showed she could play for or against Division I basketball teams. On the boards, Tennessee pulled down 40 rebounds to Army's 21, and the team was 20-for-28 at the free-throw line to Army's 5-for-8. The statistics bore out the final score: Tennessee 102, Army 54.

The locker room stood quiet, tears rolling down the cheeks of nearly every player. No one will know for sure, but many of the tears were related to one simple fact—it was the end of the greatest season in the history of women's basketball at West Point. It was also the greatest season of basketball for most of the players. The four firsties would be graduating in two months, and each knew she had just competed in her last Division I basketball game. The other tears were because of the game itself. Everyone knew the Volunteers would be virtually impossible to stop, but a 48-point blowout was intolerable. They felt their performance was beyond embarrassing; it was devastating for them, for West Point, and, most of all, for their coaches. The firsties, in particular, knew the loss itself was almost as bad as knowing their organized basketball days, going back to elementary school, had just ended.

Maggie walked into a room full of players who needed consoling. As should have been expected, Maggie was completely upbeat. She told the players they were beaten by a bigger, faster, better-skilled team. At the same time, Maggie told everyone in the room what a great season they had experienced.

She then told them they would use the 2005–2006 season to get them to another Patriot League championship the next year.

She said, "Each one of you played as hard as possible, and that's all I need."

Maggie also congratulated the firsties for the leadership they displayed during the season. The leadership Maggie had shown the team for more than five months had clearly rubbed off on every member of the squad.

Donna Brazil watched and remembers the mood switching with every word said.

"We've had a great ride. Keep your heads up," Maggie demanded.

Maggie's words for the Army team did provide a good perspective for the players. In fact, Tennessee was bigger, faster, and more talented than Army. Yet, for 10 minutes, Army battled on an even basis with the Volunteers. The entire team deserved to feel proud. The underclass players knew they would be better the next season. They envisioned being a higher seed in 2007 and pulling off the upset of the tournament. The firsties longed to have one more season with Coach Maggie Dixon.

A final "WE WILL" was belted out, and the players returned to their lockers and the showers. Maggie, Cara Enright, and Stefanie Stone headed for the postgame interview.

The postgame interview found Tennessee very respectful of Army, in terms of both how well they were coached and, more importantly, who they were as people and what they were prepared to face in the future. Senior Shanna Zolman, who hit five 3-pointers, made the strongest comment of the night concerning the Army team.

> We knew coming into the game that it was going to be hard-fought in the sense that they are competitive and hardworking. They fight not only in terms of on the court, but also for our country. When I was looking up at the beginning of the game and saw the band in their fatigues, and a lot of the fans with their Army gear on, I knew this game was a lot more than basketball and starting off the NCAA Tournament. Our opponents not only play basketball, but more importantly, they are fighting for and serving our country. We were talking a lot about what it means for them, as members of the Army, what all they have to go through, and we knew they would be well-conditioned athletes just because of being in the Army and going through boot camp. It's definitely an honor to play against them, because they are serving our country for a much more important purpose.

Truer words were never spoken. Little did Shanna Zolman know that her comment that the Army players were serving the country for a "much more important purpose" would take most of the players directly into harm's way in the Global War on Terror.

Coach Pat Summitt also spoke well of the Army players and their youthful coach.

> I thought they came out with discipline on the court. These young ladies understand discipline . . . they are very well coached. Maggie has done a great job, and I knew of her work at DePaul. I have tremendous respect and admiration for their head coach [Doug Bruno], and she could only benefit by being in his presence. There's coaching in her blood with her brother [Jamie], and when you have it in your family I know the feeling that you just talk basketball. You love the game and you love to teach the game, which she does very well.

They had been pounded by 48 points, yet Maggie Dixon, Stefanie Stone, and Cara Enright met the reporters with upbeat answers to the questions asked. Maggie's comments focused on Enright, Stone, and the team as a whole.

Maggie spoke first, stating,

> I just want to start by saying that I've never been so proud of a group of young women as I was in the last four months. They have been through so much and really just kept fighting back. I'm so honored and proud to have the opportunity to coach these women, and I'm looking forward to the future of Army basketball.

For those paying close attention, the word *future* brought hope to the Army faithful. A generic comment would be, "Maybe she will stay with us for a long time. Maybe."

Maggie's assessment of the game came across as spot-on. She said,

> Obviously Candace Parker is going to be Candace Parker, but the things that really hurt you is Zolman hitting three-pointers in transition. We got lost in transition a couple of times, and they got some baskets out of that. I think that's how the run really got away from us. We did win the Patriot League, we did enter the NCAA Tournament for the first time in school history, so I have to keep building these players up so they remember that. This isn't the way we want to end the season. They have accomplished too much to feel bad about this season. I think the first thing we need is to take a deep breath and enjoy the fact that we got to be here and play on this stage against a team like Tennessee, who I think is going to do very well this year. Our players are going to remember this, and we can use it for motivation next year.

Another magical pair of words was mentioned related to the future of the team: "next year."

Next up came Cara and Stefanie. It was clear to everyone in the room that both players were in awe of Tennessee, but at the same time, their nonverbal communication pointed to a small letdown in that they had not performed as well as they, the entire team, thought possible.

Cara, having scored 21 points on the Volunteers, commented, "We knew they were going to make their runs. I think we had a lot of intensity at the start, and we just kind of sat back a little bit. It's Tennessee, they are a great team. We just didn't do a lot of little things today."

Stefanie (who led the Army team with six rebounds, including three at the offensive end) added her take on the game. "We came in with the mindset today that it was just any other team, we didn't want to put Tennessee on a pedestal. When it comes down to it, we are just playing basketball."

The two young women smiled and were very polite throughout the interview. Both were West Point yearlings with two more years to play college basketball. One (Cara) played 810 minutes the year before; the other (Stefanie) played the one short minute. This year, Stefanie ended up starting every game, logging 761 minutes of playing time, scoring 289 points, and leading the team in both shooting percentage (.576) and rebounds (171). With two years to go, both were ready to get on with the 2006–2007 season. Cara and Stefanie would join a solid cohort of current players and new arrivals for the class of 2010. Most important in their minds stood the recognition that the USMA held a huge advantage over their opponents—the team had the finest coach in the country.

No differently than following the UConn game, it was time to put Tennessee in the rearview mirror, time to focus on academics, and time to prepare for summer training throughout the world. For three of the four seniors (Ashley Magnani, Adrienne Payne, and Megan Vrabel), commissioning as an officer in the United States Army and the impending duty leading the sons and daughters of the American people loomed on the horizon. For Micky Mallette, it was time to determine what she would do for her future and overcome a sense of loss at not being commissioned. She desperately wanted to join her sisters in the United States Army.

For all of the players, they had handled plenty of adversity during the season and would be ready for anything coming their way.

· 18 ·

Spring Returns to West Point

$\mathcal{I}$n an ironic twist, the Dixon sibling coaches lost on the same day, March 19, 2006. Army came into its game with Tennessee as a number-15 seed and was expected to lose. They did. On the other hand, the Pittsburgh men's team, seeded number five, was not supposed to lose. The Panthers, having beaten Kent State by 15 points, saw a major opening in their upcoming game with the Bradley Braves. As a huge underdog, the Braves pulled off a stunning upset of Kansas. For Pitt, they entered the second round against a number-13 seed, rather than the number four Jayhawks. As it turned out, Bradley upset Pitt, 72–66, becoming one of the Cinderella teams of the 2005–2006 season.

The Pitt team, from Jamie Dixon to the last player on the squad, was disappointed. They should have done better. For the West Point women's team, the loss to Tennessee was not as heart-wrenching. Sure, an upset of the Volunteers would have been the story of a lifetime, but the team had given all they had in defeat. The Army faithful, along with the team, knew a matter of raw talent, compounded by a cumulative height advantage of nearly two feet among starters, made the game a virtual "impossible dream." But all concerned were far more encouraged by knowing momentum of the West Point women's basketball team had shifted significantly. Word began to spread—Army and its phenomenal new coach were on the march.

The entire West Point community rallied around the women's basketball team. Turning a 5–7 start into a 20–11 season and winning the Patriot League and becoming Patriot League Tournament champions raised eyebrows in the women's basketball community. The leadership within ODIA reveled in the thought of new interest in young women throughout the country wanting to play for Army. Although the late winter/early spring

155

weather remained cool, "Gloom Period" seemed over and done with. Men and women's spring sports had started in February, a few sprigs could be seen on the trees, and budding flowers were springing to life. It appeared Maggie had created a surge of enthusiasm not seen at the academy in years. For the players, Gloom Period ended the night of March 8, 2006.

A few days after the Tennessee game, Maggie invited her players to her home for a dinner/get-together. She had done so many things for the team that her invitation came as no surprise. It was a chance for the players to relax, tell stories from the season, and laugh. And laugh they did.

A few days later Maggie, with the help of a few other members of her staff, began planning a team banquet to be held in a side room of the cavernous Washington Hall, only a few steps from the poop deck where she had exhorted the Corps of Cadets to come and support the team, and where the Corps had cheered the Patriot League champions with such fervor. Maggie would speak proudly of each player and the managers, describing what each young woman brought to the team. She would pass out letters in the shape of an "A" to those who had earned them. For Army and Navy, in any sport in which the teams play two games a year, one of the games is designated the "Star" game. But, for Army, they had done even better—they beat Navy in both games. Every letter would have a star embroidered on it, signifying the Star game win over Navy. At Army, a Navy star is a big deal. It would certainly be a grand time for everyone. For at least one night, no one would have a care in the world. The firsties were only a few weeks from graduation, and the underclass players were still enjoying the afterglow of the just-finished season and the anticipation of playing one, two, or three more years with the inspirational Maggie Dixon as their coach.

Maggie decided to speak to all of the players in general, but she would focus on the seniors and their leadership, as well as the potential for the next season. Her plan called for the firsties and members of the coaching staff to come to her home to talk over wine and cheese. It would be different from most after-season parties. Rather than basketball, the discussions would center on life. What were their hopes for the future? What were their thoughts of staying in or leaving the Army? Knowing war raged on in Iraq and Afghanistan, what personal safety concerns did each woman have? What were they anticipating in terms of the branches of the Army they had selected? Ashley Magnani would join the Corps of Engineers; Adrienne Payne selected the Ordnance Corps; and Megan Vrabel picked Air Defense Artillery. Micky Mallette, the woman who, until this moment in her life, excelled in and overcame every challenge, would continue to face adversity in one area: Her medical problems were severe and she would not be commissioned. She felt as though she was letting the others down by not being sworn in as a second lieutenant in the United States Army. At one end of the discussion would be fears about going to war; the other end would focus on life in general, stories of boyfriends or possible boyfriends, and anything else to bring laughter to the forefront.

For Micky Mallette, the struggle with medical issues throughout the season was mitigated by the opportunity to have many life conversations with Maggie. In Maggie's office or at Maggie's home, Micky also saw firsthand the sibling bonding between Maggie and Jamie. With the short six-year difference in age, "Coach" Dixon could have been Micky's older sister or best friend. They shared stories about life and what the future could possibly hold for Micky. Nearing the end of the season, Micky confided in Maggie about her concerns regarding whether she would be commissioned. Maggie, the supreme optimist, spoke of Micky's possibilities whether she was commissioned or not. Micky cherished those memories throughout the years. Maggie was the person Micky wished to be in her own life. It would have been easy to tell Micky her playing days were over and drop her from the team back in early October. That was not Maggie's style. If the situation was out of the player's control, Maggie did not punish the player for not making all the practices. As a coach, Maggie clearly understood that Micky wanted to practice and scrimmage. As certain as night and day, Micky craved being on the court.

Maggie seemed to be one of the few coaches (and it is a terrible shame) who understood that the lowest player on a team roster works as hard as the top player. To include "team White," she rewarded the bench players with as much time on the court as possible. In the seven games decided by four points or less, 10 players saw action in one game, 11 players saw action in three games, and 12 players saw action in three games. Ten of her players ended the season with 40 points or more. Simply stated, substitutes at Army played much more than substitutes at other schools. Throughout the season, all 18 players saw action in five or more games, each player contributing with at least a field goal or an assist. Few, if any, collegiate teams can show similar statistics. Most importantly, Army won six of the seven close games and both of the overtime games. Maggie's manner of communicating to each player that she was a part-owner of the team was likely unsurpassed in collegiate basketball in 2005–2006. A fact remains: Today, 18 former players, cadet managers, and coaches, as well as an entire support staff, have a stronger sense of Maggie's take on "WE WILL embrace adversity."

Maggie's fun-loving approach to basketball was life-giving to the entire team, but her style was not a matter of being soft so you can be liked. Courtney Wright described the strength of her coach, stating, "She ingrained in us the mindset that things will go wrong—but when it happens you have the option of making excuses or you can toughen up and respond to the adversity." Courtney finished by saying, "That was her mantra. Either quit or be better."

As it turned out, in the weeks following the Tennessee game, fellow cadets, officers, professors, and anyone else who had followed the season continued congratulating the players. Several made sure the women knew the game against Holy Cross was the most exciting contest, in any sport, he or she had ever witnessed. Some of the players did harbor quiet thoughts of, "Just wait until you see us next year!" Life was good. Spring had arrived. After one season, the hounds of basketball—in the form of athletic directors—sought her out. Most of them had much larger purses than Army. Not only did Maggie field calls about taking another job, but also Jamie, who was being recruited as well, received calls concerning Maggie possibly leaving the West Point position. Since they were constantly talking to one another, and because of the phone calls he received concerning her future as a major university coach, Jamie did ask her what she was going to do.

Maggie answered—using different words but having the same meaning as when she had confided in Nicci Hays Fort five months earlier—with, "They need me." For Maggie, it was not about the money or location, the best job, or winning at all costs. She simply stated, "This is where I'm supposed to be."

Maggie's life, swaying back and forth between her duties coaching the Lady Black Knights and attending many NCAA Tournament games for both men and women, was hectic, to say the least. Following the Army loss in the first round of the NCAA Tournament, she traveled to San Antonio and watched the DePaul women's team make it to the Sweet 16. Her next stop was Indianapolis, where she and Jamie linked up to watch the men's Final Four, ending with Florida's 73–57 victory against UCLA on April 3. Next, she flew to Boston to watch the semifinals of the Women's Final Four.

The night before the women's championship game between Maryland and Duke, Maggie attended a party hosted by Nike at the high-walled baseball venue Fenway Park. Many well-known coaches and other sports dignitaries were there. As the party continued, and much to her surprise, Maggie began to realize she was not an unknown; she was well known by most of the people attending. There was a lot of talk about her being a "very hot coach." When the party ended the only ones left were Maggie; Nicci; coach Geno Auriemma of UConn; Colorado coach Kathy McConnell; and Maggie's favorite coach (next to her brother), DePaul's Doug Bruno. By the time the party ended for good, the first rays of the sun had begun to spread light above the Boston skyscrapers.

With recruiting trips on the immediate horizon, neither Maggie nor Jamie could make Tuesday's women's championship game, so they returned to West Point on Tuesday, April 4. The two siblings, equally proud of one another, relaxed and enjoyed watching the blistering game, which concluded with Maryland's overtime victory against Duke. It was a great ending to an unbelievable journey.

A joyous spring was in bloom.

· 19 ·

See You on the Court

Wednesday, April 5, 2006

$\mathcal{O}$n Wednesday morning, Maggie slept a little longer than Jamie. She had been going at a whirlwind pace during the men's semifinals and final, as well as the women's semifinals of the NCAA Tournament. The siblings enjoyed breakfast together but, given Maggie's later-than-usual awakening, skipped working out. They had enjoyed the men and women's NCAA Tournament and both were in good spirits; Maggie wished Jamie could stay for a full day or two. Unfortunately, he had a tight recruiting schedule and needed to leave for the Tidewater area of Virginia. He hugged her, gave her a kiss, and walked out the door.

Maggie conducted a coaches' meeting later in the morning, the major topic being the upcoming team dinner at Washington Hall. Many tasks, including picking out a menu and obtaining plaques for several of the players, needed to be accomplished. With predictable Dixon precision, Maggie presented a suggested list of items to be done and who needed to accomplish each task. She brought the meeting to a close and prepared to relax at a friend's home. Maggie and her friend agreed to wait until the season ended and then get together for a cup of tea and conversation. No doubt about it, Maggie had made many friends during her first six months as coach. She wouldn't change a thing from the previous six months—the long hours, the bonding of her team, the wins, the losses, and her journey from total unfamiliarity with the military culture to a place of total buy in. She finally had a chance to relax for a couple of days before hitting the recruiting trail.

A special treat would be a trip to see her fellow DePaul coach, Jana Mathis, about a week before Jana was to be married.[1] The plan was for Maggie to spend a week with Jana and be a bridesmaid. Then, following Maggie's trip to see Jana, her social life would continue with her being a bridesmaid at the wedding of her former college roommate, Jackie Liautaud.[2] A large measure of genuine camaraderie and outrageous laughter were on the menu. The only negative for Maggie was the realization that some of the coaches had to be terminated and new assistant coaches hired. She offered Nicci a coaching position and had her eyes on Dave's daughter, Maureen, at that time an assistant coach at Fairfield University.[3] Maureen, the former Division I player at Boston College and Marist, possessed great credentials in basketball, and was gifted with solid interpersonal skills. She would be slated to coach at the prep school. Given her trait of compassion, terminating the tenure of some of the current coaches would not be easy for Maggie. Whether Dave Magarity would be leaving for the NBA was still up in the air. But, at least for now, some quiet time with a good friend sounded wonderful. Maggie arrived early in the afternoon.

She sat down and was offered a cup of tea. Her spirits that week could not have been happier.

Then it happened.

Shortly after arriving, without warning, Maggie experienced a medical emergency. She said she did not feel well—and collapsed. Maggie's friend immediately called for medical support, and Maggie was taken directly to Keller Army Community Hospital at the northern end of the academy grounds.[4]

Within minutes, word reached the superintendent. General Lennox and his wife, Ann, went directly to the hospital and stood vigilant and silent, praying for Maggie to recover. The doctors and nurses worked feverishly on Maggie, stabilizing her as best they could. Given the seriousness of her condition, she was flown directly to Westchester Medical Center, in Valhalla, New York, via helicopter.

It seems so out-of-place to even consider someone at the USMA facing a life-threatening medical emergency. The vast majority of the West Point community consists of young, healthy men and women, possibly the healthiest group of college-aged people in the United States. The officers and staff, along with their spouses, are incredibly strong and revel in a fitness-first culture. Maggie was young and athletic. She was not supposed to have medical issues. But, in a split second, life at the academy changed forever. Coach Maggie Dixon had fallen into medical distress; time was the enemy. Word, and with it, fear, spread through campus like wildfire.

One at a time, in small groups, or in the team locker room, the women learned of their coach's condition. Confusion reigned, and few people knew the exact nature of her ailment.

Donna Brazil received a phone call from Kim Kawamoto at about 3:30 p.m.

"Maggie's had some sort of medical emergency. She collapsed at a friend's home and has been taken to Keller," Kawamoto said, speaking seriously but not frantically.

Brazil recalled,

> We didn't know much at the time and had no idea as to the seriousness of her condition. Not realizing the true nature of Maggie's medical issue, I went to watch the women's lacrosse team practice for upcoming games against Delaware and Syracuse. At the end of practice, the wife of one of the team physicians approached me to let me know Maggie's condition was "very serious" and Maggie had been flown to Westchester Medical Center.

The situation with cadets paralleled that of Brazil.

"I don't remember who gave me the message, but I was told to go to the team room," Smash Magnani stated in recalling the event, a wistful, sad tone to her remarks. She continued,

> Ironically, I had noticed a low-flying helicopter earlier that afternoon. I'm pretty sure it was coach's flight to Westchester. In the team room, rumors were passed back and forth until we were given the official word from the superintendent, "Coach Dixon is in a coma in critical condition." It was total disbelief. She was only 28 years old. She was young and full of life.

Smash's voice started to crack as she replayed the events surrounding their talented, exuberant, loving coach.

Adie Payne and Megan Vrabel were in Adie's room when an e-mail message arrived stating, "Coach Dixon collapsed early this afternoon. All team members need to go to the team room in Christl Arena for a meeting."

Adie explained, "But we didn't fully grasp everything until we got to the team room. When we arrived, we saw General Lennox with Coach Magarity, Mr. Anderson, the coaches, and a couple of other leaders at the academy. It was clear that we were witnessing a grave situation."

Sarah Anderson remembered,

> I received word from Megan Evans or Adrienne Payne that there was a medical problem with Coach Dixon and the whole team needed to meet in the team room. In addition to Coach Magarity and the superintendent, I remember Lieutenant Colonel Porter [Lieutenant Colonel Becky Porter, Ph.D., clinical director, Center for Enhanced Performance, USMA] and Major Kawamoto. I don't remember who told us for sure. It may have been the superintendent. He told us Coach Dixon had been airlifted to Westchester Medical Center in critical condition.

It had been three weeks since Sarah Anderson sat next to Maggie at Kimsey Athletic Center waiting to find out who their opponent would be in the NCAA Tournament. The Patriot League championship game and the lead-up to the pairings announcement for the tournament were the two highlights of her athletic career. Following the terrible news, Sarah retreated to Adie's room with Megan Vrabel.

"We shed many tears and told some hilarious stories of our short time playing basketball for Coach Dixon. I stayed with Adrienne and Megan until just before taps," Sarah recollected.

Anna Wilson found out from her company tactical NCO (noncommissioned officer). Said Wilson,

> Sergeant First Class [SFC, a senior position among enlisted soldiers] Strom told me Coach Dixon was in critical condition and I needed to go to the team locker room. It hit me hard, so hard that I collapsed into his arms. SFC Strom is a great NCO. He always came to our games and supported the team.

So much good had happened in the six months since Coach Maggie Dixon called Anna in the hospital. How could this be happening?

By the time official word was given, most of the players instinctively knew what was going on. Coach Jennifer Fleming told Cara Enright about Coach Dixon's condition. General Lennox gave the official announcement to the team. Coach Dixon suffered a heart arrhythmia and was in a coma at Westchester Medical Center in Valhalla.

In addition to suffering a loss of immense proportion, Joanne Carelus personified the quizzical nature of each player in saying, "It just didn't make sense." It never does.

Others on the team had similar thoughts of that terrible day, April 5, 2006.

Micky Mallette, whose "sandwich attack" made such an impression on Maggie during the interview process, was not certain but believed she accompanied General Lennox, his wife, and his aide to Westchester that evening. Her first family encounter occurred when Jamie Dixon arrived. In her words, "He was devastated." It was Micky who had enjoyed the wonderful view of the bond between Jamie and Maggie—especially the day when he had to break through the tentacles of military security to get on post to bring Maggie a rocking chair—an act of true sibling love. Brother and sister, mentor and mentee, great coach and great coach. "They were the perfect pair."

Donna Brazil arrived at Westchester at about 8:00 p.m. on the evening of April 5. In addition to the superintendent's group, Coach Fleming and Maggie's aunt were at the hospital. Jamie Dixon arrived later. They went in to Maggie's room together. A devout Catholic, Donna prayed for Maggie's healing but also gave in to "Thy will be done." Just as devout, Maggie's aunt did the same. Similar reverence was given by each person, either individually or in small groups.

With General Lennox's approval, a trip section (a group of cadets traveling on official business to a designated location) would take the entire team and other friends to see Maggie the next day. The 30-mile trip from West Point to Valhalla took about 45 minutes. Everyone was stone quiet, each passenger left to personal thoughts, prayers requesting miracles, and efforts to understand what had happened less than 24 hours earlier. The team members went in to see Maggie either alone or in small groups. Everyone knew the inevitable—Maggie Dixon would not survive.

Smash Magnani was devastated. She related, "When we found out there would be a trip section to Westchester Medical Center, I, and everyone else, knew coach would not be coming back. I visited with her for a few minutes alone. I told her something just between the two of us. For the time being, I will keep it confidential." In her head, Smash knew she would be writing one of Maggie's eulogies. Micky Mallette would also be asked to give a eulogy.

The other firsties joined Ashley in the visitation. Adie Payne touched Maggie's arm and told her, "Thank you so much for this season and . . ." She could barely get the words out. She added, ". . . for what you have brought to our lives." Adie ended with, "And thank you for the time you gave to me. Please know that I love you and everyone loves you." Tears streamed down her cheeks, as they did for Smash, Megan, and Micky. An overwhelming sadness pulled relentlessly at each cadet's heart. The death of a young person had never visited any of the players. Encountering the death of someone who was both young and truly loved left a dark, unending void in their hearts. The suffocating sense of despair replaced the once-happy, hardworking spirit of a team that had climbed a mountain less than a month prior.

Individuals react differently to any given situation. Anna Wilson remembered going in and actually saying something lighthearted; after all, there had been so much laughter during the season, so "Why not now?" But, even the lighthearted Anna remembered becoming serious and telling her coach, "I just hope you know how much I appreciated playing for you."

To this day, Anna fondly remembers her first phone call from Maggie and being told, "I just wanted to let you know I'll be your coach." Anna only stayed a few minutes. She kept thinking, "This is a dream." But it wasn't a dream. If it were, it would be a cruel nightmare.

After nonfamily members left the hospital, family members said their goodbyes. With an almost unfathomable burden, the decision was made to take Maggie off of life support. At 3:10 p.m., on April 6, 2006, Margaret Mary "Maggie" Dixon gently passed away.

West Point teems with life. But it must also deal with death. No other academic institution in our country has to face the reality of dying in service to the nation to the degree of the USMA.

On April 1, five days before Maggie's death, Captain Timothy J. Moshier, class of 2002, was killed in Iraq. When one of its own is killed in war, members of the Corps of Cadets, on a volunteer basis, don dress gray uniforms and meet on a concrete apron fronting the barracks and astride The Plain to honor fallen comrades with the playing of taps. The day after Maggie's death, the Corps repeated the honoring of one of "their own." Megan Evans remembered, "The team made the decision to meet at a specific spot on the apron. But there were so many fellow cadets, most having no official linkage to our team, participating that we weren't able to stand as a single group." Following a lone cadet bagpiper playing "Amazing Grace," a bugler played the beautiful, yet heart-wrenching, melody of taps:

> Day is done,
> gone the sun,
> From the hills,
> from the lake,
> From the skies.
> All is well,
> safely rest,
> God is nigh

After Maggie was honored, members of the team were invited to General Lennox's home for light refreshments and a chance to cry and laugh about incidents with their coach during the previous six months. Clearly, the superintendent was as pained as every member of the team—only he was not afforded the luxury of losing his composure.

On a rainy afternoon, Friday, April 7, a memorial service took place in the beautiful Holy Trinity Catholic Chapel overlooking the Hudson River. The service was led by West Point's Catholic chaplain, Reverend Edson Wood. Father Wood was similar to Maggie, not so much for being an athlete, but in his being a man of deep faith and complete inclusiveness. A gathering of more than 500, the majority cadets, attended the memorial. In front of the altar rested a basketball, the trophy won by the women's team the previous month, and a team photo.

An autopsy was conducted by Dr. Millard J. Hyland, the Westchester County medical examiner. His findings linked her death to cardiomegaly with mitral valve prolapse. In layman's terms, it simply meant she had an enlarged heart and a mitral valve that was not closing properly. Everyone who knew her had already surmised she had a big heart, just not in a medical sense. About as large as they come.

As soon as Maggie's condition became apparent to the academy leadership, and upon approval from Maggie's family, plans were developed for taking the team and other key personnel by charter plane to a funeral mass to be held in St. Charles Borromeo Catholic Church, in North Hollywood, California. Included were General and Mrs. Lennox; Major Jay Miseli, the superintendent's aide; the athletic director, Kevin Anderson; Bob Beretta and Gene Marshall, the coaches; Colonel Brazil; Colonel Porter and the ORs; the team physician; and the managers who had contributed to the success of the team. The contingent grew to almost 50 people, of which 23 were cadets. A special passenger seat was reserved for one of the cadets, David Lindsey, the plebe who so eloquently sang the "Star-Spangled Banner" on the night of the Patriot League championship game.

On Monday, April 10, 2006, the cadets formed up at 7:30 a.m. for a pretrip inspection at the cadet guardroom prior to leaving West Point for Stewart International Airport in Newburgh. All trip sections go through an inspection to ensure that uniforms are clean, shoes are shined, and haircuts are according to regulations. At West Point, when on duty, a cadet must be in proper uniform. In so many ways, life at an academy is a culture unlike any other academic institution in the United States. In some cases, students at other institutions see the culture of the USMA as somehow coming from another planet. From the cadet perspective, it's just a matter of knowing and accepting the myriad rules as part of the price to pay to attend West Point.

The ride to Stewart International was again quiet. Each passenger took refuge within him or herself, asking the unanswerable, pleading the irrevocable, and struggling with grief they could not understand—the tragic death of someone loved so much for so many reasons.

Seating assignments for the flight were predesignated, with General and Mrs. Lennox sitting in the front row. Kevin Anderson and Major Jay Miseli sat in the second row. The next several rows held the team, including the managers, along with a couple of coaches. The rear section held coaches and members of the staff. The flight to Burbank, California, remained quiet, with most of the noise coming from the vibration of jet turbine engines. Upon arrival at the Burbank Airport, the group proceeded immediately to a waiting bus for transfer to the Sheraton Universal Hotel. The trip had gone as would be expected of any military operation. Truth be known, this was a military operation. A media room was made available for the press to speak with West Point officials. Other members of the trip section were given free time. Upon reaching their rooms, some of the cadets opened up books for study, while others talked quietly with a roommate, and a few gathered in small groups to talk about Coach Dixon and the impossible-to-answer question, Why?

Shortly before 7:00 p.m., the team assembled for travel by bus to Sisley Italian Kitchen. The ride took no longer than 20 minutes, but, strangely, the young women became more talkative as they neared the restaurant. They needed some closure to the unabated battering of the five-day storm. The team members were aware dinner would not be a "team-only" affair, and, for that, they were glad. They were particularly pleased to find out that the DePaul women's team would be joining them.

Most national press coverage linked Maggie more to West Point than DePaul. In reality, most of the DePaul team had spent more time with "Coach Maggie" than the Army team. But that fact was irrelevant to both teams, simply because every player loved Maggie. The DePaul women wanted to know more about the women of West Point and their journey with Maggie; the West Point women wanted to know more about DePaul's women and their success in the NCAA Tournament.

Throughout the evening, subjects of discussion expanded and focused on meeting new members of Maggie's close-knit family, the DePaul women's team, and a few close friends. It may have started out uncomfortably, but inherent human walls soon came down and friendships, mostly casual, developed through conversation and shared love for a young coach who positively affected members of the two teams and everyone else she touched. Stories, mostly funny, revealed a single important theme—Maggie Dixon had not changed one iota since the day she interrupted Doug Bruno's shower and the night out with the guys almost six years earlier. But even some of the funny stories were interrupted by the storyteller's need to quench a thirst for crying.

The Army players told many stories: Maggie hiding the rest of the team from the firsties; Maggie laughing hysterically at Sarah Anderson crashing into the ball cart; Maggie throwing playbooks in the trash; Maggie having her car booted; the woman who thought Maggie was an usher; Dave Magarity and his ugly snow boots; the ice cream night in Mahwah; times spent at Maggie's home; Maggie visiting players in the hospital; Plebe–Parent Weekend and the gathering on the Supe's Boat; the bonding with Maggie's family; and Maggie's emphatic challenge—borrowed from Doug Bruno when the chips were down—"How will you handle adversity?" The players from each team saw the same woman in describing Coach Dixon—a fun-loving, energetic, organized, competent, affirming woman who each player on either team considered the finest coach—along with Doug Bruno—in the nation.

A small piece of the conversation morphed into a discussion about life at the USMA.

"You have to be up at what time?"

"How much marching do you have to do?"

"Why do you have to take so much math if you're an English major?"

"How's the food?"

"You don't get the whole summer off?"

"So, do you still have to take physical education courses in addition to basketball?"

The questions showed a real interest in the culture of an institution from which every graduate would most likely experience mortal danger in his or her service to the nation. Since 2006, most of the Army players have served in Iraq, Afghanistan, and other locations throughout the world. And, yes, most have been in harm's way. But, by far, the major topic was Margaret Mary "Maggie" Dixon.

Small opportunities also existed for the Army players to have short conversations with others, mostly family and friends, during dinner. The Dixon family, still reeling from the tragedy, was gracious; it seemed the family was giving solace to those who should have been giving it to them.

After a delicious Italian dinner, conversation exceeding expectations, and knowledge that the next morning would be tough, the leadership team brought the evening to a close. Many people hugged one another for the first time, while others hugged for the umpteenth time. Others shook hands. Everyone felt a sense of family in sharing a common grief. Returning to the hotel at about 11:00 p.m., the cadets returned to their rooms or stopped to talk with other players. Exhausted, some fell into bed immediately; others stayed up much later than would be wise.

At 7:00 a.m. on Tuesday, Megan Vrabel's room served as the breakfast bar and was open for team members to stop by and grab a bagel and a glass of juice. A little after 9:00 a.m., the team departed for St. Charles Borromeo Catholic Church in North Hollywood. Years earlier, comedian Bob Hope, a man loved by the entire military, and his wife, Dolores, were parishioners there. It would not have mattered to anyone, but the chapel is singularly beautiful; architect J. Earl Trudeau had obviously been on his game with his Spanish design of the structure. The exterior, including a high, open-air steeple to the right of the main entrance and open arches along the side, is painted eggshell beige with dark brown accenting the edges and corners.

With a beautiful blue sky, descriptive of California weather, more than 1,200 people filled the church, squeezing together in the many rows of pews on each side of a long, wide aisle. Every couple of pews, red brick columns on each side of the aisle transition into magnificent concrete arches looking down on the congregation. Light is provided either naturally through beautiful stained-glass windows or from large cylindrical lamps hanging from the ceiling. From the pews, one can see a podium for delivering a homily on the left and a large-enough-to-be-a-bathtub baptismal font on the right. In the middle stands an altar, upon which the priest carries out other segments of the Mass. But the main focal point, poignantly emphasized in bright light, is the crucifix of Jesus nailed to the cross.

The cadets of the West Point women's basketball team stood at attention in two ranks facing one another at the entrance to the church. Pallbearers selected by the family, one of whom was Ben Howland, coach of the UCLA Bruins men's basketball team and mentor to Jamie, passed through the cadet cordon and into the church, stopping in front of the altar. At the sight of the casket, most could not hold back, some crying unabashedly, with others trying to squelch both tears and that terrible, lonely lump in the throat. The Army women's basketball team entered the church slowly and took its place behind family and friends. Tears rolled down their cheeks. Each one deeply loved the woman resting in the casket.

Monsignor Robert Gallagher conducted the Mass. The monsignor and Maggie had a link in that his arrival to the parish came but two months after her baptism. Monsignor Gallagher spoke of watching her grow from being a "scrawny little kid" into a beautiful, mature, successful young woman. On a lighter tone, he cited John 14:2 from the New Testament: "In my father's house, there are many dwelling places." Father Gallagher added, "I'm not sure how many are basketball courts. But you know, Maggie would take any room that the Lord would prepare for her."

Following communion, eulogies were given by Kevin Anderson, who had led the efforts to find Maggie; Jean Lenti Ponsetto, athletic director at DePaul University; Carlos Vidueira, a longtime family friend of Jamie and the Dixon family; Micky Mallette, who years later would name her newborn daughter after Coach Dixon; and fellow firstie teammate Ashley "Smash" Magnani. Each gave a heartfelt eulogy. Collectively, the eulogies brought out Maggie's incredible ability to squeeze the best out of everyone she met.

Ashley spoke of the many events during the 2005–2006 season, providing the fabric of a life of servant leadership. Many of the stories had been told with hysterical laughter during the private dinner the night before. Speaking on an unfortunate truth, Ashley spoke of Maggie's ability to see what many coaches do not see, relating, "She constantly reminded us that basketball was fun, even when it was hard. In the middle of huddles, she would be talking to us sternly and then say, 'but don't forget to have fun,' with a smile on her face." Ashley continued with an observation of her coach's position in her life. "She may have been our head coach, but Maggie Dixon was our big sister first and foremost, sharing in the things that defined us as more than basketball players." She hesitated for just a moment to gather herself and then continued. "Her legacy will live on because of the way she touched each and every person in this room today. And that's exactly how she would have wanted it: take what she gave you and build upon it." Ashley briefly looked upon the entire gathering before continuing. "Make it into something good." Ashley's final words swept over the congregation like wind across the prairie. "Coach Dixon, our angel, we promise to make you proud. We love you, and we will see you on the court."

Jean Lenti Ponsetto spoke of Maggie's strengths in terms of inspirational leadership and the value of a fellow human being. She stated, "Like St. Vincent DePaul, she valued the dignity of every person whom she came in contact with and cared for those who were marginalized in our society."

Lenti Ponsetto, whose relationship with Maggie Dixon closely paralleled that of Doug Bruno, described both the compassion and sense of humor Maggie always brought to the table. "Maggie, in a moment's notice—in her own charismatic way—could get together more staff to join her at Kelly's or McGee's pubs than if I were to call a staff meeting to pass out bonus checks."

She closed her remarks with

Maggie girl, we'll miss the shoes (I think of you every time I buy a pair) . . . the outfits . . . the red boots . . . the green purse . . . the laughter . . . the brightness of your eyes . . . the warmth of your smile and seeing you every day. But, we'll be forever grateful that for a magical time in our lives our hearts were touched by you. Thank you, girlfriend!

Jamie Dixon's remarks were deeply heartfelt, explaining the reasons why it was so easy to love Maggie. He said,

I encouraged her to go into coaching. We would talk every day, and it was Maggie who gave me inspiration. She saw the good in everyone. She made everyone around her a better person. She made me a better person. I've said this before—when I grow up I want to be just like her.

Jamie meant every word he said.

Monsignor Gallagher ended the Mass with a blessing for Maggie and the entire congregation. Of all the scenes, Jamie kissing Maggie's coffin is probably the most remembered event. He had to say goodbye in the only way he knew how—to let her know how much he loved her.

Maggie's pallbearers, gently moving her coffin, led the procession out of the church. As the cadets, Joanne Carelus being the first, emerged into the sunlight, the depth of emotion was written on their faces. Joanne could not help but to cry, as did the other team members. They could not come to grips with the devastating shot to the stomach, taking them from the top of the mountain to a valley of despair. Each cadet knew the questions "how?" and "why?" would never be answered satisfactorily. At that moment, they did not know of her statement, "They need me." But, even if for only one season, they did need her. And she needed them as well.

The group made a final stop at Notre Dame High School in Sherman Oaks. The West Point group spent most of their time in the gymnasium, a perfect and meaningful venue, looking at many photographs and other memorabilia of Maggie's short life. Light refreshments were served, but the attendees were more interested in conversation than eating—a strange phenomenon for a cadet. Many people were there, including the two basketball teams she had so significantly affected, fellow coaches, friends of the family, and others fortunate enough to have crossed paths with her. Conversation was not locked into small cliques of "birds of a feather." Many people were interested in the players from West Point and went out of their way to speak with them and tell them how much they respected their willingness to serve the country. It also provided an opportunity for team members to converse with the Dixon family. They were gracious to a fault.

Both the DePaul and West Point players had enjoyed one another's company the night before and took advantage of the opportunity to tell a few more stories about their remarkable coach. Sarah Anderson described the event well when she said, "I remember us sharing Maggie stories with the DePaul players, much like we did the night before. They had a different experience of her but similar views of Coach Dixon. Everyone loved her just as we did, and that was evident." It did not take her death to evoke words of praise. During her tenure at each school, the players of Army and DePaul had many opportunities to sing her praises. The time passed too quickly; it seemed they had barely arrived at the venue, and it brought Maggie a little bit closer to each person. But the hour passed in the blink of an eye—it was time to leave and return to West Point.

The flight back to Stewart International was uneventful. Fortunately, there were no passengers other than the contingent from West Point. Whereas the flight to California had been quiet, the flight back featured a few more conversations and a lot of homework being done. The plebes were fortunate enough to have Major Michelle Isenhour as a tutor. She sat with the players and gave them "additional instruction." Given the rapidity of the lessons in the mathematical sciences, falling behind is an absolute "no-go." Major Isenhour and other professors saved many a plebe, athlete or not. Given Maggie's death and the activities associated with the NCAA Tournament, almost every player was existing on borrowed academic time. After a couple of hours in the air, with the lights off, most of the group nodded off to differing degrees of sleep.

During the flight home, General Lennox and Dave Magarity had a conversation concerning West Point's need for a new coach. The topic of discussion was straightforward and went to the heart of the matter. Said the superintendent, "I spoke to the athletic director—he wants you to take the job, and I agree."⁵ General Lennox invited a couple of the cadets to take his seat to convince Magarity to take the position. Dave Magarity originally planned to serve one year to help Maggie get her feet on the ground. Early on in their dual tenure with the team, Dave let Maggie know of his situation with the New Orleans Hornets. He shared that he would probably be with the team for a single year and then head for New Orleans and the NBA. During the next few days, he would give in to the realization that the USMA was exactly where he should coach for the remainder of his professional life.

The flight landed at Stewart, and the group arrived at West Point shortly after midnight on Tuesday morning, April 11, 2006.

In the days immediately following Maggie's death, General Lennox made the decision to seek permission from the Dixon family to have Maggie laid to rest in the West Point Cemetery. It was a unilateral decision by Lennox—but he did give a "heads up" to Lieutenant General Buster Hagenbeck, his West Point classmate and army deputy chief of staff for personnel. General Hagenbeck would follow General Lennox as superintendent of the USMA. General Hagenbeck had no intention of opposing the plan.

As for a civilian being buried at West Point, regulations exist making it rare for a non-West Point graduate, especially a civilian, to be buried at the institution. But, to clear the record, many reports to this day state that only "high-ranking officials" are authorized for burial at the West Point Cemetery. That statement is incorrect. At the time of Maggie's death, standing regulations limited the cemetery to graduates of the USMA or military personnel and their spouses and children who died while assigned to the academy. If ever an exception to an Army regulation was appropriate, this was it.

As for the Dixon family members, Jim, Marge, Jamie, and Julie were a little confused when approached with the idea of a West Point burial. Fortunately, General Lennox made it clear as to the degree of Maggie's impact on West Point. One by one, the family members came to understand that Maggie, who spent most of her young life in California and most of her adult life at DePaul, had such a profound effect on not only 18 female basketball players, but also on an entire community and, to some degree, a military society, that it would be the proper thing to do. The family originally came from the New York area, so visiting her would not be overly difficult. And a drive in the Lower Hudson Valley, with all its natural beauty, is always an enjoyable experience.

As an athlete and a leader, Maggie had everything on her side. Her resting place was selected in the shadow of the Old Cadet Chapel, the first house of worship at the academy. Constructed in 1836, the chapel was initially built in the cadet area, and upon completion of the new, much larger Cadet Chapel in 1910, it was moved stone-by-stone to the West Point Cemetery. Although much smaller than the newer Cadet Chapel, it remains just as beautiful and still serves to host marriages of former cadets (in some cases, "former" could easily mean "within an hour of graduating"), funerals, and religious services. A few feet from Maggie's resting place are the grave sites of legendary football coach Earl Henry "Red" Blaik (class of 1920) and 1946 Heisman Trophy winner Glenn Davis (class of 1947). But, well beyond the great athletes of Army sports lore, Maggie was to be laid to rest among those military men and women who had served our nation for more than two centuries, along with members of their immediate families. The headstones carry such names as George Armstrong Custer (killed at the Battle of the Little Bighorn, Montana, June 25, 1876), General William Westmoreland (commander of U.S. forces in Vietnam), Lieutenant Colonel Ed White (the first American to make a space walk), Colonel Ted Westhusing (a senior officer who died in the Iraq War), General H. Norman Schwarzkopf Jr. (commander of U.S. forces during the First Gulf War), and many others of all ranks.

April 14, 2006, Good Friday, began as a dreary day. The forecasted rain had not arrived, but dampness permeated anything and everything gray. "Gloom Period" returned with a vengeance. The original plan for the burial service called for a private gathering, but there were too many people who wanted, and needed, to say goodbye to Maggie. It turned out that 500 people, mostly cadets, were in attendance. The clouds thickened, and rain was on the way.

Those attending the funeral stood in honor as six military pallbearers carried Maggie's coffin toward the burial site. They marched between two ranks of women cadets, the cadets she led into battle on the "friendly field of strife" known as basketball. Maggie loved basketball, and she loved every cadet standing at attention. Separated by about six feet, the two ranks faced one another. The young women were dressed in white short-sleeved military shirts, each having gray epaulets with the stripes and shield signifying her cadet rank and class, and gray trousers with the well-known black stripe down the sides. Their military caps and shined shoes finished out the uniform. In the coming years, each one would tell stories of the coach who led them beyond their wildest dreams. The pallbearers weren't other coaches, family, or close family friends. They were U.S. soldiers. They were soldiers with multiple ribbons placed on crisp dress uniforms; they were soldiers having served in Iraq and/or Afghanistan. Finally, they were exactly the type of soldiers the young women Maggie coached would lead in the years to come. It was only appropriate.

Maggie's casket was not covered by the American flag, a tradition reserved for those who have served in the U.S. armed forces. But Maggie Dixon had been a "warrior," plain and simple. She took her team into battle 31 times; led the players through personal crises on many occasions; and taught each player, manager, and young officer how leadership is manifested. Coach Maggie Dixon was the personification of the inspirational, transformative servant leader.

At 12:30 p.m., Father Wood solemnly bid farewell to a person who was universally loved by others. When an old soldier or officer dies, mourners will be sad, but they are consoled by the knowledge that the person had experienced a life "lived completely and lived well." When a young soldier or officer is killed in combat, grief comes in waves. For Maggie Dixon, the grief blanketed everyone at the gravesite. She died much too soon.

"May her soul and the souls of all the faithful departed through the mercy of God rest in peace." Father Wood concluded the burial rites, and the burial service ended. In the distance, a bugler once again played the beautiful and ever-so-lonely taps. Deep guttural sobs and tear-stained faces completed a mosaic of sadness. A sense of despair continued to crush those struggling to accept her death and wishing to turn back the clock. To see her sister Julie kiss Maggie's coffin was both beautiful and overwhelmingly sad.

Almost on cue, a small fall of rain began right after the mourners departed. The cemetery workers slowly broke down the appurtenances of the service and lowered Maggie's casket into the burial plot. The raindrops fell cold on their clothing, adding to the chill of the day. But, if she would have been able to, Maggie Dixon would have called out to them, "Don't worry. Keep your heads up. This falling rain will make the flowers grow." She always looked for rainbows in a storm. Maggie Dixon knew how to embrace adversity.

A

Dear Gene—

Thank you so much for your continued support and guidance. I know that you had a great deal to do with me being here, and I hope that you know that you are also one of the reasons I took the job. To have the opportunity to work in a program where the administration that supports me the way that you and Kevin do, is a dream come true! Thank you!

ARMY BASKETBALL

Sincerely,
Maggie

ARMY BASKETBALL

United States Military Academy
639 Howard Road
West Point, NY 10996-1589

Gene Marshall
ODIA

Note from Maggie to Gene Marshall following the end of the season. *Courtesy of Gene Marshall*

Team members stand at attention as U.S. soldiers carry Maggie to her final resting place. *Army Athletics Communications*

· 20 ·

Leadership, Love, and Legacy

$\mathcal{A}$nd so we have it. A young woman swoops down onto the grounds of the USMA with a plan to take a college basketball team to a place they had never been. In six months, she resurrected the fortunes of a group of frustrated, but willing, young women and, in doing so, captured the love and admiration of an entire community. Maggie's time spent as a head basketball coach was much too short, but during her remarkable short tenure at West Point, she taught many cadets—well beyond the women's team—about leadership and how to overcome the obstacles of life. For that matter, her sphere of influence was gigantic. Part of her legacy today rests in her players knowing how to define, reach, and surpass goals while affirming everyone on a team.

Maggie was more about the human spirit than wins versus losses; however, no one should get the wrong impression of the previous statement; Maggie Dixon was a fierce competitor—she was the "woman in the arena." She performed her duties with distinction, taking her team far beyond what anyone, player or fan, thought possible. She was honest, accessible, organized, energetic, and knowledgeable. She took responsibility for things that did not go well but shifted the accolades to others for achievements gained.

Maggie may not have looked at it this way, but her example of how to live life rubbed off in varying degrees on everyone with whom she came in contact. It is not proposed that Maggie Dixon was the only inspirational leader in existence. But it would be accurate to state that she, through her actions, never took away from a person's sense of honor or ability to accept a challenge. Long before Maggie arrived on the West Point campus, she led a life of leadership and service to others. High school friends and teammates, fellow players at the University of San Diego, other coaches and players at DePaul University, family, friends, and much of the community at the USMA were also fortunate recipients of the Maggie Dixon mystique.[1]

In defining a person's legacy, time is a significant measuring device. It has been more than a decade since Maggie's untimely death. Yet, even on a national level, virtually anyone with an interest in women's basketball will recognize the name Maggie Dixon.

She impacted everyone she met. There is no greater fan of Maggie than her DePaul coach, Doug Bruno. Mention her name and he will react on both the upslope and downslope. He laughs and cries in tune with those little vignettes of the intersection between her life and that of the DePaul University women's basketball team and community.

Bruno remembers the five years Maggie spent at DePaul. He commented,

> The way she handled herself, I always felt like I was working with someone in her 40s. And she would hang with the guys. But she had multiple circles of friends. You know, like one of those little electrons. She had her coaching friends, and my guy friends, older guys, all adopted her. We were cross-pollinating friendship circles along with busting our butts coaching.

He finished by saying, "It was a magical time."

The Maggie Dixon Classic was initiated in the fall of 2006, in honor of her contributions to women's basketball and her inspirational leadership qualities. The first Maggie Dixon Classic, a doubleheader, was held at West Point. Because Jamie was her brother, the University of Pittsburgh men's basketball team played Western Michigan (Pitt won, 86–67), and the Army women played Ohio State (losing, 41–77). The subsequent doubleheaders have been played only by women's teams. In 2006, and for most of the following Maggie Dixon Classics (three other venues since the event's inception have been DePaul, St. Johns, and Texas A&M), the doubleheaders have been played at Madison Square Garden. The 2017 Maggie Dixon Classic occurred on 17–18 November, at the Wintrust Center in Chicago. Maggie's DePaul Blue Demons won both of their games, against Delaware State (110–71) in the opener, and Saint Louis (86–78) to win the championship.

In 2007, although designed for individual players, the entire Army team received the V Foundation Comeback Award. The basic criterion calls for the award to go to the basketball player who best shows triumph in the face of adversity. The "V" stands for former coach Jim Valvano, who died of cancer at the age of 47. In a 1993 address in front of a huge audience at the ESPYs awards show (held in Madison Square Garden), Valvano spoke about adversity with the words, "Don't give up. Don't ever give up." Although still reeling from their loss, none of the players gave up; instead, the team dedicated the next season to Maggie. With Dave Magarity at the helm (and yes, the team still made use of the "WE WILL" messages), the team won 24 games, losing just six. She may have used different words, but the message from Maggie Dixon to her players—"Embrace adversity"—was the same as Jim Valvano's—"Don't ever give up!"

Also in 2007, the Women's Basketball Coaches Association (WBCA) initiated the Spalding Maggie Dixon NCAA Division I Rookie Coach of the Year Award. The award is based on season records, tournament records, team improvement, and the ability to enrich the lives of others (which Maggie would love).

Then, in 2009, the Maggie Dixon Courage Award was initiated. The award is given to an individual exhibiting courage in the face of adversity and exemplifies Maggie's mantra of never letting adversity keep any person from achieving a dream. The award is presented by Maggie's siblings, Julie and Jamie, at the Maggie Dixon Classic.

Returning to the year 2006, it became painfully clear that Maggie died at a time when everyone who knew her saw a healthy young woman in possession of an effervescent personality. Her medical situation was masked to her friends and players by her energy and, to a significant degree, her lack of realizing she had a medical condition at all. While trying to escape the apocalyptic sting of her death, the Dixon family made the decision to go a step further than the Maggie Dixon Classic. Jim, Marge, Jamie, and Julie initiated the Maggie Dixon Foundation to support the Classic and educate people about heart health, particularly sudden cardiac arrest (SCA), and be able to do something about it. It turned out that a linkage with the Sudden Cardiac Arrest Foundation (SCAF) would be a benefit to everyone.

Training programs by SCAF have reached many college campuses, and Jamie Dixon was instrumental in bringing the program to the University of Pittsburgh. Numerous states have requirements for coaches to undergo SCA training. Hundreds, if not thousands, of high schools require CPR training, but not training on the use of automated external defibrillators (AEDs). Training in both is needed. Many young athletes' lives have been saved by CPR training. According to a 2017 study by the Korey Stringer Institute at the University of Connecticut, North Carolina leads the nation for the most comprehensive health and safety policies, with a participatory rate of 79 percent, while Colorado has the lowest rate, at 23 percent.[2] The message is clear: More training is needed in the collegiate and secondary school systems.

When Maggie used the phrase "*Our* alma mater" in the postchampionship interview, she hit the proverbial nail on the head. She may not have graduated from West Point, but if ever a nongraduate earned membership to the Long Gray Line, it was Maggie Dixon. It wasn't just her manner of interacting with the team; Maggie Dixon was a magical woman for all seasons and all people. Always with a smile, Maggie put people at ease. Few people understand the human condition sufficiently to know which buttons to punch based on the traits of the person encountered. Maggie did. While she worked with players on an individual basis, she concurrently worked with the entire team as a single entity. Always positive, but with an ability to let the team know when it was not performing to its potential, Maggie Dixon was the poster girl of what each woman on the team could be and had to be.

How do we measure Maggie Dixon's legacy as basketball coach, mentor, friend, and leader? Many examples of Maggie's attributes stay affixed to the personas of those she coached and those she touched in other benign ways. To this day, her manner of living and leading is embedded in the psyche of the members of the 2005–2006 women's basketball team. Each one of those women carries the spirit of Maggie—and Maggie's approach to leadership— with her. In her eulogy at Maggie's funeral Mass, DePaul athletic director Jean Lenti Ponsetto spoke of Maggie's legacy:

> If I had to choose from all Maggie's strengths, it would be her legacy of caring for family and the human spirit. She saw the good in everyone. And if your spirit was low or your heart was hurting or your focus was in a wayward bent, Maggie would wrap her soul around you and hug your troubles away.

More than a decade has passed since Maggie's death, and articles are still being written about her being an inspirational leader. To quote Melissa Triebwasser, writing on the TCU website Frogs O' War, "In the years that followed, I adopted many of her practices—cooking dinners for my teams, telling terrible jokes during tersely called timeouts in the tensest of moments, trying to turn teams into families—focusing on the people, not just the score-boards."[3]

Coach Maggie Dixon is interred in the West Point Cemetery—another resounding statement of the utter respect she commanded. More than bas-ketball, her ability to understand and respond to the needs of others on any level was her strongest attribute. Rightly, her resting place is near the entrance to the singularly beautiful cemetery; it says much of this singularly beautiful woman. Many stories speak of her legacy through human contact.

In early 2011, Micky Mallette Piasecki called Jim and Marge Dixon with a heartfelt request. Micky and her husband, Todd, were expecting a girl in May and wanted to name their daughter Maggie May Piasecki. The name Maggie would be used instead of Margaret, and the name May would come from the fact that Maggie Dixon entered the world in May 1977. Marge and

Jim were thrilled at Micky's request and enthusiastically gave their blessing. Today, a young girl—who will grow to maturity much faster than her parents would like—is named Maggie May Piasecki because of Maggie Dixon. And, as Maggie May grows, she will learn the stories of her namesake. Someday she will understand firsthand the legacy passed on to her from her mother and father. It will be her responsibility to pass on the message to a third generation. And the fourth, the fifth . . .

During my research for this book, I asked a question concerning the players' current relationship to the "spirit" of Maggie Dixon and her personal qualities as a leader.

Sarah Anderson stated she had recently returned from a mini reunion for the team; each of the former players placed flowers on Maggie's headstone.

Adrienne "Adie" Payne Sherk commented, "I visit her whenever I return to West Point. I usually just stand or kneel in silence and think back to my time spent with her. I talk with her, say some prayers, and let her know that we'll never forget her." As a leader in the game of life, Adie added,

Maggie brought out the best in us as players, people, and cadets. Ultimately, that is the best thing a leader can do. We were beat down before coach arrived. It took very little time for her to turn everything around. We were seniors and wished we had more time with her coaching us. She was a civilian, but she was as good a leader as the best at West Point. I learned so much from her in such a short time. She was a great example of what genuine and positive leadership is all about. She was so kind and generous. Nothing fake about her. If she made a promise, regardless of the subject, she would follow through.

Says Ashley "Smash" Magnani,

Every time I return to the academy, I visit Coach Dixon. I make it seem as though I'm just stopping in to say, "Hi!" I tell her how life has been after basketball, thank her for the tremendous impact she had and still has in my life, pray, and usually cry. It might seem strange, but the more I reflect on it, the more I realize visiting her serves as a form of therapy; talking to her is always what I need to put things right again. It's not much different than it was when she coached me.

Smash and Adie's remarks link perfectly with Jean Lenti Ponsetto's eulogy, during which she said, "And if your spirit was low . . . Maggie would wrap her soul around you and hug your troubles away."

On a lighter note, as fun-loving as they usually are, cadets and young army officers tend to be more conservative than most millennials. Most are relatively adamant about resisting tattoos. Today, most—maybe all—of the players from the 2005–2006 team have a small tattoo of an Irish shamrock on a hip, stomach, or ankle, with "MD" lettered into the artwork. The four firsties went for their tattoos together. Today, every player from the 2005–2006 team is older than Maggie was when she died; for the most part, they still call her Coach Dixon or Coach Maggie.

Returning to the concept of time as a ruler with which to measure one's true legacy, many basketball coaches, both male and female, still know of Maggie and what she accomplished at an unfamiliar military institution. One can only guess how many coaches have gone from a "tyrant" to a "compassionate" model in his or her relationships with players. Be careful how you define "compassionate." Nowhere in a dictionary will you find the word "substandard" or anything even close as a synonym. Maggie inspired her team by treating every member with absolute dignity, while concurrently demanding a level of play be met or exceeded.

Insight from a different perspective helps define the overall legacy of Maggie's life. General Lennox's aide, Major (now Colonel) Jay Miseli, had not played high school basketball, nor was he a fervent follower of women's basketball at West Point. But, because his boss was strongly supportive of women's basketball (General Lennox was actually a strong supporter of every sports program at the academy), Miseli found himself in contact with the women's basketball team, especially Maggie Dixon, on numerous occasions. He did not have many interactions with her, as his view tended to be from "outside the bubble"; however, the more he watched her and how she dealt with the team, other coaches, and community members, the more impressed he became. He attended the Patriot League Tournament and made the trip to Norfolk, Virginia, to watch the Army–Tennessee game. Along with General Lennox, Major Miseli came to the game wearing BDUs and face paint. Since Lennox had done so earlier in the game, the cadet band (also in BDUs) started a chant to urge Miseli to give a "Supe's Aide" rocket. He did, the Supe joined in, and the Army fans were "fired up." In his eyes, Maggie was the ultimate example of the transformational leader. The following year, Miseli volunteered to serve as an OR for women's basketball.

When asked what her legacy meant to him, Miseli hesitated briefly, then responded with, "She solidified the role of women as leaders at the academy and throughout the United States Army." And for the reader, never forget: There is no more important mission in the United States Army than that of being a compassionate, competent, and decisive transformational leader.

In the years since Maggie's death, the members of the 2005–2006 women's basketball team have served throughout the world, including in combat operations in Iraq and Afghanistan. Those whom I have interviewed strike me as having followed Maggie Dixon's model of leadership very closely. Margaret Mary "Maggie" Dixon was, is, and always will be the personification of the inspirational leader. Because of the manner in which she worked for the good of the team, worked with the coaches and players, and led others on a daily basis, Maggie Dixon represents the leadership model to be achieved in the core values of West Point: Duty—Honor—Country.

Maybe it is Coach Magarity who made the most striking analogy regarding Maggie. A man whose life was dramatically changed by a young, brilliant, loving coach, he said of her, "And then she gave me this incredible gift, a ride I'll never forget." Of her death, rather than speaking in a helpless, sad manner, he described her the way she would want to be remembered: "Maggie went out like a comet."

A magnificent comet is exactly what she was.

Epilogue

To Support and Defend

Commanding soldiers in combat is one of the most dangerous and physically demanding professions in existence. Today, there are no "front" lines and no identifiable uniforms. In the Global War on Terror (GWOT), officers must be village mayors as much as they are combatant commanders. Just as it was when they were being recruited, the members of the 2005–2006 Army women's basketball team were made well aware that there are no special deals for officers who happened to play basketball at the USMA. When they raised their hands as far back as June 2002, each of the players was sworn in with, "I (state your name) do solemnly swear that I will support the constitution of the United States . . ." When they graduate, the oath is a little bit different, with two additional words: "I (state your name) do solemnly swear that I will support *and defend* the constitution of the United States . . ." The small addition of "and defend" is the final blank check given to the United States.

While Micky Mallette would have served immediately if not for her medical problems, the others were commissioned and served with distinction. Most of them served time in such places as Iraq and Afghanistan, places where the U.S. government cashed too many of the checks signed by officers and soldiers. Aside from the war, each one has achieved much in their chosen profession and in dealing with other people in many differing situations. The following paragraphs provide biographical sketches of 16 of the 18 players from the women's basketball team of 2005–2006.

CLASS OF 2006

Ashley "Smash" Magnani was commissioned into the Corps of Engineers. Prior to graduation, she, along with Adrienne Payne, received the Army

Athletic Association 2005–2006 Maggie Dixon Award. While waiting for her basic officer training to start, she served as a graduate assistant in the ODIA. Beginning in March 2007, Ashley attended the experimental Basic Officer Leadership Course (BOLC), phase II, at Fort Sill, Oklahoma, and the Engineer Officer Basic Course (EOBC), at the home of the Engineers, Fort Leonard Wood, Missouri. Her first unit assignment was as a platoon leader and an assistant executive officer in the 937th Engineer Route Clearance Company. She was heavily involved in training for clearing improvised explosive devices (IEDs). The training served her well; she deployed in April 2008, with the 937th, to Camp Fallujah, Iraq.

Ashley returned to the United States in March 2009. In 2010, she attended the Combined Logistics Captains Career Course and subsequently transferred to the Quartermaster Corps as a logistician. Her follow-on assignment, in October 2010, was to Fort Stewart, Georgia, as Assistant S-4 (Supply) in Headquarters and Headquarters Company, 1st Armored Brigade Combat Team. During her service, she received the Bronze Star, two awards of the Army Commendation Medal, the Army Achievement Medal, and the Meritorious Unit Commendation. Having spent well in excess of the required term of service, Ashley left the United States Army in May 2014, accepting a position as a deputy project manager/project manager with CACI-ISS, Inc., in Lexington Park, Maryland. She moved up to the Integrated Project Team (IPT), as a logistics engineering manager for the company.

Today, she is employed by CRL Technologies, Inc., as an IPT Lead. As for CRL Technologies, Ashley recently remarked,

> I absolutely love it! They have made me feel like family, as if I had been working for the company for years; that's something that I haven't experienced in the workforce since the Army. This change has given me renewed energy and has helped me remember how healthy it is for the soul to enjoy the place you work and love the people you work with and for.

Ashley met her former husband, Daniel Evans, at the USMA Preparatory School in 2001, but they did not start dating until second semester cow year. In her own words, she put the experience in proper context. "Although many times were challenging being a dual military couple, I do not regret the life we had together, and we have three beautiful children to show for the love we once shared." She deeply loves Hunter David, Austin Donald, and Emma Joy. She keeps fit by helping her parents on their organic fruit and vegetable farm.

When asked about her life since graduation, she wrote,

I look back often and cannot believe the enormous amount of life I have experienced in just a few short years. The pace was fast and the hurdles were endless, but the learning, growing, and loving continue always. Along the many paths I have followed, I have to thank my God-given family, my basketball family, my Army family, and my civilian friendships for their support, guidance, and positive reinforcement that were always given to me when I needed them most. I cannot wait to spend the rest of our lives together.

Finally, Ashley has deep feelings about Maggie Dixon. In her own words, she answered,

"You must do the thing you think you cannot do." This was Eleanor Roosevelt's quote, but we saw Coach Maggie Dixon live this out in every day she spent with us. She accepted the impossible as a challenge, and she made us better in basketball and in life by challenging us to do the same.

Michelle "Micky" Mallette was not commissioned upon graduation; however, she did remain at West Point for a year, serving as director of basketball operations for the Army women's team through the 2006–2007 season. Her next move led her to Procter & Gamble (P&G), where she worked as a marketing purchases manager and technical engineer. She succeeded at P&G but always wanted to pursue a law degree. She decided to attend Albany Law School of Union University. Accepted in 2010, Micky successfully completed the requirements for her law degree in three years. During her third year in school, she served as a legal intern for the Third Judicial Department Town and Village Courts. She also worked as a summer associate for Couch White, LLP. Today she serves as executive editor for state constitutional commentary for the *Albany Law Review*.

Micky joined the law firm Harris Beach, PLLC, in Albany, New York. According to her biography shown on the website LinkedIn, she practices law in the areas of energy, environmental law, and the U.S. collegiate sports industry. She has represented clients in cases related to statutory and regulatory matters in front of state and federal agencies.

It was Micky who called Marge Dixon, asking permission to name her soon-to-be-born daughter after Maggie. The Dixon's were thrilled and enthusiastically agreed. Young Maggie May Piasecki was born in May 2011.

Reflecting on her personal interaction with Maggie and viewing Maggie's handling of the entire team, Micky said,

There are a lot of superlatives you can throw out there—passion, loyalty, organizational strengths, and on and on. For us, it was about us as people. There's a cliché about if you're a good leader, others will run through a wall for you. And that's the way it was with Coach Dixon. At the end of the day, we all wanted to make her proud.

Micky also spoke of Maggie and Dave Magarity, relating, "Coach Dixon and Coach Magarity had a dynamic relationship that was unique. They complemented each other very well. They were a team within a team."

Adrienne "Adie" Payne (Sherk) received the Army Athletic Association 2005–2006 Maggie Dixon Award, along with Ashley Magnani, just prior to graduation. She was commissioned into the Army Ordnance Corps. Following initial training at the Ordnance Officer's Basic Ordnance Course in Aberdeen Proving Ground, Maryland, she served as a platoon leader, maintenance officer, and company executive officer while serving with the 215th Brigade Support Battalion (BSB), 3rd Brigade of the famed 1st Cavalry Division, Fort Hood, Texas. She deployed to Baqubah, Iraq, with the division. Unfortunately, the subscapular tear she suffered during her yearling summer military training at Camp Buckner led to her being medically discharged in May 2009.

One year later, Adrienne married Corey Sherk, a 2005 West Point graduate and former football player, in St. Vincent de Paul Catholic Church, Petaluma, California. They have two children, a boy (Dylan) and a girl (Avery). Adrienne has been employed by Dell; Booz Allen Hamilton; and Taylormade–Adidas golf, in the Global Operations department, where she was responsible for supply chain planning. Because of her experiences as a combat veteran, Adrienne accepted a position as Pacific regional director for Team Red, White, and Blue (RWB), a veteran nonprofit organization with the mission to "enrich the lives of America's veterans by connecting them to their community through physical and social activity." For health and fitness, Adrienne says, "We hike, play at the beach, ride bikes/scooters, and play at the park." The Sherk family currently lives in Half Moon Bay, California. When asked about her life's journey since graduating from West Point, she stated, "I am so blessed; I have a loving husband, two beautiful children, an incredibly supportive family, and a group of amazing friends."

After more than a decade, Adrienne still speaks of Coach Dixon with great respect. She declared,

> There's so much to say. Coach Dixon brought out the very best in us as players, cadets, and human beings. To be honest, we felt beat down and rudderless when the search was going on. From the first day we met her, she changed everything for the better. She may have been a civilian, but she was as good a leader as the best of West Point. I learned so much from her about how to lead others. Her example was that of a genuine, positive leader. Finally, Coach Dixon was kind, generous, and real. Her impact on my leadership skills has not waned one bit over the years.

Megan Vrabel was commissioned into the Air Defense Artillery (ADA) branch. Her first assignment, from May 2006 to May 2007, was serving as the athletic intern for the West Point women's basketball team. Her basic branch schooling first took place at Fort Benning, Georgia, and later at Fort Bliss, Texas. Her first unit assignment was as a launcher platoon leader in the 43rd ADA Battalion. In October 2009, Megan became the executive officer for headquarters battery. In late 2009, she made a branch transfer into the Adjutant General Corps. She remained with the battalion, serving as the personnel officer and battalion adjutant. Among Megan's decorations are the Army Commendation Medal and the Army Achievement Medal.

In May 2011, Megan left military service and moved into the health care industry. She rapidly moved from account manager to director of business services. She then took a position with a private security services company, this time moving from client manager, to director, to regional vice president. Today she is senior vice president for the AAA of Northern California, Nevada, and Utah.

In December 2012, Megan married Zac Maodus, USMA class of 2007, at the idyllic National Hotel in South Beach, Miami, Florida. They have two little girls. She enjoys playing basketball, taking bike rides, and hiking with the kids. They live in Walnut Creek, California. Looking at her life since graduating from West Point, she remarked,

> I've been fortunate enough to be surrounded by amazing people, both in my professional and personal life. I continue to expand that group by taking new opportunities and never being afraid of change. For all people, my mantra would be, "Get out there and make your life what you want."

When asked about Maggie Dixon's influence on her life, Megan replied, "Sometimes in business, women think they need to be tougher than everyone else to be successful. Maggie treated everyone with respect, was the ultimate team player, and was, most importantly, kind. Striving to emulate her in my career has always led me in the right direction."

CLASS OF 2007

Erin Begonia was commissioned into the Chemical Corps. Her first tour of duty was as an assistant basketball coach for USMAPS. Following her attendance at the officer basic course, she was assigned as the chemical, biological, radiology, and nuclear officer for the Headquarters and Headquarters Company (HHC) with the 3rd Battalion, 25th General Support Aviation Battalion (GSAB) at Wheeler Army Airfield, Hawaii. She deployed with the unit to Iraq. Following a year in Iraq, Erin attended the Telecommunications

Systems Engineering Course at Fort Gordon, Georgia. She then assumed duties as the telecommunications systems engineer with the 5th Signal Command in Wiesbaden, Germany. In 2014, she was individually tasked under the Worldwide Individual Augmentation System (WIAS) and served in a similar capacity for the Joint NETOPS (Network Operations) Control Center (JNCC-P)/Communications, Office of Defense Representative, Pakistan (ODRP), U.S. Embassy in Islamabad, Pakistan. Among her numerous awards and commendations are the Joint Commendation Medal, three Army Commendation Medals, and the Army Achievement Medal.

Erin speaks gently when thinking back to her days as a player, saying, "It was a night-and-day difference from before. Coach Dixon had so much enthusiasm, it was like shining a light on the entire team. In some cases, she was just a silly person, but when it was time to prepare ourselves, she could be tough."

Jillian Busch (Borque) was commissioned into the Ordnance Corps following graduation. She attended the Ordnance Officer Basic Course in Fort Lee, Virginia. Following her basic schooling, Jillian served in various assignments in the United States (Fort Lee, Fort Hood, Texas, and Fort Bragg, North Carolina). In 2008, she deployed to Iraq. Upon returning to the United States, she served as the brigade ground maintenance officer in the 4th Combat Aviation Brigade. In June 2008, while in Iraq, she met Captain Brian Borque. They were engaged in 2009, and married in 2010. Additional information was not available at the completion of this book.

Joanne Carelus (Fantroy) was commissioned into the Adjutant General Corps. Following the initial entry basic officer's course, she was assigned to Fort Stewart, Georgia, with the 3rd Infantry Division (ID). She served as the personnel officer (S-1) for the logistics component for the 3rd ID. Her next assignment was battalion S-1 with the 3rd Battalion/69th Armor. Joanne was deployed to Iraq as the personnel officer to the 3rd Brigade Support Battalion (BSB). She spent eight months at Forward Operating Base (FOB) Falcon in Baghdad. During her five years of active duty, she found herself taking on more and more responsibilities related to human resources. Her knowledge of different human resource information systems (HRIS) served her well as she prepared recommended human resource policies and procedures. Because of her background in HRIS, her transition to civilian society in May 2012 went smoothly.

Joanne performed well working in the field of human resources with Macy's (St. Petersburg, Florida); as a human resource manager; and with Linden Care, where she directed and coordinated such human resource functions as recruiting, employee relations, benefits, compensation, and employment services. In 2015, she broadened her skills with her appointment as manager of talent and organizational performance with Northwell Health. Added challenges include leadership development, accountability, and achieving organizational goals. She interacts closely with union representatives and employees concerning employee and labor relations.

Joanne looks back on her life and sees a glorious time, commenting, "What a ride I have been on. I am blessed."

Joanne's thoughts on Maggie Dixon are as follows:

> I'm proud to have played on her team, making history. She was a special person, coming from a great family. I recall many laughs with her. I will always remember her leadership style—she cared for us, was always prepared, and raised the level of our competitiveness. It wasn't just the team; her touch reached to many different areas of the academy. The whole community loved her. She had great relationships with the academy leadership. Her death opened my eyes as to what may happen. She made me want to live each day to the fullest and to be able to say, "I love." She absolutely made me a better person.

CLASS OF 2008

Cara Enright received her commission into the Air Defense Artillery (ADA). Her first year of active duty was spent as a graduate assistant at USMAPS. She supervised 18 cadet-candidate athletes and assisted the USMA's athletic department and women's basketball program with logistical, operational, and recruiting requirements. A year later, she attended the Basic Officer Leadership Course (BOLC) branch qualification schools at Fort Sill, Oklahoma, and Fort Bliss, Texas. Upon graduation from the BOLC, Cara was assigned as executive officer of the 2nd Battalion, 43rd Air Defense Artillery Regiment, Fort Bliss, Texas. During that period, she deployed to Bahrain. Upon returning to the United States, she served as assistant battalion operations officer (S-3) for the regiment. In spite of her rank, she was selected over 20 other officers to serve as the battalion S-3. Following her tour, she attended the ADA Career Course at Fort Sill. Her next, and final, assignment was as future operations planner for the 3rd Battalion, 4th ADA Regiment. In this position, she was responsible for the planning, coordination, and operations of the 700-soldier battalion.

In May 2014, Cara returned to civilian life and a position at General Mills as a logistics planner for Yoplait. Being successful, she was elevated to the position of management coordinator for General Mills in Murfreesboro, Tennessee. Cara took a project manager position with Hospital Corporation of America in April 2016. She lives in Nashville, Tennessee.

Cara once remarked, "Coach Dixon wasn't just a basketball coach. She invited the players over to her house quite often. She talked to us about so many things. She cared about us more as people than basketball players."

Margaree "Redd" King (Richard) was commissioned into the Ordnance Corps. Prior to graduation, she was selected as Defensive Player of the Year for the Patriot League. Her basic schooling led her into the dangerous arena of explosive ordnance disposal (EOD). As of this writing, she served as a captain and, in January 2018, was selected for promotion to major. She currently holds the position of assistant professor of military science at Austin Peay State University in Clarksville, Tennessee. Other key assignments include service with the 716th EOD Company at Joint Base Elmendorf-Richardson, Alaska (June 2011–June 2012).

Following her graduation from the Ordnance Career Course in 2013, Margaree was assigned to the battalion staff of the 184th EOD Battalion. In September 2013, she was given command of the 723rd EOD Company. In November 2013, she deployed with her company of 47 soldiers (44 men and three women) to Bagram Airbase, Afghanistan, where the unit provided EOD liaison to the Combined Joint Special Operations Task Force Afghanistan. She found the assignment critically important and extremely exhilarating. Her biggest goal was to bring everyone home without serious injury—and she did.

Upon returning from Afghanistan in March 2014, King was assigned as assistant operations officer (assistant S-3) in the 184th EOD Battalion. From February 2016 to September 2016, she served as the battalion S-3 as a captain, a position normally slated for more senior officers (making it a plum assignment for her). Among her awards and decorations are two Bronze Stars, the Meritorious Service Medal, the Army Commendation Medal, the Army Achievement Medal, and the Senior EOD Badge.

Margaree married Captain Cleve Richard on October 31, 2015, at the beautiful Destrehan Plantation outside of New Orleans. Bridesmaids for the wedding included teammates Anna Wilson, Cara Enright, Stefanie Stone, and Alexys Myers (team manager). Margaree and Cleve met while both were cadets. Although she did take the name Richard, many still use the last name King. As a dual military couple, they have the fortunate situation of being stationed together. Cleve is assigned to the famed 101st Airborne Division (Airmobile) at Fort Campbell, Kentucky, only 10 miles from Clarksville.

Of her life since leaving the academy, Margaree commented in 2018, "I have a much greater appreciation for every moment, be it during times of stress or relaxing at the breakfast table. Hanging with my teammates was great. I would not change it, good days or bad days, for the world."

Thinking back to Maggie Dixon, Margaree said,

> I want to be like Maggie Dixon when I grow up (Redd was 32 years old when she made the statement). To a small degree, I am working with kids just as Coach Maggie worked with me. I coach high school and middle school girls' basketball teams. I love it. She made me believe in myself. I want to eventually coach collegiate basketball because of Coach Dixon. Finally, I can still remember the way she helped me out of a deep, dark hole. Her hammering away at embracing adversity has always stuck with me. When I had a bout with cancer, I took it head-on, and she was the reason I was so positive. Without question, I am where I am today because of Coach Maggie Dixon.

Natalie Schmidt (Ryan) was commissioned into the Transportation Corps. Unfortunately, she suffered a broken neck (three broken vertebrae in her cervical spine and spinal degeneration throguhout time) and was medically discharged in March 2009. Three months later, in Warrenton, Virginia, Natalie married Tommy Ryan, a 2006 graduate of West Point. Tommy was a football player, and they were both assigned to the same cadet company. Because he remained in the United States Army, Natalie has traveled quite a bit, including assignments to the Air Force Academy, University of Arizona, and a return to where it all started—West Point. While Tommy teaches in the Department of Systems Engineering, Natalie serves the Association of Graduates as director of donor engagement for the Johnny Mac Soldiers Fund.[1] They have two children, a six-year-old daughter and a four-year-old son.

Considering her time spent at the academy and with Maggie, Natalie says,

> I have West Point to thank for my professional career, my husband, my kids, my basketball sisters, and lifelong friends. I have Maggie to thank for the way that I approach all of those endeavors, and for her I am eternally grateful. Being now older than Maggie was when she died, I am in even more awe of her maturity and leadership of our team. In my time working in both the Army and private sector, I have been hard pressed to find leaders willing to take full accountability for their actions. Maggie did.

Stefanie Stone was commissioned into the Air Defense Artillery (ADA) and, following a short period of leave, attended the four-month ADA

Basic Officer Leadership Course (BOLC) at Fort Bliss, Texas. From there she went directly to Delta Battery, 1st Battalion, serving as a platoon leader until January 2009. At that point, she deployed with her battalion for a one-year tour of duty to Kuwait, where she served as the officer in charge at the Fire Direction Center for the battalion. Upon returning to the United States, she was assigned to the 69th ADA Brigade. Her stay was interrupted by a nine-month deployment to Qatar and the United Arab Emirates.

Stefanie was selected to attend the ADA Career Course (a school to prepare ADA officers for increasing levels of command) from January to June 2014. Upon graduation from the Career Course, she was assigned to one of the best tours of duty in the military—the USMA. In her case, Stefanie served from August 2014 to August 2016 as an instructor in military science and the branch advisor for the ADA. She returned to civilian life in August 2016. For her performance during her time in the military, Stefanie received the Meritorious Service Medal, two awards of the Army Commendation Medal, the Army Achievement Medal, and many service medals.

Stefanie works and lives in New York City, and holds a position as a financial services consultant.

To the dual question concerning how life has treated her and her current thoughts on Maggie Dixon, Stefanie replied,

> My life has been full of travels to various places around the world, different adventures, hardships, and fond memories—trying to work as hard as I possibly can and enjoying life a bit at the same time. I often look back at my times at West Point with great sadness but also happy memories, especially during our times with Coach Dixon. I will never stop remembering the glorious season of 2005–2006 and the amazing things our team accomplished under the leadership of the person who led us there—Coach Maggie Dixon.

Anna Wilson (Christen) was commissioned into the Adjutant General's Corps upon graduation. Her first assignment was as graduate assistant/coach of the USMAPS women's basketball team. Following basic officer's school, she was assigned as the battalion personnel officer (S-1) with the 14th Military Intelligence (MI) Battalion at Fort Sam Houston, Texas, and deployed with the battalion to Camp Cropper, Iraq. Upon her return to the United States in July 2010, Anna was assigned as the Brigade S-1 of the 470th MI Brigade, also at Fort Sam Houston. She left active duty in 2013 but joined the Army Reserves and currently holds the rank of major, and serves as assistant professor of military science at Texas A&M–Corpus Christi.

Among Anna's awards are the Iraqi Campaign Medal, the Defense Meritorious Service Medal, the Joint Service Commendation Medal, the Army Commendation Medal, and the Army Achievement Medal. In 2015, at Saint Isaac Jogues Church in Marlton, New Jersey, Anna married Sam Christen, a fighter pilot in the United States Navy and a graduate of the USNA. Of her marriage, Anna wrote, "Sam and I dated through high school and college; he attended the Naval Academy, so it was always an added bonus to beat Navy. After switching to the reserves, we finally got the chance to live in the same zip code, get married, and last season, we watched Army beat Navy in football (one of us was more excited than the other)!" Anna and Sam maintain a high degree of fitness by snowboarding, wakeboarding, running, and playing basketball with the Navy pilots. She can more than handle the competition with the men.

Anna summed up her four years at the academy by saying, "West Point provided me with many fulfilling opportunities and lifelong friendships with some of the most caring, genuine people alive. Though I was never stationed in the same places as my basketball classmates, those girls are still my closest friends." She loved Maggie Dixon, and Anna's staying at West Point rested heavily on the compassion and leadership of her coach. Through Anna's eyes, "Coach Dixon was able to read people and relate well to her players. Based on the situation, she was able to switch from coach to teacher, enforcer, friend, and sister, with ease. Much of my decision to stay at West Point came from the wisdom of Coach Maggie Dixon."

CLASS OF 2009

Sarah Anderson received her commission into the Air Defense Artillery (ADA). She attended the Basic Officer Leadership Course (BOLC) branch qualification schools at Fort Sill, Oklahoma and Fort Bliss, Texas. Upon graduation from the BOLC, Sarah returned to Fort Sill, where she was selected for duty as a battery executive officer of Alpha Battery, 4th Battalion, 3rd Air Defense Artillery (ADA) Regiment, 31st ADA Brigade, a proud unit with a lineage dating back to 1821. While stationed at Fort Sill, she held numerous positions, each leading to more responsibility, including command of Alpha Battery and commandant of the Fires Center of Excellence Resiliency Training Campus.

During her time in the United States Army, Sarah received three awards of the Army Commendation Medal and three awards of the Army Achievement Medal. She left the Army in December 2014 and moved to the Kiewit Company, a major international construction firm. Her current title is regional talent development lead. Sarah works with the programs providing training and development of employees in technical, management, and leadership areas of focus. Her geographical area of responsibility includes eastern Canada and the eastern United States. She lives in Denver, Colorado.

As for leisure, Sarah enjoys traveling, outdoor activities (fishing, hiking, learning to ski), and spending time with friends and family. When asked about life since graduation from West Point, she replied,

> One of the larger lessons I have learned from West Point, the Army, the civilian sector, and life so far is that change is always happening, but how we react to it is most important. It shows our true character and that of others. I am grateful for all the opportunities and lessons I have experienced; I continue to learn something new every day.

Concerning her time spent at West Point, Sarah added,

> I learned so much about myself at West Point and am better equipped to tackle the challenges that come my way professionally and personally. I also learned from those I was surrounded by at West Point (teammates, peers, instructors, coaches, and many others), and I carry those lessons with me in everything that I do. I have an immense sense of pride for being part of that community and family.

Without a doubt, Maggie Dixon's legacy lives on in Sarah Anderson's heart. Sarah commented,

> Maggie was fearless and strong. She challenged me every day to be my best and yet showed compassion and genuine care for others' well-being. She was our coach and always will be. She left a part of her with each of us, and the impact she had will never be forgotten. We continue to carry with us her wisdom. "There are no limits to what we can do" and "'We Will' take on anything that comes our way and turn it into a positive."

Megan Ennenga was commissioned into the Military Police Corps (MP), and her first assignment was attending the Military Police Corps basic officer's course. Her first duty station, in December 2009, was Schofield Barracks, Hawaii, where she served as a platoon leader in the 58th Military Police Company. In October 2010, she was advanced to the position of company executive officer. In June 2011, Megan deployed with her unit to Kandahar City, Afghanistan. She excelled in her duties and, upon her return to Hawaii, was assigned the position of assistant S-3 (Operations) for the 728th MP Battalion. Her next assignment was also as an assistant S-3 for the 94th Military Police Battalion at Camp Humphreys, Daegu, South Korea. Megan was particularly pleased with her assignment, as she was born in Kyonggi-do, South Korea, and adopted by Mark (a former Army first sergeant) and Carol Ennenga. Megan soon was given command of the 188th MP Company. After successful command, she was reassigned to the position of antiterrorism officer, Multinational Force and Observers, at Forward Operating Base (FOB) North, Sinai. Continuing to "see the world," Megan returned to the United States with an assignment as instructor at the Military Advisor Training Academy (MATA).

Among her awards and decorations are the Bronze Star Medal, the Meritorious Service Medal, the Army Commendation Medal (twice), the Army Achievement Medal, and the Basic Parachutist Badge. It does not matter where she is located, Megan loves to play sports and travel.

Of her life, she says,

> Having been adopted, I have always wanted to give back to my country. As for West Point, playing sports was a major factor in my journey to the academy. Just as I was on the basketball team, I feel honored to be part of a team known as the United States Army. I've seen both good and bad leadership, but we always have a team. And, by the way, I still love to play sports.

Megan recently spoke of Maggie Dixon, stating,

> What Coach Dixon symbolizes to me is togetherness—it has been more than a decade since she's been gone, but immediately I know I can call, out of the blue, each one of my teammates from the 2005–2006 team and feel like it was yesterday that we last talked. We all share something because of Coach's eternal light.

Megan Evans was commissioned into the Military Police Corps. Her early military schooling included the Officer Basic Course (OBC) at Fort Leonard Wood, Missouri, the Military Police Captains Career Course, and Anti-Terrorism Basic Course. Her early assignments included service as a platoon leader and then executive officer of the 66th MP Company at Joint Base Lewis-McChord, Washington. She progressed through numerous important assignments, including Brigade Provost Marshal, 4th Infantry Brigade Combat Team (IBCT), 1st Infantry Division, Fort Riley, Kansas. She also served as the Future Operations Officer for the 97th MP Battalion at Fort Riley. Her assignments culminated with her selection as a company commander of the 977th MP Company of the 97th MP Battalion. She deployed to Iraq in support of Operation Iraqi Freedom during the period 2009–2011. Her awards and decorations include the Meritorious Service Medal (MSM), Army Commendation Medal with three oak-leaf clusters (3 OLC) reflecting four separate awards of the ACM, the Army Achievement Medal (2 OLC), the Iraq Campaign Medal, the National Defense Service Medal, the Global War on Terrorism Service Medal, the Army Service Ribbon (ASR), and the Meritorious Unit Commendation (MUC). At the publication of this book, she is serving as the director of operations for the West Point Women's Basketball Team. Of her personal life, Megan says:

> I'm single and have a 3-year-old Yellow Lab named Hank. I still love being active! Working out, lifting (taking full advantage of having access to the amazing facilities in the weight room in Kimsey), running, hiking with Hank, yoga, and snowboarding. I also love to cook and bake. I don't play basketball anywhere nearly as frequently as I used to, but I do find the chance every so often.

When asked about Coach Maggie Dixon, Megan responded:

> I'm sure it's been said by almost everyone, but Coach Dixon had the ability to light up a room the moment she stepped in and put those around her in such a great mood. Her passion and energy for the game and her positive attitude were infectious and so uplifting. Practices were challenging and tough physically and mentally; but, those hours and minutes ticked away quickly and were so enjoyable because the excitement/buzz/energy/passion (whatever you want to call it) in the gym was pervasive and ever-present throughout the course of season—all of it stemming from Coach Dixon and her approach to the game, leadership, and our team.

Alex McGuire finished her career at Army with her second selection to the Patriot League first team and a final scoring record of 1,467 points. Upon graduation in 2009, she was commissioned in the Adjutant General Corps. She immediately was assigned as the basketball intern to the women's basketball team until proceeding to her basic officer's course at Fort Jackson, South Carolina, in February 2010. Her first full assignment was to the 172nd Support Battalion, Schweinfurt, Germany, as the personnel officer. She deployed with the battalion in May 2010, to Forward Operating Base (FOB) Sharana, Pakitka Province, Afghanistan. Other assignments include serving as personnel officer for the Maneuver Enhancement Brigade, Fort Polk, Louisiana. Alex then served as assistant professor of military science at the University of Wisconsin–Stevens Point. She subsequently served as deputy of the Personnel Accountability Division at Fort Shafter, Hawaii; she barely had time to see the scenery before being assigned to the same position at Camp As Sayliyah, Qatar.

Among her many decorations, Alex has received the Bronze Star, the Meritorious Service Medal, two Army Commendation Medals, three awards of the Army Achievement Medal, and the Afghanistan Campaign Medal.

Alex recently commented on her life in sports and the military:

> Sports and the Army have played a central role in my life. My dad was in the Army for 20 years (USMA '81), and he and my mom encouraged my brother (USMA '14) and me to play sports at an early age. Since graduating from West Point, I have had the opportunity to live and travel all over the world and meet people from diverse backgrounds. Some of those people have become lifelong friends. I would have never imagined growing up, that I would get to have such amazing experiences, to include playing for a German basketball team while I was stationed in Germany.

In looking back at her time spent under the tutelage and mentoring of Maggie Dixon, Alex remembered, "Coach Dixon saw the best in people and had the ability to get them to see that as well and exceed their expectations. That is something I have tried to do as well."

Courtney Wright (Razon) was commissioned into the Ordnance Corps. In an 18-month period, she attended the Ordnance Officer Basic Course in Fort Lee, Virginia; EOD training, Phase 1, at Redstone Arsenal, Alabama; and EOD training, Phase 2, at Elgin Air Force Base (AFB), Florida. Her first permanent assignments included two years as an EOD platoon leader in Fort Lewis, Washington, and in southern Afghanistan. While in Afghanistan, Courtney was wounded in action by an improvised explosive device (IED). In the same incident, her future husband was also wounded. Courtney returned to the United States and was given a company commander assignment at the Naval School, Explosive Ordnance Disposal (NAVSCOLEOD), at Eglin AFB. She served for two years as executive officer and operations officer at the 21st EOD Weapons of Mass Destruction (WMD) Company at Kirtland AFB, New Mexico. Based on performance, she was selected for a master of business administration degree (MBA) at the University of New Mexico.

Courtney met Jarrett Razon in 2011, while both were stationed at Fort Lewis. They were married on August 10, 2013, on the North Shore of Oahu, Hawaii. In between, the wrath of war dictated some, but not all, of their future. While on foot patrol—and yes, women were often exposed to danger—they came across indications of an IED. While trying to move other soldiers out of the way, an infantry platoon sergeant accidently stepped on the IED. Both Courtney and Jarrett were severely wounded in the explosion, and the infantry sergeant lost both legs and an arm but did survive. Because of their wounds, having a family was thought to be impossible.

Defying the odds and predictions, the young couple underwent in vitro fertilization (IVF). [NOTE: Initial funding for the IVF procedure came from the EOD Warrior Foundation charity.] Arriving two months early, a little (two pounds, seven ounces) girl—Finley—joined the Razon family in 2017. Finley and parents are doing well. Quoting Courtney, "She's a constant reminder of how grateful my husband and I are to have each other and how blessed we are to have her. We love to ski, hike, camp, paddleboard, raft, road bike, and cannot wait to teach our daughter to do all of these things!"

Among Courtney's awards are the Purple Heart (for wounds received in combat), the Bronze Star, the Army Commendation Medal with "V" device (for valor), and two Meritorious Service Medals. She also has been awarded the Senior Explosive Ordnance Medal and the Combat Action Badge. In the real sense of the word, Courtney and Jarrett are American heroes. Finley has shown herself to be a fighter as well.

Of Maggie, Courtney wrote, "Maggie is my constant reminder to not dwell on adversity you face; instead, face it head on and attack it!"

To the last player, the inherent values of West Point have held great personal value. All the players have succeeded in either military (most having led American soldiers in combat environments) or civilian society. The inculcation of "Duty, Honor, Country" plays out in their daily lives, regardless of their chosen profession.

The mission statement of the USMA includes the following wording: "The mission of the United States Military Academy is to educate, train, and inspire the Corps of Cadets so that each graduate is a commissioned leader of character." The players on the 2005–2006 West Point women's basketball team were fortunate to have played under a coach who educated, trained, and inspired each one of them. She loved them, and they loved her. She never berated players; she made players better. She never quit; she would not let her players quit. She set high standards and challenged them to achieve and surpass those standards. She built in each one a desire to enjoy every day to the fullest. Maggie Dixon was truly a once-in-a-lifetime inspirational leader.

Acknowledgments

*M*aggie was an inspirational leader taken away from us much too soon. When she died, I thought about her quite a bit during the next two years and decided to write an article for *Assembly Magazine*, published for graduates by the West Point Association of Graduates (AOG). I titled the article, "Remembering Maggie." My task was to verify everything I heard about her. Based on my discussions with two players (they were still cadets at the time), Cara Enright and Redd King, and doing a little research, I realized she was better than advertised. Throughout the years, I could not get her out of my mind—so I decided to capture as much of her persona as possible—thus, this book. I am not a natural-born writer, but I have been compelled to tell at least some of her story. I have but scratched the surface. The final product came from the eagerness of many people wanting to help an old soldier capture the unvarnished character of Maggie Dixon and her accomplishments in six months at the United States Military Academy.

I'll start first with Jamie Dixon, the current head men's basketball coach at Texas Christian University (TCU). He took time during the season, a time when travel, preparation, and playing games are intense and lead to many 14-hour workdays, to speak about his youngest sister. I received great insight from Jamie concerning the little nuances of who she really was. He loves her deeply. Thanks Jamie.

Coach Doug Bruno of the DePaul University Blue Demons, also in the crucible of a basketball team in season, nevertheless made time for me to grab two hours of his remembrances of Maggie. His insight is a proverbial goldmine—and he was the source of the "WE WILL" cards used during Maggie's time as head coach at West Point. It is clear he will treasure the days Maggie spent at DePaul. Thank you, Doug. Although through very different lenses, both men painted a beautiful picture of Maggie.

Next, and since they scored the baskets leading to the phenomenal 2005–2006 season, I want to say thank you to the West Point women's basketball team. Each player I talked to was more than delighted to provide input for the manuscript. So, thanks and a tip of my hat to those who are the fabric of the best of American society: Sarah Anderson, Erin Begonia, Joanne Carelus, Megan Ennenga, Cara Enright, Megan Evans, Margaree "Redd" King, Ashley "Smash" Magnani, Micky Mallette, Alex McGuire, Adrienne "Adie" Payne, Natalie Schmidt, Stefanie Stone, Megan Vrabel, Anna Wilson, and Courtney Wright. I could not find Jen Hansen or Jillian Busch, but I'm certain they would have wanted very much to speak about coach Maggie Dixon. Extra kudos to Sarah Anderson (for photographs, the "WE WILL" cards, photos, and background notes) and Micky Mallette (for her many photographs and background information). Speaking of Micky, let me add in Jim Mallette, Micky's dad, for speaking with me—and for the support he and Kathy Mallette gave to our team. We can add kudos to Ashley Magnani, Erin Begonia, and Stefanie Stone for significant additional background information. Each player I interviewed displayed nothing but reverence for Maggie. I wish I served at West Point when the 2005–2006 women's team took to the court.

Coach Dave Magarity helped not only in speaking with me for several hours, but also, as I mention in the book, he invited me into the locker room during pregame, halftime, and postgame sessions. It was evident how much Dave respected Maggie. He also told me to contact Gene Marshall, which turned out to be a great recommendation. Gene was most helpful both in talking to me and in his efforts to bring Maggie and Dave together as a team unto themselves. Unsung heroes include Steven Schoon, associate director of communications at TCU; Laura Griggs, administrative assistant to coach Doug Bruno at DePaul University; and Harrison Antognioni and Matthew Tedino, assistant directors for athletic communications at the United States Military Academy. All four assisted me with documents and/or setting up times to interview Jamie Dixon and Doug Bruno.

My agent and longtime friend Rob Wilson has supported book projects and given me sound advice concerning getting a book published. My first reader of the manuscript was John Raymond, my close friend since we were army privates in 1959, and classmates at West Point. He did not hesitate to tell me what needed to be changed. I owe thanks to former superintendent Lieutenant General (Ret.) William J. Lennox Jr. for his insight into hiring Maggie Dixon and her being laid to rest at West Point. To General Lennox's former aide-de-camp, Colonel Jay Miseli, many thanks for discussing (the day before he was to take his brigade to the National Training Center) the interactions between General Lennox and Maggie, and for his recollections of the atmosphere at West Point during Maggie's tenure.

Janis (Mathis) Balis, Nicci Hays Fort, and Jackie (Liautaud) O'Neill provided much information on Maggie's fun-loving and infectious attitudes about life. The operative word they used in describing Maggie's personality is "laugh." Brigadier General (Ret.) Maureen LeBoeuf, a friend of many years, helped me with accuracy related to her interactions with Maggie. Colonel (Ret.) Donna Brazil, also a close friend, and who spent many years at West Point, was the officer representative (OR) of the team; she provided a clear look at the team and their coach. She also spoke enthusiastically about her memories of the championship game. Both Maureen and Donna were mentors to many cadets during their tenure at the academy.

To my editors at Rowman & Littlefield, I give thanks for guiding me through the maze of "things to be done." Both Christen Karniski, my acquisitions editor, and Andrew Yoder, my production editor, made sure I did not go too far astray at the beginning and at the time for the final copy to be placed "in stone." Christen was insightful and professional—and she held the line, always with great politeness, when it came to meeting my timing requirements. When Christen took a hiatus for maternity reasons, Bethany Davis stepped up to the plate to keep me "on target" and "on time." Stephen Ryan, senior acquisitions editor, gave me sage guidance during the final stages of the manuscript. Jessica DeFranco and Kelly Quarrinton brought me out of the wilderness in terms of marketing. All the folks at Rowman & Littlefield were genuinely professional and most enjoyable in helping me complete this project.

And to my family. To my wife of 54 years, Judy. Hon, I have no idea how you did it, but thanks for inspiring me to "get the job done," while concurrently reading everything I put on paper. I love you, yes, I do. To my daughters #2 and #3—thanks Kim and Kory for pushing me forward. Finally, to daughter #1, Kelly Petrillo, I can only say, "Thank you, thank you, thank you." Your insight into the topics and characters was exceptional. Your editing every page of my manuscript, including the photographs, resulted in at least 200 corrections, deletions, or additions. And your expertise in all things computer kept me from going stark raving mad when mine crashed about 10 minutes before I was going to submit my initial manuscript. You are one smart, energetic, and beautiful woman by any measure. "To the Moon" young lady.

Notes

CHAPTER 2

1. Douglas MacArthur, *Reminiscences* (New York: McGraw-Hill, 1964), 82.
2. 94th Congress. Public Law 94-106, Section 803, Title VIII, General Provisions, as pertains to Chapter 403 of Title 10, United States Code, October 7, 1975.
3. The author was assigned to the USMA from 1973 to 1976. He watched the first woman enter the academy in July 1976.

CHAPTER 3

1. Brian McQuarrie, "Fewer Applying to U.S. Military Academies," *Boston Globe*, June 13, 2005, www.archive.boston.com/news/education/higher/articles/2005/0613/fewer_applying_to_us_military_academies (February 17, 2018).

CHAPTER 5

1. United States Military Academy, *West Point Catalogue, 2007–2008* (West Point, NY: USMA, 2007), 24.

CHAPTER 6

1. The "Supe's Boat" is a boat taken from a drug raid and used by the superintendent for social occasions. It is generally open for use by any activity on post. It is rented in order that it does not cost the American taxpayer any money.

CHAPTER 9

1. Glen P. Graham, "McGuire Never Stops Driving: Talent and Work Ethic Have Produced Something Special in Arundel's West Point-Bound Star," *Baltimore Sun*, January 13, 2005.

2. Department of the Army, Army Doctrine Publication (ADP) 1, "The Soldier's Creed and the Warrior Ethos," Army Publishing Directorate (superimposed on photograph at beginning of ADP 1 [no page number]), September 2012.

CHAPTER 13

1. Captain Philip Egner, United States Army, "On Brave Old Army Team," 1910.

CHAPTER 16

1. Margaret Cobb and Bruce Channel, "Hey Baby (I Wanna Know If You'll Be My Girl" (LeCam Records, Fort Worth, Texas, 1961). Numerous versions.

2. Paul S. Reinecke, *The Alma Mater* (1908).

CHAPTER 19

1. Jana Mathis is now Jana (Mathis) Balis.

2. Jackie Liautaud is now Jacqueline "Jackie" (Liautaud) O'Neill.

3. Maureen Magarity spent four years (2006–2010) with the Army women's basketball team. At the time of this writing, she is head coach at the University of New Hampshire.

4. Maggie's friend requested that I not mention her name or specific events prior to Maggie's arrival at KACH. I have honored her request.

5. Harvey Araton, "The Hearth Beckons, So a Coach Stays on, with No Regrets," *New York Times*, February 13, 2007, https://mobile.nytimes.com/2007/02/13/sports/ncaabasketball/13araton.html (February 17, 2018).

CHAPTER 20

1. Elizabeth Merrill, "Maggie Dixon Still Revered for Her Impact," *ESPN.com*, April 8, 2011, *ESPN.com*, April 8, 2011, http://www.espn.com/espnw/blogs/news/article/6300857/magie-dixon-revered-impact (17 February 2018).

2. Adam Williams, Samantha Scarneo, and Douglas J. Casa, "State-Level Implementation of Health and Safety Policies to Prevent Sudden Death and Catastrophic Injuries within Secondary School Athletics," *Orthopaedic Journal of Sports Medicine* 52, no. 6 (2017): 6.

3. Melissa B. Triebwasser, "The Legacy of Maggie Dixon," *Frogsofwar.com*, March 28, 2017, https://www.frogsowar.com/2017/3/28/15069876/the-legacy-of-maggie-dixon (January 6, 2018).

EPILOGUE

1. The Johnny Mac Soldiers Fund is in honor of Colonel John Michael McHugh, class of 1986, among the most senior-ranking officers killed in Afghanistan. He was captain of the USMA soccer team, an aviator, and an officer respected at every level of command.

Bibliography

Araton, Harvey. "The Hearth Beckons, So a Coach Stays on, with No Regrets." *New York Times*, February 7, 2007, https://mobile.nytimes.com/2007/02/13/sports/ncaabasketball/13araton.html (17 February 2018).

Berkow, Ira. "Coach Finds Awakening at Army." *New York Times News Service*, February 13, 2007 (17 February 2018).

Berkow, Ira. "Memory Softens a Brother's Sadness," *New York Times*, NYTimes.com, April 24, 2006.

Department of the Army. Army Doctrine Publication (ADP) 1, "The Soldier's Creed and the Warrior Ethos." Army Publishing Directorate (superimposed on photograph at beginning of ADP 1 [no page number]), September 2012.

Fittipaldo, Ray. "Seasons of Change/An interview with Jamie Dixon." *Pittsburgh Post-Gazette*, http://post-gazette.com/sports/pitt-basketball/2006/10/08/Seasons-of-Change-An-interview-with-Jamie-Dixon/stories/200610/08, October 8, 2006 [no page number].

Graham, Glen P. "McGuire Never Stops Driving: Talent and Work Ethic Have Produced Something Special in Arundel's West Point-Bound Star." *Baltimore Sun*, January 13, 2005.

Greenberg, Mel. "Maggie Dixon Burial a Solemn Day at West Point." *Knight Ridder Newspapers/247sports.com*, April 14, 2006, https://247sports.com/college/depaul/board/103824/contents/maggie-dixon-laid-to-rest-54249960 (17 February 2018).

Grubbs, John H. "Remembering Maggie." *Assembly Magazine*, March/April 2007, 22.

Litsky, Frank. "Maggie Dixon, Army Women's Basketball Coach, Is Dead at 28." *New York Times*, April 8, 2006.

McManus, Jane. "Sadness, Success Bond Army Women's Basketball Team." *Journal News*, January 30, 2007.

McMillan, Ken. "Army Enlists Dixon." *Newburgh Times Herald-Record*, October 6, 2005 (17 December 2010).

Merrill, Elizabeth. "Maggie Dixon Still Revered for Her Impact." *ESPN.com*, April 8, 2011, http://www.espn.com/espnw/blogs/news/article/6300857/magie-dixon-revered -impact (17 February 2018).

O'Connor, Ian. "West Point Burial Locks in Dixon's Legacy at Army." *USA-Today.com*, April 15, 2006, https://usatoday30.usatoday.com/sports/columist/ oconnor/2006-04-14-dixon_x.htm (17 February 2018).

Whiteside, Kelly. "Dixon Relit Successor Magarity's Love of Coaching." *USAToday. com*, October 4, 2008 (17 February 2018).

———. "They're Playing for Maggie—Dixon's Presence Hovers over Army Women." *USAToday.com*, October 4, 2006 (17 February 2018).

INTERVIEWS

Anderson, Sarah Eila (team)
Begonia, Erin Grace (team)
Brazil, Donna Marie (officer representative, colonel [ret.])
Bruno, Doug (head coach, women's basketball, DePaul University)
Carelus, Joanne (team)
Dixon, Jamie (older brother, head coach, Texas Christian University)
Ennenga, Megan (team)
Enright, Cara (team)
Evans, Megan (team)
Hays Fort, Nicci (close friend)
King, Margaree "Redd" (team)
LeBoeuf, Maureen (friend, brigadier general [ret.])

Magarity, David William (associate coach, currently head coach)
Magnani, Ashley Ann (team)
Mallette, James (father of Michelle "Micky" Mallette)
Mallette, Michelle Katherine (team)
Marshall, Eugene (deputy athletic director, USMA)
Mathis (Balis), Janis (team)
McGuire, Alexandra Claire (team)
Miseli, Jason Augustus (former aide-de-camp to the superintendent, colonel, United States Army)
Payne (Sherk), Adrienne Noel (team)
Schmidt (Ryan), Marie Natalie (team)
Stone, Stefanie Rachel (team)
Vrabel, Megan Ashley (team)
Wilson (Christen), Anna May (team)
Wright (Razon), Courtney (team)

Index

About the Author

Jack Grubbs retired as a brigadier general, following 35 years in the United States Army. He served two combat tours in Vietnam. He has seen leadership, both good and bad, up close and personal. A graduate of the United States Military Academy, he holds a master's of science and engineering degree (MSE) from Princeton University and a PhD in civil engineering from Rensselaer Polytechnic Institute. Following military retirement, he served on the faculty and senior administration at Tulane University in New Orleans. In 2006, he founded Simon-Meyer, Charlotte, a construction consulting company. Grubbs has spoken widely on the topics of leadership, team-building, and ethics. This is his sixth book and the second addressing inspirational leadership. He and his wife Judy live in Charlotte, North Carolina.